California Desert Miracle

The Fight for Desert Parks and Wilderness

California Desert Miracle

The Fight for Desert Parks and Wilderness

Frank Wheat

SUNBELT PUBLICATIONS
San Diego, California

Sunbelt Publications, Inc.
P.O. Box 191126
San Diego, CA 92159-1126
(619) 258-4911

02 01 00 99   5 4 3 2 1

"Sunbelt Natural History Guides"
A series edited by Lowell Lindsay

Library of Congress Cataloging-in-Publication Data

Wheat, Frank, 1921–
        California Desert Miracle: The Fight for Desert Parks and Wilderness
        by Frank Wheat—1st ed.

                p.   cm.—(Sunbelt Natural History Guides)
        Includes index.
        ISBN 0-932653-27-8

1.   United States. California Desert Protection Act of 1994.
2.   Desert Conservation—Law and legislation—United States.
3.   Wilderness areas—Law and legislation—California.
4.   Desert conservation—Law and legislation—California.
                I. Title.   II. Series.

KF5635.A314A168 1999
333.73'616'09794—dc21   98-30452
                                              CIP

To Nancy

Enchanting companion
in desert and mountain

TABLE OF CONTENTS

Acknowledgements

Many of those whose names appear in this book were asked for an interview and almost without exception all responded—some more than once. Many also provided particular documents or larger files for research. To all of these, a hearty thank you.

Dr. Edgar Wayburn, Honorary President of the Sierra Club, drew upon his vast experience in conservation campaigns to write the generous foreword. Doyce B. Nunis, Jr., Distinguished Professor of History Emeritus at the University of Southern California and veteran editor of the quarterly of the History Society of Southern California, reviewed the manuscript and offered invaluable comments. Vicky Hoover graciously applied her good judgment in preliminary editing of the text, which benefited substantially from the final editing of The Marino Group. My former partners at Gibson, Dunn & Crutcher put at my disposal an office, office services and (when her other duties did not preempt) my long-time secretary Judith Phillips, who typed innumerable letters and could magically turn scribbled foolscap into reliable text. To all, I am indebted beyond measure.

FOREWORD

The long campaign to win protection for the remote, undeveloped wild lands of large expanses of the California desert, which occupies fully one quarter of the State of California, was an extraordinary, almost unique chapter in the annals of the preservation movement in our country. For those who lived through its daily, ongoing events and actions, it seemed at times as though it would go on forever. But it had a beginning, a long, accelerating sequence of events and finally—at least as far as the legislation went—an end. Frank Wheat has undertaken and successfully carried out the complex task of documenting the story of this major conservation campaign.

Such campaigns need certain essential elements to succeed. The proponents must have a vision of the big picture. They must also have strong local knowledge and be able to juggle competing interests, both of friends and foes. They must be able to withstand both relevant and irrelevant criticisms and attacks. Above all they must have staying power—the ability to come back year after year to renew the fight. And even when victory is apparently gained, there must be readiness to remain on the alert to defend it. In safeguarding the environment, victories are usually temporary but losses are permanent. Many of my own campaigns, such as those for open space in the Bay Area, for Redwood National Park, and for the wildlands of Alaska, still require constant vigilance.

Wheat was close to the events of the desert campaign and is especially qualified to act as the campaign's historian. He and his wife Nancy are also true denizens of the desert, retreating when they can to a hideaway surrounded by the playas and mountains of Anza-Borrego Desert State Park to soak up its spirit. The story he tells should be of overwhelming interest to all those who were involved in one or another aspect of the long fight for the desert. In addition, it will serve as an instructive and inspiring account for anyone interested in helping to carry out any major conservation campaign involving public education and promotion of legislation over an extended period of time—something significant legislative campaigns require.

The author does much more than take apart the techniques of campaigning and provide the anatomy of a legislative campaign. He gives us a narrative of individual effort and dogged persistence that is at times breathtakingly exciting as he focuses on the essential role of the individual principals in the campaign. At various times, the fate of desert protection seemed to hang by a thread. The narrative lets the reader share closely in the excitement of such moments and the sometimes excruciating suspense when activists truly did not know what would happen next. The more detailed his accounts, the more interesting they seem. His interrelated stories of people and of the enactment of key laws are remarkable. This would not have been possible had the book been written by someone not so involved in the affairs of the campaign.

As the book shows, the eventual success of the desert campaign demonstrates what can be accomplished by positive, close working relationships between forward-thinking legislators and volunteer citizen advocates. Wheat has woven the threads of cooperation between advocates and legislators involved into a solid, closely knit drama. The willingness of politicians to seek the advice and to respect the knowledge of the citizen volunteers, together with the volunteers' readiness to respect the considered judgment of the legislators on the political accommodations they felt had to be made, immensely facilitated final passage of the bill.

The California desert attracted my attention soon after my 13-year effort to enact the Alaska National Interest Lands Conservation Act of 1980. Looking back, I am struck by some remarkable parallels between the situations we faced in Alaska and in the California desert. Both cases dealt with Bureau of Land Management (BLM) lands on a vast scale, and at an early stage in both there were regional BLM directors who, with a remarkable vision rarely found in bureaucratic officials, comprehended the need for more protection of these lands than their agency could provide under existing laws and regulations. In the late 1960s,

Burt Silcock, then Bureau of Land Management State Director for Alaska, foresaw the need for more authority to empower his agency to provide protective management. His grasp of these needs was analogous to that of Russ Penny, BLM California State Director during much of the same period, whose story is told in this book on the California desert. The campaign for the Federal Land Policy and Management Act of 1976 evolved in part from these felt needs. Silcock showed me some of the sensitive areas that had extraordinary resource values which the BLM could not adequately care for—areas such as Nizina and Chitistone Canyon and Skolai Pass in the Wrangell Mountains, and the Arrigetch Peaks and Walker Lake in the Brooks Range. We then campaigned to protect those places that later became part of the core areas of new national parks—Wrangell–St. Elias National Park and Preserve and Gates of the Arctic National Park, respectively.

Shortly after the successful effort to pass the Alaska bill came the campaign to pass the California Wilderness Act of 1984, which dealt with National Forest lands. Meanwhile, as this book shows, the BLM had increasingly shied away from effective measures to protect its desert lands. Based on the facts, the California citizen volunteers made the case for a desert bill to Senator Cranston and his aides. My own part in this effort was small but I hope significant. I helped to convince him that much time and energy could be saved, that we would have the same supporters, the same opponents, and that the ultimate goal was more likely to be attained, if he would sponsor one bold bill on which the campaign could concentrate, rather than a series of small bills. Thus the California Desert Bill, when introduced, was a truly visionary piece of legislation.

Up until that time no national park established in our country was large enough to afford its area all the protection it deserved. Size matters. National parks and other reserves must encompass large areas to provide lasting ecosystem protection. The desert bill has managed to accomplish this. It is notable that Death Valley National Park is now the largest national park in the Lower 48. And the Mojave National Preserve, with its over 1.5 million acres, outdoes Yosemite and Grand Canyon National Parks by a substantial amount. Like Alaska, the California desert is an immense and wonderful place.

What will be the next massive land conservation battle? Already we are engaged in a major legislative campaign to preserve the wildlands of Utah, and we hear rumblings of wilderness to be proposed in Nevada. Then there will be New Mexico, Montana, Idaho, Wyoming—all states that have much wild and roadless public land that needs to be protected for the future from careless, needless human impacts. Wheat's book is timely indeed. I'm sure citizen advocates gearing up to work on these campaigns will be inspired and will learn much from its story of the monumental and successful campaign for the California desert.

Edgar Wayburn, M.D.
Honorary President
Sierra Club

AUTHOR'S PREFACE

This book celebrates the California Desert Protection Act and its significance for future protection of wild lands in our country. The historic conservation measure, passed by Congress on October 8, 1994, established two new desert national parks and a national preserve under National Park Service management. It also designated as protected wilderness over seven million acres of land both inside and outside the parks and preserve.

When word finally reached supporters that the Senate filibuster had been broken without a single vote to spare and the Act had been adopted, it seemed to them a miracle had occurred. Both events *had* taken place *after* the scheduled final adjournment date for the 103d Congress—quite possibly the last Congress for a very long time in which the Act could have been passed.

This book relates the story of that miracle, a story which begins almost thirty years ago. Many events, large and small, had to happen during those years to set the stage for the final miracle. First, it took a remarkable California state director of the Bureau of Land Management (BLM) to initiate the earliest studies of desert management in the late 1970s. Volunteers from the conservation community simultaneously began development of a constituency for the desert with an intensive program of desert study trips. A hole in the Wilderness Act was closed, after much effort, by legislation requiring the BLM to examine its public lands for possible wilderness designation and to prepare a California Desert Plan. Experience with that plan led volunteer conservationists in California to conclude that the plan failed to protect treasured wildlands in the desert; their efforts turned to developing a Desert Protection Act. Sponsors were found in Congress and the battle began. Supporters of the new legislation finally carried their fight to the cusp of victory by October 5, 1994.

There remained barely three days before the 103d Congress would adjourn. Neither House nor Senate had yet scheduled votes on the Conference Committee's Report and one last filibuster loomed in the Senate. A cloture petition to cut off debate would be necessary. That petition could not even be *filed* before the House had acted and only on the third day after the filing could a cloture vote be taken. If cloture succeeded, the Senate's rules allowed 30 more hours for opponents to talk before a vote on the Conference Report could be held. How could this possibly take place in the short time left, particularly in an election year when many legislators were desperate to get home to campaign? It seemed impossible.

For those who can't wait, the final miracle that occurred in those desperate days is described in Chapter Eleven, the book's last chapter.

No such miracle would have been possible without the work of hundreds of volunteers who distinguished themselves in the long fight for the desert. Herein lies the truth behind most seeming miracles. A particular light shines on the work of several men and women named in the book's chapter titles. None of them sought or gained material benefit. All kept the fires of their dedication aflame for years, demonstrating how effective individual Americans can be if determined to carry on and never quit the fight. Human courage takes more than one form. In moments of great physical danger, it may be aided by adrenaline the body produces under such conditions. No such wondrous substance supports the courage of those who see their efforts come to naught time and again and, though tempted to give in, find the courage to persist. This book honors that kind of courage.

The legislative process in the U.S. Congress is the book's second major theme. Two statutes were involved, the Desert Protection Act of 1994 and the Federal Land Policy and Management Act of 1976 (known as FLPMA). Both were landmarks in the long campaign to achieve better protection for the California desert.

Much has been written about the fundamentals of our Federal system of government, about the "checks and balances" conceived by the authors of the Constitution, and about the process of lawmaking in a Congress divided into separate Houses with markedly different terms and constituencies. The story of the Desert

Bill illumines some of the more complex inner workings of that process. One encounters here the time-consuming impact on legislation of the short, two-year life of each session of Congress, the tradition-bound rules and customs of debate in each House, the remarkable powers vested in committee chairs, the Speaker of the House and the Senate Majority Leader, the uses of the filibuster and other procedures to stall legislative action, and how all these roadblocks can sometimes be overcome.

The story also demonstrates how small events in the history of a piece of legislation can either cause that legislation to fail or propel it toward success. Shakespeare put into the mouth of Brutus, "there is a tide in the affairs of men which, taken at the flood, leads on to fortune." More often one might say there are a multitude of small tides which, if *each* is taken at the flood, may lead to fortune. Thus it was with legislation to protect the California desert.

An old adage tells that sausage—and legislation—are the two things one should never watch *being made*. After a major piece of legislation is adopted, however, there can be great value in examining *how* it was made. Sometimes this will involve incidents good for a laugh, bits of theater or even moments of high drama. All three are a part of the history of FLPMA and the Desert Bill. The author hopes that this story of what volunteers can accomplish will lend encouragement to those who labor today to protect precious public lands in Nevada, Utah, Colorado and elsewhere in our country.

★ ★ ★ ★

The question remains: Was it worth it? What is this California desert that so many labored so long to protect? It is a desert of 27 million acres, the size of Connecticut, Massachusetts and Rhode Island combined, the greater part of which is public land belonging to all Americans. Once (like other deserts) it was thought to be mainly barren, hostile, and dangerous to humans, lacking the familiar beauty of forests, plains, and snow-capped mountains—to be avoided if possible. This attitude changed gradually after World War II. People who had joined the postwar migration to southern California, footloose and supplied with transportation by the largest vehicle market in the world, were drawn to this last large area of wildland left in the state. After the war hundreds of thousands of relatively inexpensive motorcycles poured into California from Japan. Where could these new machines be used without restriction, without speed limit, and with the steepest hills to challenge? In the desert, of course.

People discovered magnificent scenery in the desert: then as now windblown sand dunes up to 700 feet high could be found, their stark beauty enhanced by perfection of contrast and line. Mountains appeared on all sides, one range rising to over 14,000 feet. Nestled within it were groves of bristlecone pines alive long before the birth of Christ. Lower down, on a vast desert dome, stood the world's largest forest of Joshua Trees—giant lilies which John Charles Fremont, crossing the desert in an earlier era, referred to as "the most repulsive trees on earth."[1] ("Strange" might be a better term—it would be hard to call them ugly after seeing the tip of every branch decorated in spring with an armload of creamy white flowers.)

The history of lost parties of '49ers trying to reach the Pacific coast drew visitors to Death Valley National Monument, as did the chance to stand at the lowest elevation in the country, surrounded by marvelously painted canyons. Illustrating unexpected contrasts in the California desert is an exquisite waterfall, hidden in mountains not far from the place in Death Valley where record-high temperatures have been recorded.

A prehistoric Indian trail, one of many, traverses the California desert westward from the Colorado River, touching rare desert springs on its way and managing to cross or skirt range after range of mountains. In the last century it became a wagon road for pioneers and traders along which the Army, for protection against Indian attack, established small forts. Today it is a popular route for latter-day adventurers in 4x4 vehicles.

In the California desert there are over 1,000 sites with petroglyphs and pictographs, the ancient rock art of prehistoric peoples. Dr. Sylvia Broadbent, of the University of Southern California-Riverside, calls it one of the largest concentrations of prehistoric art in the world, surpassing even the paleolithic cave paintings in France and Spain and the valleys of Northern Italy. Before the Desert Bill was introduced, she testified: "The tragedy is that at the rate this heritage is being destroyed [by souvenir hunters and vandals] it may be gone before the majority of our citizens even know it exists."[2]

Travelers newly exposed to the desert learned that in spring many of its valleys are carpeted with wildflowers. Zoologists and botanists had long known that the California desert is amazingly rich in both plant life and wildlife. It is home to over 350 species of vertebrate animals—ranging in size from a tiny lungless salamander to the mountain lion and desert bighorn—plus thousands of invertebrates. There are over 1,200 species of higher plants, some rare or endangered, some found only in California, some embodying chemical substances developed for their own survival, that furnished an entire pharmacopoeia to desert tribes of Indians. As Dr. Robert Stebbins, Emeritus Professor of Zoology at the University of California-Berkeley, put it: "The desert is a storehouse of still untapped scientific information. We are in the process of burning bridges to new medicines, crop plants…and a more informed future." [3]

It is beyond the scope of this book to attempt to capture in words those special aspects of the desert's beauty—dark mountains in the vast distance, white playas (called "sand mirrors" by one of the author's friends, a poet), tiny, life-saving oases sometimes shielded by native palms, the colors of naked rocks, the clarity of light and the depth of the desert night in which planets and stars glow with unmatched brilliance. Other writers have done this. Others, too, have spoken of a closeness to the Master of Creation found only in wilderness, *desert wilderness*, untouched by the presence or works of man, where God spoke to Moses. These are among the values that inspired the volunteers to whom this book pays tribute, who won their battle at last.

September 13, 1998
Frank Wheat

PREFACE TO MEMORIAL EDITION

In *California Desert Miracle,* Frank Wheat wrote the definitive history of the fight for desert parks and wilderness in California. Almost the definitive history. He left out his own role and that of his wife, Nancy, in making the miracle happen. Wheat does not appear in the Index or anywhere in the text and definitely should. This preface to the memorial edition of *California Desert Miracle* is an attempt to flesh out the record.

Though Frank was born and raised in Los Angeles, his father, Carl Wheat (1893-1966), wrote monographs on Death Valley, giving Frank early exposure to, and love of, the desert. Many years later, Frank and Nancy Wheat made their second home in the Anza-Borrego Desert area where Frank nurtured a truly extraordinary cactus garden. Frank's energy and interest encompassed all things of the desert from the belly flower to the mountain peak and how to protect them.

Earthjustice (formerly the Sierra Club Legal Defense Fund) provided Frank an avenue to foster this protection. As a trustee, he encouraged the organization to provide counsel for desert protection leading to two monumental victories. The first was stopping the enormously destructive Barstow-to-Vegas motorcycle race. Each Thanksgiving, as many as 3,000 motorcycles took part in what was essentially a cross-county race. The scars are yet on the land and will be there for a hundred years, but the race is no more and the scars are beginning to heal.

The second victory was the permitting process for the Viceroy Mine in the Mojave Desert. The Viceroy Mine was originally approved by the Bureau of Land Management, based on a simple environmental analysis of fewer than 100 pages. Earthjustice said "Whoa." Hundreds of pages and years later—and after two environmental impact statements—the Viceroy Mine was given permits with the most stringent restoration requirements of any public lands mine. It was another decade before Frank's research and relentless advocacy, along with that of others, taught the Bureau of Land Management it had the right and authority to say no to the most egregious mines.

California Desert Miracle centers on winning passage of the California Desert Protection Act of 1994, which Senator Alan Cranston had introduced in 1986. In 1987 the Sierra Club Foundation brought a group to the Mojave. Patty Carpenter Hughes served as hostess: "I remember the first time I met Frank Wheat. We had invited the members of the Sierra Club Foundation on a tour of the East Mojave, hoping to win their support for the Desert Protection Act. We were at Kelso Dunes and I was in charge of food. I prepared a feast. Then the van pulled up and out stepped five men. The sixth, tall, lanky, wearing a tan outback hat, with the vigor of a young boy and a smile the size of the sun, jumped out. He marched straight to the table, all smiles and full of praise. I was flattered. Then he looked me straight in the eye and asked me why I wasn't out working for gun control. Never to be outdone, I argued back. He walked away with a gleam in his eye. A gleam that I would see many times again. Always a challenge, always a rebuttal."

Frank and Nancy Wheat were a team. While he was a trustee of Earthjustice, Nancy was a trustee of the Sierra Club Foundation and the National Parks and Conservation Association. For the California Desert Protection Act, it was their combined efforts that brought the NPCA from faint support to staunch leadership.

A retired senior partner of the largest law firm in Los Angles, Frank's specialty had been corporate law and his former practice had frequently taken him to the East Coast. In Washington, D.C., he became a most effective lobbyist for the California Desert Protection Act in his retirement years.

Debbie Sease, Sierra Club Legislative Director, remembers one trip east. "As everyone knows, Frank was one of the most persistent and indefatigable lobbyists the desert bill ever had. One day he was in D.C. seeking cosponsors and encountered a particularly difficult House office where despite his entreaties, he had not been able to secure a meeting with the member, or even with the staff. As he was waiting in the office late one afternoon, the chief of staff walked into the reception area wearing a tuxedo. He tried to make it past Frank, but Frank nabbed him. The staffer said he would love to talk with Frank, but he was headed to a black tie dinner. Frank simply climbed into the taxi with him and lobbied all the way to dinner."

"He was a Democrat with many big-ticket Republican friends," recalls Jim Dodson, another key figure in the desert campaign. "He encouraged them to write to their legislators at critical times. They responded. Passage of the desert bill required this bipartisan support. When a picture book on the 116 wilderness areas was needed, Frank and Nancy were the first to contribute. When a desert video was needed, he contributed and hit up his friends. The video was produced and circulated nationwide."

That kind of persistence was typical of Frank Wheat. I remember learning of a remarkable technique pioneered by Joshua Tree National Park. It involved rooting cacti and other plants and propagating them in tall pots 30 inches long and six inches in diameter, letting them grow long enough to develop strong root systems. One of the most daunting and difficult tasks in this dry landscape is to restore vegetation damaged by livestock or motorized vehicles, and the survival rate for these plants, once transplanted in the desert, was a phenomenal 80 percent. It was a simple, elegant, and effective technique, but to take proper advantage of it, one needed a tractor equipped with an augur. The people who would do the restoration work needed $10,500. Frank raised the money in nine days. Thousands of plants now grow throughout the desert thanks in part to Frank's vigor and persistence.

That vigor was physical as well as mental, and Frank loved hiking in the desert. "On my February trip [only a few months before his death] he was as strong as could be, and as usual a joy to hike with," said Steve Tabor, president of Desert Survivors. "I figured he'd outlast a lot of us. I never suspected he was 79, the way he trooped up and down the hills and across the plains."

My own special memory of Frank was a letter he wrote to Interior Secretary Bruce Babbitt. This letter contained very sensitive political information. An underling opened the letter and proceeded to draft a reply; meanwhile, the letter was routed to people who should never have seen it. When Frank realized what had happened, his considerable fury reached a towering peak. He drafted a second letter to Mr. Babbitt and then faxed it to me with two questions: Should he change it? Should he send it? I was in DC and shared his letter with the Sierra Club staff. It was agreed he should send it and change not a word. Secretary Babbitt, upon reading the second letter, realized how inept his staff had been with the first letter. Thereafter, Secretary Babbitt always returned Frank's calls personally.

Frank understood and loved the interplay of law and land protection. Deborah Reames, the Earthjustice attorney who litigated the cases involving the motorcycle race and the gold mine among many others, said, "You may wonder where Frank gathered the information he used in California Desert Miracle. I can tell you about the legal documents. Those he found mostly in my files. He practically lived in my office for days at a time, then would disappear for a few months, usually toting my only copies of various critical documents, later deny he had them, still later return them to me—in other words, driving us quietly nuts. No other trustee of the Legal Defense Fund was more deeply involved in any of our campaigns than Frank was in the fight to preserve the California desert. He was immensely curious, wanting to know every detail of every case we brought, whether to challenge the Barstow-to-Vegas motorcycle race, to keep throngs of cattle and sheep out of tortoise habitat at critical times in the spring when the grasses grow, or to force the Viceroy mining company to invent a whole new way of covering its ponds to protect birds and to guarantee total reclamation of the site once the lode is used up. He was an indefatigable ally."

Buck Parker, Executive Director of Earthjustice, tells of Frank's participation as a trustee, "When you look for people to serve on the board of trustees of a nonprofit environmental law firm, you find that the pool of potential candidates is not exceptionally large. You want a person with a passion for the work, an unapologetic environmentalist. You want a lawyer, or at least someone with a profound understanding of how the law can and must be used in the conservation cause. You want an individual who will devote a considerable amount of time and effort to making your organization survive and prosper. And you want someone who is personable, helpful, friendly, and will get along with his or her fellow trustees. Frank Wheat was all those things and many more. No trustee was more devoted to the Legal Defense Fund, more generous with his time, or more responsible in his duties. When he disagreed with someone on a point he thought was important, he said so, but his criticisms were always constructive and never hurt. When he supported you on a point, any doubts you had were removed. Frank's logic was matched only by his passion. Earthjustice has always been blessed with a magnificent band of trustees. None was better than Frank."

In 1989, the Sierra Club Legal Defense Fund published an illustrated book titled *Wild by Law*. Frank gave me a copy with great pride. The author, Tom Turner, shared this tidbit with me years later. "About fourteen years ago, I set out to write *Wild by Law*, a book about the Sierra Club Legal Defense Fund and the places and critters it had gone to court to defend. A year and a half later, the manuscript was finished, the photographs made and selected, the typesetter ready to turn the typescript into elegant letters, the designer poised to make beautiful pages, the printer getting the presses warm. The phone rang on the desk of Rick Sutherland, our executive director. It was Frank.

"Would you please ask Tom to send me a copy of the manuscript? I'd like to read it before it goes to press.' My blood drained to my ankles. I could see our precious schedule going up in smoke. In 300 pages anyone could find something to quibble with if he tried hard enough. I printed what I had nervously hoped was the final version of the manuscript and called FedEx. Two tense days dragged by, then three. At the end of the third day Rick's phone jingled again. 'I wouldn't change a single word,' said Frank."

Upon his death, the Associated Press described Frank's activities as follows, "Wheat, a prominent securities lawyer, served on the Securities and Exchange Commission during the Lyndon B. Johnson administration. Wheat also was a founding director of the Center for Law in the Public Interest and the founder and a past president of the Alliance for Children's Rights, which provides free legal assistance to poor children and their caretakers. Several environmental groups claimed Wheat as a trustee, including: the Sierra Club Legal Defense Fund, Earthjustice Legal Defense Fund, the California Desert Protective League and the Anza Borrego Foundation.

Following the death of Frank Wheat, Mary Martin, Superintendent of Mojave National Preserve, wrote to Nancy Wheat, "Without Frank Wheat there would be no Mojave Preserve."

Finally, a word from a man now entrusted with preserving what Frank and Nancy worked so long and hard to protect, Ernest Quintana, the superintendent of Joshua Tree National Park.

"Over the years the fight to protect our California desert landscape has been waged by many with a select few individuals leading the way. Frank Wheat was one of those leaders. He understood and respected the unique beauty of our desert. His vision of the desert encompassed more than the natural wonders found there. He understood the healing value the region has on the human spirit.

Mr. Wheat was an extraordinary person who gave of his time and energy to protect our special place on this earth. The National Park Service desert units of Death Valley, the Mojave Preserve, and Joshua Tree are better places today because of his efforts."

Elden Hughes
Chair, Sierra Club
California/Nevada
Desert Committee
January 2003

"It is tempting
to believe that
what the desert holds
uppermost for man
is not a raceway
for his engines
but a crucible
for his spirit."

—John Waugh in the *Los Angeles Times*

RUSS PENNY

The
Desert
Shall
Not
Die

CHAPTER ONE

"What's this?"

asked Russ Penny. He was looking at a crude diagram handed him by Hall McLean, Manager of the Federal Bureau of Land Management's Riverside District.

"It's a motorcycle race course out in the desert." McLean responded.

"On whose land?" Penny asked.

"Ours and some private land."

"Any official program for this?"

"No, they just go,"

"How many go?"

"Oh, maybe two or three hundred."

"Go out there and see what's happening.
Take pictures. Send me a report."

The year was 1967, and Penny had just arrived in Sacramento as the new State Director of BLM. He was making the rounds of his district offices. McLean and his people in Riverside were responsible for the major part of the huge California desert.

McLean's report and photographs soon came in. Six-hundred and fifty motorcyclists had participated in what would eventually grow into "the largest motorcycle race in the world" with as many as 3,000 riders. The photographs showed substantial damage to the desert vegetation and soils, the kind that often leads to serious erosion. Penny understood the portent of the photos. He had once been in charge of soils and moisture conservation in the Rawlins, Wyoming, regional office of the Federal Grazing Service in the late '30s, almost a decade before two agencies in the Department of the Interior, the Grazing Service and the General Land Office, were merged to form the BLM in 1946.

Penny concluded that he had a problem on his hands. Something significant was happening on public lands in the desert. Very little was known about it apart from the fact that tens of thousands of new motorcycles, mostly from Japan, were pouring into California and being quickly sold to people who found the nearby desert a handy place to use them. There was no management. The BLM had no enforcement authority. It seemed vital to Penny to move swiftly to study the uses being made of the desert and its varied resources in order to determine what, if anything, should be done. Penny took the Riverside District's report and photos to the next meeting of the state directors of the BLM, where he asked the National Director for $25,000 to make such a study. In his usual no-nonsense style, Penny presented his case. He got the money.

Thus began what was probably the first project in the history of the BLM and its predecessor agencies to study what could be called "management of people"—the tens of thousands who use the public land but have no other connection with it. Historically, the BLM's job was to manage grazing on leased public land, to conserve the range, and to sell and dispose of public lands where buyers could be found. It was said that the BLM possessed the land nobody wanted, the land left over after the rest had been homesteaded, patented or reserved for national forests or parks. "People management" was foreign to the BLM. It might not be an acceptable concept to Penny's superiors. He adopted the phrase "recreation management" and found it less likely to raise hackles in Washington, D.C.

It was more than a stroke of luck to pry loose that $25,000 from the BLM's budget. Here was the beginning of organized attention to the question of what the BLM's desert lands offered to people in general—not just to miners and grazers, but to motorcyclists and thousands of others who sought the desert for all kinds of recreation. What resources never before inventoried by the BLM, did California's desert lands contain—resources such as unusual animals, plant life, scenic beauty, solitude, and historic or prehistoric artifacts? All might be in danger of damage or destruction by what people were doing in the desert. Few understood what riches might be lost.

What Sort of Man Was He?

J. Russell Penny was born in a North Dakota country farmhouse in 1913, one of six children. In 1931 he hitchhiked to Fort Collins, Colorado, to enroll in Colorado College of Agriculture (later

Russell Penny, visionary Director of the California State office, BLM, who first saw the need to protect the sensitive resources of the desert.

Courtesy of Russell Penny

Colorado State) and graduated in 1935. While in high school and college, all his summers were spent on his family's farms, some during periods of drought and depression when farmers couldn't pay their taxes. Soon after graduation he joined the Federal Resettlement Administration, running surveys in Colorado and Wyoming of range lands which the Federal government bought or planned to buy from farmers who were broke.

Two years later he was Range Conservationist and Assistant to the District Grazier of the Grazing Service in Green River, Wyoming. By the late '30s he succeeded his boss as District Grazier, later moving to the regional office in charge of its soils and moisture conservation program.

Then came World War II and the Marine Corps. He was a Marine rifleman on Okinawa when the war ended and spent another ten months in China before returning to the States and his wife Jacqueline in 1946. Jackie had spent the war years as a "Wave" yeoman in U.S. Naval Intelligence. Russ proudly recalls that she wrote the lyrics of the song "Waves of the Navy," which every Wave knew by heart.

A fellowship at Harvard resulted in a Master's degree in public administration, after which Russ rejoined his old outfit, now the BLM's Division of Grazing in Washington, D.C., as Assistant

Chief of Range Management. In 1954, a troublesome problem came to Penny's attention. An influential Wyoming cattleman had shipped his steers across the state, unloaded them and turned them loose on an open range that the cattleman neither leased nor owned. He had no permit and, when charged, defied the BLM and refused to settle, obviously expecting the matter to be quietly dropped. It was, however, a significant instance of illegal trespassing. Penny believed the BLM had to stand up to the man and he prepared the case for the U.S. Attorney in Cheyenne. That lawyer's name was Sackett, the name adopted by author Louis Lamour for his toughest character. Not surprisingly, Sackett moved on the case. The influential cattleman soon decided that his best bet was to plead guilty.

An Assistant Director of the agency gave Penny hell for what he'd done. Another Assistant Director told him: "That case was one of the real stepping-stones for the BLM. It's the first time the agency stood up to a well-connected trespasser. It hardened our stomachs. I think you deserve a lot of credit." The next day, Penny was appointed State Director of the BLM for Idaho. Appointments followed for directorships in Montana, Nevada, and finally, California in 1966.

Penny is admired by many who were once his subordinates: "He could get people in the organization to do what he wanted them to do, sometimes at substantial personal sacrifice, since he genuinely respected those under him," according to Bert Stanley, his former chief counsel in Sacramento. "They knew he was sincerely dedicated to the land and to making changes he felt the situation demanded, but he could let you know quite emphatically if he was unhappy with your work." Del Vail, Manager of the Riverside District of the BLM in the first half of the '70s, said: "He was a visionary and a go-getter. He took the initiative on a lot of things. If people [in the Bureau hierarchy] didn't agree, he'd find a way over or around them. He was not popular with a lot of people in Washington." Bob Jennings, Range Conservationist and a member of Penny's original Desert Plan staff, described his former boss as "a wiry guy, a dominant presence, a driver, decisive, and not easy to work for. But he had a knack for picking good people for tasks he felt important." He would need them in the times ahead.

Studying People Management in the California Desert

As soon as he got his hands on that $25,000 for a study of the California desert, Penny considered his needs. No one in his organization had experience in people management and most had no experience in protection of endangered natural resources. Knowing he could gain valuable insights from the National Park Service, Penny called his friend John Rutter, Western Regional Director of the National Park Service, and proposed that the Park Service join with his staff in this first-ever desert study. He assigned people from his own staff, including representatives of each of the two districts, Riverside and Bakersfield, with responsibility for parts of the desert. An extensive field investigation was conducted. Experts from the University of California at Berkeley and Los Angeles, San Diego State College (later University), and the San Diego Museum of Man were asked for their assistance.

The product of this effort, published in 1968, was a 378-page document entitled "The California Desert—a Preliminary Study." Its recommendations to the BLM were unique in the history of the agency. The report called on the BLM to

- Begin work immediately on development of a comprehensive plan covering all the resources of the California desert.

- Undertake an aggressive public information and education program to make the public aware of the needs of the desert.

- Move forward with studies of the natural and scientific resources of the desert.

- Establish an adequate ranger force with enforcement authority.

- Construct "way stations" on primary highways in the desert to provide rest and information to desert visitors.

- Designate areas for cross-country motorcycle riding.

- Undertake control of off-road vehicle use where necessary to protect desert resources.

- Classify for retention in public ownership 19 areas found by the study to have "significant recreation values," and "develop plans to insure those values are not impaired or destroyed."

The 19 "recreation lands" identified "as a start" in the report totaled 2.441 million acres and included many areas later recommended for wilderness designation. Special warnings were included in the report for two of these areas: for Red Rock Canyon, "intensive day and overnight use is rapidly ruining remaining natural values" and for the Yuha Desert in Imperial County, "the assortment of natural, scientific, historical, and recreational values cannot long endure present intensive, uncontrolled, and promiscuous use."

Significantly, the report described the Whipple Mountains just west of the Colorado River and stated: "These lands are the best examples of wilderness area remaining in the California Desert and they should be so managed." This was possibly the *first* mention anywhere of the idea of protecting a part of BLM lands in the California desert as "wilderness." Paradoxically, it is contained in a document published by the only Federal public land agency left completely out of the Wilderness Act of 1964. In that Act, Congress directed that lands managed by the Forest Service, National Park Service, and those lying within National Wildlife Refuges be reviewed to determine if they were suitable for wilderness designation. The Secretaries of Agriculture and Interior were required to report such determinations to the President, who would make the appropriate recommendation to Congress. The BLM held by far the largest portion of the nation's public lands. Either no one thought there could be any land of wilderness quality under an agency like the BLM, or, as has been suggested, the BLM was purposely excluded from the Wilderness Act in the attempt to persuade the powerful Wayne Aspinall (Democrat, Colorado), chairman of the House Interior

Committee, to allow the bill for the Wilderness Act to come to a vote in his committee. Probably both reasons were to some extent true. Now, possibly for the first time, someone in the BLM had been permitted to dip a finger in the water to test its temperature for BLM wilderness. It was Russ Penny who allowed it to happen.

The Uncomfortable Notion of "Planning"

There would be no pause in the process that had now been set in motion. "Planning" on any scale approaching what Penny had in mind was entirely new to the BLM. There had been legislation back in 1964 proposing that regulations be adopted to classify all BLM lands for disposal or retention based on their potential uses. Little had come of it, however. Now Penny's fellow state directors, bemused by what he seemed to be doing, were happy to let him act as a guinea pig.

Penny moved swiftly but carefully. First, he kept together the small Desert Plan staff that had helped to prepare his 1968 report. Early in 1969 he engaged a respected planning consultant and architect from Pasadena, Simon Eisner, to assist his staff. Over the next year, Eisner and the staff held many seminars on how best to create a plan for the desert. Reports prepared by Eisner covered such subjects as the many facets of land use plans, the testing of concepts, public participation, base and other mapping, implementation and plan maintenance. Meanwhile, Penny could not resist the opportunity for a "first." In May 1969, he and his Desert Plan staff, with local support, officially recognized and provided some protection to a group of hills at the foot of Mt. Whitney, far older than the Sierra Nevada and hence of special geological interest. The "Alabama Hills" became the first BLM-designated "Desert Recreation Land."

"Penny's Law"

Early in 1969 the BLM in Washington published regulations on motor vehicle use not previously published as *proposed* rule making because they "involved matters relating to public property." These unusual regulations authorized the requirement of a special land use permit for motor vehicle races and rallies on public lands.[4] Applications had to be accompanied by a map and an estimate of the number of participants. A bond could be required to insure clearing of litter and repair of damage and the permit was required to contain provisions "to minimize damage to the land and its resources." Areas could be restricted to a specific use or no use.

When *Cycle News*, a major publication for motorcyclists, got wind of the new rules, they were promptly dubbed "Penny's Law" in its issue of April 15, 1969. "If we are to believe that anti-motorcycle bureaucrats can get away with such a hoax, it means you cannot legally ride your motorcycle on any public land and if you have done so since January 18 you have already broken the law," the *News* wrote. Penny avoided taking offense at the attack. He believed in a gentler approach than that proposed in the regulations, which might well be subject to challenge for side-stepping the public comment requirements of the Administrative Procedure Act. With the cooperation of the better-organized motorcycle clubs, he proposed an arrangement under which the Riverside District office would issue, on application, an informal "letter of authorization" rather than a "permit" for any organized motorcycle event that did not threaten injury to botanical or archaeological resources known to the staff. In the few instances where groups were advised that a letter of authorization could not be issued, they backed away or revised their plans.

Penny knew he had to plan carefully before he could go farther. In June 1969 he organized "ORVAC," or Off-Road Vehicle Advisory Council, asking it to advise him on how best to manage off-road vehicle use in the desert. He asked desert user groups to nominate the members, designating himself as a co-chair, a representative of the California Farm Bureau Federation as the other co-chair, and Ron Sloan of the American Motorcyclist Association as vice-chair. Although only three of the 15 council members could be said to represent the conservation community, ORVAC published, after only nine months of work, "Operation ORVAC," a report recommending radical changes in the way the BLM did business with the off-roaders.

Ron Sloan was a major factor. Known to be hostile to the idea at first, he gradually became convinced that some limitations on off-road activity in the desert were needed. A growing public outcry could otherwise cause such activities to be more severely limited. He joined in the report's four critical recommendations.

First, all public lands should be classified into three groups: "open" areas for unrestricted off-road play; "restricted use areas" where there would be appropriate limitations on off-road vehicle use; and "non-use areas" where, to protect resource values, off-road vehicles would not be allowed at all.

Second, the BLM must have law enforcement authority or it could not carry out its responsibilities for public land management. Such authority should be provided by legislation, and enforcement personnel should be distinctively uniformed, be highly trained in enforcement procedures, be highly mobile, be authorized to carry sidearms under certain circumstances and be designated peace officers authorized to enforce both local and Federal laws.

Third, off-road vehicles should be registered on a no-fee basis to promote safety and aid in educating their users.

Fourth, the Federal government must provide the funds to carry out this program.

A Second Desert Report

While ORVAC was meeting and preparing its recommendations, Penny's Desert Plan staff was hard at work on its next report. In October 1969, it published a preliminary volume of technical data on desert resources and related issues and the report itself in January 1970. Smaller in size and easier to read than the 1968 report, the new document, "The California Desert—a Critical Environmental Challenge," announced completion of desert planning guidelines. It estimated the total costs of planning at $18 million over several years. It observed that long before planning could be completed management action would be necessary to preserve rare desert values in imminent danger. As Penny put it in his report to the 1970 Annual Meeting of his Desert Advisory Board: "The

California desert, your desert, is on the brink of an environmental disaster."5 He was not one to mince words. He was not challenged.

The First Bill in Congress for a Desert Plan

Early in 1970, Bob Jennings of Russ Penny's Desert Plan staff left the BLM to accept appointment as District Assistant in Bakersfield, California, for Republican Congressman Bob Mathias. (Mathias was famous throughout the land as winner of the Olympic decathlon for the United States in 1948 and 1952.) At the time, Mathias's district crossed the Sierra to include such northern desert valleys as Saline and Eureka and the mountains around them. Jennings had in mind a piece of legislation his new boss might like to sponsor. He described the BLM's need for authority and money to draw up a plan for the California desert and to enforce its regulations there. He informed Mathias that the BLM

Secretary of Interior Rogers Morton and California Congressman Bob Mathias, author of the first bill in Congress for a California desert plan, review Russ Penny's Desert Report in 1971.

Courtesy of California State office of the BLM

presently had only enough staff in the desert to assign one person to every million acres. Mathias was interested and told Jennings to go right ahead. Jennings called on his old friends at the BLM, including Russ Penny, to discuss it.

At first, Penny was very doubtful about working directly on a piece of legislation affecting his agency and thought it should go through the Bureau's Washington staff. Jennings argued to the contrary, stretching the point a little by telling his old colleagues at the BLM that Mathias was sufficiently concerned about delay that he would be likely to draft and introduce the bill without their input. The group somewhat reluctantly agreed to work with their old colleague to draft the first piece of legislation designed to benefit the California desert.

Drafting continued through the rest of 1970. Penny's first desert report of 1968 had contained a rough outline of the study area, confining it to the broad southern reaches of the California desert. These boundaries were substantially refined during the 1970–71 drafting discussions to include the northern portion. The draft legislation proposed that this entire area be established as "the California Desert National Conservation Area." It required the Secretary of Interior to prepare a long-range program for management of the desert. As recommended in Penny's Second Desert Report, the Secretary was to execute an immediate interim program for protection of endangered resources. Somehow, Russ Penny had managed to scrape up funds to hire Development and Resources Corporation, a national planning and engineering firm, to recommend a management framework for his proposed desert plan and to estimate the costs involved in both long-range and interim programs. Early in 1971, the firm submitted an estimate of $28.6 million. That figure was added to the Mathias bill. Other bill provisions authorized acquisitions of land by purchase or exchange, issuance of regulations, and protection of mining claims. Mathias was leery, however, of asking Congress to give the BLM enforcement powers.

The Mathias bill, H.R. 9661, was introduced July 8, 1971. Mathias succeeded in adding 29 California co-sponsors, both Republicans and Democrats, well over two-thirds of the entire California Congressional delegation.

Mathias's fellow Congressman, Jerry Pettis (Republican, California) represented a major part of the California desert. "Aha," thought Pettis to himself when his staff told him of the Mathias bill. "I seem to have a colleague who would poach on *my* territory." His swift reaction was to whip up a bill of his own, H.R. 10305, and introduce it three weeks later on August 2, 1971, without co-sponsors. Not having time to be original he had no choice but to copy both the structure and, to a large extent, the language of the Mathias bill. His bill established the same national conservation area but with a slightly different name. It also ordered preparation of a long-range plan for the desert within a specified time. It added provisions for an advisory commission, authorized grants for research plus assistance to local government units, but left the appropriation amount blank. He probably had no idea where Mathias had gotten his figure of $28.6 million.

Both bills were referred to the House Interior Committee where they quietly languished.

All was not quiet, however, in the other chamber. California's senior Senator, Alan Cranston (Democrat), found out about the Mathias and Pettis bills and was taken with the idea of authoring such a bill in the Senate. He spoke with Mathias about it. Mathias and Jennings knew the Senator could move the bill faster than they could and would therefore get the credit for it. Jennings reports Mathias as saying, "Senator, the bill is the important thing so as far as I'm concerned—take it and run with it."

The Senator took the framework and much of the language. He borrowed the provision establishing an Advisory Commission from the Pettis bill. His deadline of June 30, 1978, for completion of the California Desert Plan and the appropriation authorization of $28.6 million were both taken from the Mathias bill. He asked his newly elected junior colleague in the Senate, John Tunney (Democrat, California), to join him in introducing the bill, S. 3874, in August 1972.

When the 94th Congress opened in 1973, the three Congressional proponents of a California desert plan introduced new bills identical to their original bills. Pettis moved first with a January 3, 1973, introduction of H.R. 890, again without co-sponsors, followed the next day by Cranston and Tunney with S. 63. Mathias was not about to lie low—he rounded up the Republican and Democratic co-sponsors of his 1971 bill before introducing his new bill, H.R. 5288, on March 7, 1973. By August 2, Pettis had persuaded most of the same members of Congress to co-sponsor his bill.

Of what value was this side lines competition between the two Congressmen? In later House hearings it might well have been important. Both Congressmen had demonstrated that most of the

California delegation, including those members who represented the areas involved, was solidly behind the legislation.

Now the influence of the two Senators from the most populous state in the nation was felt. Cranston was able to schedule a hearing in February 1974 before the Interior Committee's Subcommittee on Public Lands. This hearing was a crucial event for the California desert. The Administration opposed the bill as unnecessary, urging that the BLM was already dealing with damage by off-roaders and was progressing with a long-range plan for the desert. However, the great majority of those who testified strongly favored the bill. Larry Moss of the Sierra Club effectively countered the Administration's position. He noted that the BLM was unable to enforce any of its interim planning for the California desert, could not get any money for the purpose out of the Office of Management and Budget, and would probably never get such money without passage of a specific monetary authorization like that contained in S. 63. He also testified that the deadline in the Cranston bill was important if a desert plan was ever to be completed. Mathias was not present but submitted a strong statement at the hearing. Pettis provided effective testimony, as did Cranston. Both wisely suggested that the Cranston bill be added as an amendment to the pending Senate bill for a BLM "organic act," the Federal Land Policy and Management Act (dubbed FLPMA and pronounced "flipma"). FLPMA had nationwide significance and at the time was slowly wending its way through Congress. It was intended to provide a charter for the work of the BLM.[6]

The suggestion to tack Cranston's Bill onto FLPMA was more persuasive than anyone could have hoped. The subcommittee met after the hearing, resolved a few technical problems, and *unanimously* agreed to recommend to the full Committee that S. 63 be incorporated in the full Committee's bill for the BLM's organic act. It rejected the Administration's objection that this amounted to special legislation for a single state and hence should not be part of the larger bill. The full Committee also acted unanimously. By the time the Senate was ready to vote on its version of FLPMA, S. 63 was firmly ensconced within the Senate bill. It appeared in both the House and Senate bills when these were introduced at the opening of the next session of Congress in 1975. It was included when both bills passed in 1976. And it was still there when the FLPMA Conference Committee agreed at the last moment to a report that both Houses passed in October 1976.

Here is an example of the familiar saying that begins, "For want of a nail, the shoe was lost" turned on its head. In all likelihood, FLPMA would never have reached the President's desk with provisions for a California Desert Plan had not each of the following events occurred:

- 1967—Penny put Jennings on his Desert Plan staff.

- 1970—Jennings unexpectedly went to work for Congressman Mathias.

- 1970—Based on his knowledge of the desert's needs, Jennings suggested legislation for the California desert to Mathias.

- 1970–71—Penny was persuaded to help Jennings, his former employee whom he trusted, draft a careful bill for Mathias to introduce which stood the test of time when it was copied and re-copied by other legislators.

- 1972—Senator Cranston was stirred into action by the introduction of the Mathias bill (and probably also by the Pettis bill, itself stimulated by Mathias's action) to introduce a Senate bill which largely copied the Mathias bill.

- 1974—While Mathias and Pettis, both Republicans, could get nowhere with their legislation in a House dominated by Democrats, Cranston (a Democrat) got a subcommittee hearing in the Senate.

- 1974—Testimony at the hearing persuaded the subcommittee to recommend that the Senate's much larger FLPMA bill be amended to include Cranston's desert bill.

- 1975—Even though Mathias was defeated for reelection in 1974, Pettis won reelection and the House inserted the Pettis bill in its own version of FLPMA.

- 1976—Whereas a *separate* desert bill might never have become law, being strongly opposed by the Administration, FLPMA was critically needed with or without the allegedly extraneous California desert provisions. With them, it was passed and signed by President Ford.

One final episode in this sequence of events remains to be told. The House champions of desert plan legislation had both left the scene when FLPMA went to Conference Committee. In November 1974, Congressman Mathias lost to a Democrat in his

Shirley Pettis succeeded her husband Jerry, representing California's 37th District; both worked successfully for a California desert plan.

Courtesy of Shirley Pettis Roberson

redrawn district. Congressman Pettis died in a tragic plane crash in February 1975. His wife, Shirley Pettis, took his seat that same year, winning a special primary election so conclusively that no runoff was needed. She was devoted to the passage of FLPMA because it contained the California Desert Plan provisions so dear to her late husband.

A violent disagreement broke out on the Conference Committee in the last hours prior to the scheduled adjournment of Congress in 1976. Congressman Teno Roncalio (Democrat, Wyoming) and Senator George Hansen (Republican, Idaho) were at each other's throats over an issue involving grazing fees. Shirley Pettis was on the House Interior Committee and undertook to try to resolve the dispute, shuttling back and forth between the antagonists.

At last she achieved a compromise. Although the clock was stopped at midnight on October 1, the day of adjournment, the final vote to adopt the Conference Report took place just before 2 A.M. in the morning of the next day, October 2, 1976! On October 2, the *Washington Post* reported that compromise had been achieved by "the lady in red." It was Shirley Pettis.

President Nixon Lends a Hand

To the surprise of many, on February 9, 1972, President Richard Nixon published Executive Order 11644 entitled "Use of Off-Road Vehicles on the Public Lands." The stated purpose of this short and straightforward document was to provide for procedures to control the use of off-road vehicles so as to protect the resources of public lands, promote safety, and minimize conflicts among users. It ordered all agency heads with jurisdiction over public lands to issue regulations designating "specific areas and trails on public lands on which the use of off-road vehicles may be permitted" and areas where such use "may not be permitted" for the general purposes stated but also to "minimize damage to soil, watershed, vegetation and other resources," to "minimize harassment of wildlife or significant disruption of wildlife habitat," and to "minimize conflicts between off-road vehicle use and other existing or proposed recreational uses...taking into account noise and other factors." Agency heads were, "where authorized by law," to prescribe penalties for violation of their regulations and to enforce them. The language of this Executive Order leaped far ahead of anything that had been written or contemplated before its publication. It may have been prepared in response both to the ORVAC Report and to testimony submitted to the Senate subcommittee chaired by Alan Bible (Democrat, Nevada), which had been studying the effects of off-road driving and had held a hearing on the subject in May 1971.

The Nixon order gave agencies six months to issue regulations in accordance with its terms. When six months had elapsed but no action seemed to be pending in the Interior Department, Russ Penny was concerned. His legal officer had advised Penny that he had no authority to issue "letters of authorization" for sizable off-road events in the desert, as he had been doing for the past three years. The action message conveyed by the Nixon order was crystal-clear, as was the authorization to require permits for such events contained in the January 1969 regulation previously referred to, which he had not been following. It was time to switch to permits for off-road events.

In August 1972, Penny published an instruction memo to his District Directors to issue permits for events where more than 25 vehicles were involved, and to include appropriate conditions if deemed desirable.[7] The instructions stated that a permit application could be rejected where its issuance might involve "unacceptable, significant damage to natural, cultural or aesthetic values."

Russ Penny—"The Baron of the Desert"

Immediately, *Cycle News* in its issue of August 22,1972, labeled Russ Penny "baron of the desert," first cousin to the old robber barons of the Rhine River, for his effrontery in requiring permits and charging fees. The *News* trumpeted: "What Penny hopes to do with this tariff treasure is pretty clear from his futile demands on the U.S. Department of Interior the past couple of years. He wants more BLM cops, wants to buy guns for them, wants to raise an army to protect his domain from vandals, hippies and motorcyclists." Within days, the off-road community filed suits against the BLM, seeking unsuccessfully to enjoin all permit requirements.

It was certainly true that Russ Penny had been unable to pry loose significant funding for his desert plan project. The writer from *Cycle News* chose not to mention that Penny had as yet no enforcement authority whatever—one could hardly call any BLM ranger a "cop" in those days. Penny needed help, and the *Cycle News* story gave him the idea to invite the Secretary of Interior, Rogers C.B. Morton, to come to the desert to solemnize the setting aside of the 19 special recreation areas identified in Penny's 1968 desert report, and at the same time to become better acquainted with the problems Penny was encountering. Perhaps the visit would persuade the Secretary to allocate to California a few more dollars from Interior Department funds.

Secretary Morton Relaxes from the Cares of Office and Boosts the Desert Program

Jack Horton, Assistant Secretary for Land Management in the Interior Department, had been a supporter of Penny's efforts and gladly helped to persuade the Secretary to make the trip. A gala party was arranged in May 1972 in El Centro, California, followed by a field trip to the Algodones Dunes in Imperial County, part of which had for years been a favorite ORV playground. Del Vail, then Director of the BLM's Riverside District, recalls picking up BLM personnel, people in local government, and others from all over the state and transporting them to El Centro, along with an Air Force band. The Secretary made a speech. Penny recalls his pleasure hearing the Secretary say: "If we err, we should always err on the side of conservation." If *this* was to be the policy, he could confidently go forward. The Secretary signed a symbolic order, prepared by Penny in advance, withdrawing all land in the 19 special areas—a significant total of over 2.4 million acres—from disposition. At the Algodones Dunes, a local dune buggy owner caught the Secretary's ear for a moment. Without an instant's hesitation, the Secretary hopped into the spectator's classy dune buggy and together they roared off, disappearing over a tall dune. The Secretary had a bit of unscheduled relaxation (or was it terror?) while his coterie of assistants suffered an anxiety crisis. All in all, a very successful party.

The Secretary couldn't promise much in the way of tangible help but was clearly impressed by the program for a Desert Plan. A few extra dollars did come to California in 1973 for an addition to the ranger force, but BLM rangers still had no enforcement powers. Penny got out an attractively printed Visitors' Guide to the newly designated special desert recreation areas. Emboldened by the Secretary's warm comments, he also expanded his Desert Plan staff, absorbing the cost from his budget. Neil Pfulb, Director of Planning for San Bernardino County, a member of

Penny's State Advisory Board, was hired as its chief. Wes Chambers, formerly Director of Planning for The Southern California Association of Governments, became second-in-command. Pfulb and Chambers thought the Pasadena consultants' guidelines on "how to plan" were too cumbersome and, of course, the $28.6 million estimated by the consultants to do the job, was nowhere in sight. But both agreed with Penny on the need to adopt an immediate, interim protective program while a long-term plan remained on the drawing boards. They told Penny, "The thing we need most is an interim off-road vehicle plan. Let's do that and forget the rest for the time being." Penny said, "Go ahead, and get it done fast."

The Growing Threat of Off-Road Vehicles (ORVs)

Chambers recalls that from that point on, he spent every weekend in the desert. They "bled the universities" for data to help decide which areas of the desert should be closed to vehicles, sought to determine which areas already severely damaged should be classified "open," with vehicles in all other areas limited to "designated" or "existing" roads. Known as the "ICMP," the Interim Critical Management Program, it was widely published in draft form, receiving over 18,000 written comments. A final version was ready for Penny to adopt by November 1973. He acted, as he was wont to do, on his own motion.

The ICMP project, though limited in scope, was a huge undertaking for the small staff Penny could deploy, particularly in view of his instruction to complete it swiftly. Perhaps by necessity, perhaps by design, it turned out to be a model of unbureaucratic conciseness. Instead of a wordy, multipage regulation, it consisted of a single large sheet of paper, one side containing a map of the desert with 71 open, closed and restricted areas in different colors, each with a number. On the other side were printed descriptions, by number, of each area along with useful notes. It survived with relatively little change for seven years, until publication of the final California Desert Plan in 1980. The conservation community was not particularly happy with the ICMP. Twelve areas were closed to vehicles, involving only a small portion of what were considered the most sensitive desert lands. Areas open to unrestricted vehicle use amounted to about the same total acreage. Equivalence appeared to be the order of the day.

During the period when the ICMP project had priority in staff time, adequate attention had not been focused on the rapidly growing popularity of off-road desert racing events. It was widely believed that off-road racing, more than any other activity, irretrievably damaged sensitive desert resources. The BLM's District Managers found issuance of the newly authorized permits for such events a troublesome assignment. Permits were often granted without adequate assessment of the likely impact of the event. In 1972 alone, permits were issued for 151 events, drawing an estimated 67,000 participants and 189,000 spectators. Frequently, permits were issued only a few days before the event was to be held.

The conservation community was alarmed. Larry Silver, a senior lawyer for the Sierra Club Legal Defense Fund—later renamed Earthjustice Legal Defense Fund—recalls the frustration of attempting to stop some races with temporary restraining orders on very short notice, with no time to develop evidence sufficient to win the case. Cases were often lost—judges did not like to countermand the administrative interpretation of the law and were put off by the brief notice frequently given the court. On other occasions, however, negotiations with the BLM or a motorcycle club led to beneficial changes in the course of a particular race. (The Legal Defense Fund is a nonprofit legal services organization entirely separate from the Sierra Club, although its origin goes back many years to the original voluntary legal committee of the club, and the club is frequently one of its clients.)

The ultimate frustration for the conservation community lay in the annual Thanksgiving weekend Barstow-Vegas motorcycle race, for which permits had been granted by the BLM in 1972 and 1973. This event had become more popular and more destructive every year after the first race was organized in the latter half of the 1960s. Following the 1973 race, Penny ordered his staff to prepare a full-scale environmental impact statement on the effects of the race. It was a huge undertaking, resulting in a document 450 pages long with close to 100 additional pages of maps and charts. Its findings were ominous. Since it was published barely a month before the 1974 race and because no prior official race-monitoring data had been accumulated, the BLM considered it impossible to reach a decision on the event that year. The 1974 race was monitored by dozens of BLM personnel in order to gather the data necessary for decision. The impacts tabulated by the monitoring report led to denial of permits for the race in 1975 and for the next seven years. We shall encounter Barstow–Vegas again in later chapters.

Penny Passes the Baton

A friendship grew between Secretary Morton and Russ Penny as both approached the end of their years in office. On one occasion, when the Secretary was in the hospital, Penny had a chance to visit him. It was springtime. He asked the Secretary if he could plan to come to the desert to see the flowers. "Can't do it," Morton said, "but my wife Ann would love it." In 1967, a small Desert Lily Sanctuary had been established near Desert Center. In 1972 Secretary Morton had enlarged it, and it was permanently set aside as a Preserve by the California Desert Protection Act at the urging of its long-time proponents, southern Californians Beulah and Tasker Edmiston. Penny, Del Vail, Bill Flint and his staff, and their wives agreed on a spot for a picnic next to the Lily Sanctuary. Russ called on his friend "Pinky" Brier, known throughout the desert as the lady who sported a leather pilot's jacket trimmed with mink, to fly Mrs. Morton to the party in Pinky's single-engine Cessna. She had been a favorite pilot of the writer Erle Stanley Gardner on his expeditions to Baja California to seek "the desert whale." Pinky and Mrs. Morton landed on a dirt road and taxied up to a table in the desert covered with a red-checked cloth, laden with picnic delicacies, and surrounded by lilies in bloom. Mrs. Morton's delighted comment: "You people put on the most unusual party I've ever attended."

During his reign as Director, Penny was known for such dramatic moments. Jack Horton, Assistant Secretary of Interior, had occasion to experience it. Penny once drove Horton out across the East Mojave to Hole-in-the-Wall, an unusual rock structure now a featured attraction of the Mojave Natural Preserve. On the way he commented several times on the numbers of people who lost their way or suffered injury in accidents on rough desert tracks and the urgent need for more rangers to patrol the area. As they rounded a corner near their destination, before them in the middle of the unpaved road was a car upside down with two elderly occupants unable to get out, though neither was seriously hurt. Horton to Penny: "Did you *arrange* that?"

In December 1974 Russ Penny retired. For six months his Assistant Director Jim Ruch was Acting State Director until Edward ("Ed") Hastey took office as State Director in June 1975. At his retirement party, the American Motorcyclist Association presented Penny with a magnificently mounted photo taken at the start of a permitted, competitive race. It showed a burly, bearded motorcyclist giving an "in your face" lecture to the smaller Russ Penny. Another large, burly man stood next to them in the picture, gazing at the ground trying, as it turned out, to suppress his laughter. Unknown to the motorcyclist, the other man was Penny's friend Jack Horton, the Assistant Secretary of the Interior.

Russ Penny was one of the first individuals, inside or outside of government, to recognize the need for protection of the California desert and its urgency. Moreover, he was in a position to act, and he did so. His actions bore strongly upon what was to come. Russ Penny was unique. The BLM could not expect to see his like again.

" Here you may find
the elemental freedom
to breathe deep
of unpoisoned air,
to experiment with
solitude and stillness,
to gaze through
a hundred miles of
untrammeled atmosphere…
to make the discovery of
self in its proud sufficiency
which is not isolation
but an irreplaceable part
of the mystery
of the whole."

—Edward Abbey

BILL HOLDEN
AND
LYLE GASTON

The
Sierra
Club
Becomes
Interested
in the
Desert

CHAPTER TWO

It was the fall

of 1970. Russ Penny, California State Director of the BLM, and his staff had already produced two strong reports on the escalating need to protect sensitive desert resources. Penny had even floated, in supplementary statements written by his staff, the revolutionary idea that there were parts of the desert deserving *wilderness* protection. Penny's Off-Road Vehicle Advisory Council, ORVAC, had recently produced a report containing the equally revolutionary recommendation that in some parts of the desert off-road vehicles should not be allowed.

Bill Holden, founder of the Sierra Club Desert Committee and first of the dedicated desert volunteers.

Courtesy of Bill Holden

Bill Holden was in the office of the Angeles Chapter of the Sierra Club talking with his friend Alan Carlin, who chaired the chapter. Bill, who was on the Chapter's Executive Committee, was annoyed, to put it mildly. He was generally mild-mannered. "What's going on in San Francisco?" he asked. San Francisco was the club's national headquarters. "Last week, the California desert didn't even make the third level of the club's conservation priorities! Maybe we'll have to take this ball into our own hands."

Carlin asked, "What do you propose we do?"

"At least we could form a desert committee down here where there are lots of members who would be interested," said Holden. "I don't mean the usual committee that would meet and pass resolutions, but one committed to a study of issues leading to recommending some action to protect the desert. Would you support that?"

"Go to it," said Carlin.

Bill Holden—
First of the Extraordinary Desert Volunteers

E.B. (Bill) Holden, Jr., came from Michigan, where his great-grandparents were homesteaders. Following the war years he went to the University of Michigan for a degree in industrial engineering. His first love affair was the automobile, and his first jobs were in the great automobile plants of Detroit. After stints with Kaiser-Fraser, Borg-Warner, Ford, and Chrysler he found another interest and obtained a Master's degree in human factors engineering. In 1963 Douglas Aircraft hired him and sent him to its Long Beach, California, plant.

He was a stranger to southern California but not to the outdoor life. He began hiking in the nearby southern California mountains. Observing this, a fellow employee introduced him to the Long Beach Group, a subdivision of the Sierra Club's Angeles Chapter. Its leader was Pauline Hubbard, a public health nurse and enthusiastic hiker and camper. Less than a year later they were married.

It was enough at first to join the short camping excursions that the group sponsored to wild places of notable scenic beauty. But there were those who had their eyes on Bill Holden. He found himself increasingly involved in the conservation mission of the club.

The Long Beach Group was part of the largest Sierra Club chapter in the country. After serving on the Long Beach Group's Management Committee (later as its chairman), Holden was appointed as the Group's Representative to the Angeles Chapter Advisory Council. He then filled a vacancy on the chapter's Conservation Committee, becoming its chairman in 1969. In the same year he became a member of the chapter's Executive Committee. The chapter had its own small paid staff, its own monthly periodical, its own array of committees covering everything from outings to legislation. Conservation activities were coordinated among all chapters in southern California by the Southern California Regional Conservation Committee, known as SCRCC. Such acronyms, the more obscure the better, are favorite methods of shorthand communication among active Sierra Club members. Bill Holden became one of two chapter delegates to SCRCC.

By this time Bill and Pauline Holden had discovered a new world of interest—the desert. He recalls the special pleasures of camping in the desert with their friends Robin and Lori Ives and the intensity with which the latter communicated their belief that the desert needed help to survive without unacceptable damage. Holden learned a great deal more as the club's appointee in 1969 to Russ Penny's Off-Road Vehicle Advisory Committee, widely known as "ORVAC." When he undertook to form a desert committee in 1970, he was ready for a labor of love that would soon take all the energy he had to spare.

The author first met Bill Holden in 1995. Erect and slender with iron gray hair, his appearance belied his 69 years. Recalling his days as a Sierra Club leader seemed to afford him modest relief from the consuming sorrow of his wife Pauline's death only two months before. Pauline Holden had been his constant companion ever since they met in the mid-1960s. Her progressive and increasingly debilitating illness had lasted ten years before it killed her.

The Astonishing Popularity of Desert Study Trips

Holden wanted to expose as many people as possible to the desert through a program of "study trips." One motivating reason was the sheer pleasure of sharing, but another was to focus attention to areas of the desert needing protection. He hoped to develop a constituency for the desert. The committee he chaired, in the technical hierarchy of club committees, was a subcommittee of the SCRCC; thus all southern California chapters of the club were involved and the entire desert was encompassed. It came to be known simply as the Desert Committee.

Holden was familiar with Russ Penny's 1968 desert study report including its recommendation that 19 areas in the southern desert be set aside as "recreation lands." He had personally camped in or near several of them. The BLM could help the committee with an analysis of the process it used in choosing these 19 areas and the committee could then sort out its own priorities. Holden contacted Jack Wilson, Manager of the BLM's Riverside District, and asked for more detailed information. Wilson immediately offered to have his people personally go out with Holden's new committee to show them the 19 areas and anything else which interested them. The man he delegated to do this was Bill Flint, Riverside District Public Information Officer. A few months later, preparing his first Desert Committee Report, Holden wrote:

> *I suppose my exposure to civil servants is only somewhat greater than average, but I have to say I've never run into a civil service employee like Bill Flint. He has approached the problem of the California desert with all the dedication of a Sierra Club volunteer. I'm not saying he's an "every flower" person, but he fully reflects the concern of Russ Penny and Jack Wilson for the California desert.*

The first study trip took place in March 1971. It did not start auspiciously. As Holden described it, "We left the coast in weather more suited to scuba gear and by 11 a.m. were standing in snow. By 4 p.m. we were in a sandstorm on the way to Palm Desert." But at the campfire that evening in the Mecca Hills, now a wilderness area, enthusiasm for the study trip concept began to flower. Bill Flint was there with desert stories. Bill Holden had asked Lyle Gaston to be co-leader. A long-time explorer of the desert, Gaston was a fountain of information. Benjamin and Miriam Romero of Montrose, California, were among the participants in this first study trip and volunteered that night to write to more than 100 of their friends soliciting their help in identifying areas that needed protection. A month later, when the second trip took place, attendance had doubled to 40.

An important feature of the study trips program was the identification of leaders for future trips. Holden and Gaston together led the first four trips in March, April, and May of 1971, each attended by Bill Flint. During the hot summer, trips were not scheduled but scouting work continued to identify routes, campsites, potential hikes, prehistoric Indian sites, damage that needed to be observed. By the time the trips resumed in October 1971, more than 35 new leaders had been recruited and trips were scheduled almost every weekend. Twenty-five trips to different desert destinations took place in the first year. Almost the same pace was kept up in the years that followed; for example, a total of 69 trips had taken place before the end of June 1973. When the total reached 235 in the 1980s, the Desert Committee ceased counting. Holden reports that Bill Flint or one of the BLM area managers usually came along, more often than not accompanying the trip members on his own time.

Holden was a tireless organizer and indefatigable advocate for the California desert. He wrote numerous articles on the Desert Committee's work, he and Gaston developed a planning guide for trip leaders, and he corresponded with dozens of people interested in desert study and advocacy. He wrote to Congress urging support for Russ Penny's desert plan project and for granting the BLM enforcement authority, as recommended by ORVAC. He asked committee members to write in support of the Mathias bill. In 1974 he testified before the Subcommittee on Public Lands of the House of Representatives. He urged his trip leaders to write reports of their findings so he could pass on useful data to Flint and Wilson.

One such report, on the natural resource values of the Amargosa River Gorge, was a remarkable and influential piece of work, and has since become a collector's item. Miriam Romero, with her husband Ben, led a study trip to the Amargosa River Canyon in October 1971. The historic Tonopah and Tidewater (T & T) Railroad, built in 1907 to carry gold ore from Nevada mines to a junction with the Southern Pacific in the Mojave Desert, once traversed the Canyon, and Ben had once been a member of a T&T construction crew. Miriam fell in love with the area—an "island" in the desert with an isolated, year-round stream flowing between colorful, strikingly eroded canyon walls and inhabited by rare desert pupfish, survivors of the ice age. The stream ultimately reaches the southern end of Death Valley, where it disappears.

Starting with a survey of the pupfish, Miriam began to seek scientific assistance for preparation of a detailed report on the area's natural values and the need to preserve them from further vandalism and vehicle damage. Her efforts came none too soon—the BLM was reported to be considering opening up the Gorge to off-road vehicles. Miriam organized "The Desert Pupfish Habitat Preservation Committee." Members of the committee made at least five scheduled trips to the area, and individual scientists conducted additional surveys. The result was a 126-page printed report dated May 10, 1972, including many photographs and an extensive appendix. Letters of support from scientists, professors and others were included. The text featured extensive data on soils, water quality, geology, archaeology, history, paleontology, plants, fishes, birds, mammals, reptiles and amphibians. More than 30 scientists contributed the results of their work in these areas. The water in the stream turned out to contain a high concentration of fluorides, sulfates and chlorides but was still critical to plant, animal, and bird life. The report urged the BLM to set the area aside as a protected "natural area" as authorized by the Bureau's own manual. Assisted by Bill Holden, Miriam collected donations from over 100 people and organizations to finance publication of her report.

Russ Penny brought together representatives of the BLM's Bakersfield and Riverside offices for a formal presentation of Miriam's report in June 1972. It was wholly successful. No further consideration was given to allowing ORVs in the Gorge. The next year's "ICMP" (the Bureau's Interim Critical Management Program) officially closed the area to ORV travel. The description of the area in the ICMP highlighted "Outstanding natural values, rare and endangered wildlife, colorful canyon scenery,... rich historic and archaeological values—all sensitive to damage by vehicles."

Predictably, the off-roaders quickly ripped off the BLM's signs. The BLM had not yet acquired any enforcement authority. However, although the extent of privately held land in the area was thought to prevent its consideration for wilderness designation, the area was made an "Area of Critical Environmental Concern" (ACEC) in the BLM's 1980 California Desert Plan. Subsequently, Wells Fargo Bank acquired through foreclosure 10,000 acres of the ACEC. Later the bank donated the land to the California Nature Conservancy. This combination of actions gives reasonable assurance that the pleasures of discovery, once enjoyed by Miriam Romero and those she called on to assist her, will continue to be shared by those who seek out the Amargosa River Gorge today.

In March 1972, with the first 25 study trips completed, Holden, with help from Gaston, put together a "Desert Symposium" held on Gaston's campus at the University of California-Riverside. The committee held at least two more such symposia in subsequent years. Each trip leader was encouraged to use a room with a projector to show slides of and talk about his or her chosen area of the desert. The first symposium attracted more than 250 participants including many representatives of the BLM. Jim Dodson, an early study trip leader, had led his group to the Cima Dome area in the East Mojave. In his slide show he used many slides he had taken of the radiantly blooming Joshua Tree forest on the Dome. He recalls explaining to the audience that there appear to be two species of Joshua Tree in the Eastern Mojave Desert, the "Jaeger" variety on the Cima Dome which he had photographed and a more common variety found elsewhere, but he wasn't sure of the differences between them. An older man in the back of the room spoke up: "The one you photographed is generally shorter and branches bilaterally closer to the ground." At the end of the show Dodson asked who it was who had spoken. It turned out to be Dr. Edmund Jaeger—himself the preeminent authority on California desert plants and wildlife. He told Dodson he believed that the blossoming of the Joshua Trees and other desert plants that spring had been the finest seen in 50 years.

By this time it had become a major objective of the study trips to identify areas the committee believed needed special protection—areas which might have been missed by the BLM's initial surveys—and to call them to the attention of the BLM. In addition, through the medium of the study trips, hundreds of people discovered the desert for the first time, learned to love it, and were ready to help when the time came for action to insure its protection.

Lyle Gaston—A Scientist-Outdoorsman Heads the Desert Committee

By 1974 Bill Holden had turned over many aspects of the committee's work to Lyle Gaston, and now Gaston agreed to succeed him as its chair. The timing was fortunate; early in 1974, a sizable layoff of engineers occurred at the Long Beach plant of Douglas Aircraft and Holden was caught by it. He had to retool himself. He enrolled in California State Polytechnic University, Pomona to obtain a Master's degree in Urban Planning. By early 1976 he had undertaken a demanding new job at North American Rockwell's El Segundo plant. During the remainder of the '70s, Holden stayed much involved but could not keep up his former pace. He later served as a conservation appointee on two BLM Desert Advisory Councils, one in the late '70s and the second following completion of the California Desert Plan in the early '80s.

Lyle Gaston, chair of the Sierra Club's Desert Committee and an apostle of the need to "experience" the desert.

Courtesy of Lynne Foster

Meanwhile, Gaston, the Desert Committee's new chair, was persuading more and more of his fellow academics and scientists to consider what should be recommended to improve management and protection of the desert. This began a process that ultimately resulted, a decade and a half later, in more than 1,600 scientists and educators endorsing the California Desert Protection Act.

Lyle Gaston grew up in a small town in Iowa. He recalls the hard times before World War II when the younger members of his family worked the acre or so of land adjacent to their home to produce all of the family's food. During summers when he was still in high school, he roamed the hill country on foot and cut wood for winter on timberland owned by his grandparents.

Like Bill Holden, Gaston was a confirmed outdoorsman when he first reached California in the mid 1950s, following graduation from Iowa State, to enroll at University of California, Los Angeles for post-graduate study in chemistry. This was followed by post-doctoral study at the University of Colorado, Boulder, and a return to California to accept a job as Assistant Research Chemist at the University of California, Riverside. Soon promoted to Research Chemist, with a sidelight as lecturer in entomology, he remained at U.C. Riverside until his retirement in 1993.

A new field of chemistry was opening up in the late 1950s. It was stimulated by the assertion of the Dean of the College of Agriculture at U.C. Riverside, an entomologist, that "there's lots of chemistry going on in bugs." Gaston, his assistants, and a group of University biologists were able to isolate the chemical used by male cotton-boring insects to attract females. Suppress its production by the male insect and you make unnecessary the poisonous pesticides previously used by cotton growers to protect their crops. But, says Gaston resignedly, farmers are notoriously set in their ways and it was hard to induce them to give up pesticides and try something new.

To ease his frustrations over stubborn farmers and faculty politics, Gaston climbed the mountains of California with the Sierra Peaks section of the Sierra Club's Angeles Chapter. To keep in shape for the Sierra in summer he had to find somewhere to climb in winter. He discovered more than enough mountains in the California desert for this purpose. He also found that many of his fellow faculty members, especially the biologists, were using the desert as a laboratory, studying along with their graduate students the many biological feats of desert plants and animals. He joined his colleagues and acquired a background of desert lore and science that made him an ideal successor to Bill Holden as head of the Desert Committee.

Gaston's Wide Ranging Contributions

In 1975 the National Park Service was attempting to finish its required Wilderness Act inventory of recommended wilderness areas in national parks and monuments for transmittal to the

President and Congress. The Superintendent of Joshua Tree National Monument had recommended a bare one-third of the Monument's area for designation as wilderness. Gaston, who considered this abysmally small, had his San Gorgonio Chapter of the Sierra Club send him back to testify before the House Committee with jurisdiction over national parks and monuments. No one from the staff of Joshua Tree National Monument showed up at the hearing, and the representative of the Washington office of the National Park Service hardly knew where Joshua Tree National Monument was. As a result, the committee—and the Congress in 1976—accepted Gaston's carefully reasoned proposal that 80% of the Monument be made wilderness. Not quite two decades later, in 1994, Congress followed this precedent by designating an even larger percentage of the new Death Valley National Park as wilderness. In both instances, roads were left open between wilderness areas that provided ample access for the visiting public to almost all popular sites in both parks.

Gaston also went back to Washington several times to try to persuade the BLM that it did not have enough base-line information on desert lands to manage them effectively. Not surprisingly, as a scientist he wished to promote good scientific research. The BLM, he suggested, should designate appropriate lands, which he had in mind, for university research stations, to be managed by the University of California's Natural Lands Committee. Thus the Granite Mountains Research Station in the East Mojave, managed by the university, came into being. Not to be outdone, a group of institutions in the California State University system sought a location for their Desert Studies Center. In 1976 they formed it at Soda Springs in the Mojave, former site of "Zzyzx," a health and self-improvement resort with a 60-room hotel operated by the colorful and exuberant Curtis "Doc" Springer for several decades before the BLM evicted him in 1974. Doc had unfortunately attended to higher things and not to the technical rules pertaining to public land use.

In the mid-1970s, Gaston carried word to the BLM that it had to control an increasing population of feral burros which were damaging the scarce water sources available to wildlife in the desert.

He thought the fact that the burros were an annoyance to grazing cattle would help to attract the BLM's attention. The answer of the Sacramento office was: "Sorry, we have no money." But Jack Horton, Assistant Secretary of Interior, directed the BLM to control the burros. The Agency has been attempting to do so ever since, with mixed results.

Although always on the best of terms with his good friends Jack Wilson and Bill Flint, when it came to the BLM's failure to enforce its own regulations Gaston could be sardonic, even caustic. As quoted in the *Los Angeles Times* on March 2, 1975:

> The BLM may be doing a good job keeping vehicles off the vertical cliffs of the Turtle and Whipple Mountains, but in other areas they [the ORVs] are going all over the place. [The Bureau] has not tried to enforce its Interim Critical Management Plan even when it knew it was going to be violated.

One must remember that this comment was made somewhat more than a year before Congress finally gave the BLM the basic authority to enforce its own rules.

Both Lyle Gaston and Bill Holden had long been active and involved with an active and vigilant organization of scientists and other friends of the desert. This was the Desert Protective Council, Inc., founded originally in 1954 for the purpose of protecting Joshua Tree National Monument from political interests seeking to reduce its size. It is still going strong. Gaston became its president, Holden its treasurer, later succeeded in that office by Gaston who guarded DPC's finances for many years. Among the many younger trip leaders they discovered and pressed into service during their years as early chairs of the Desert Committee were Jim Dodson and Judy Anderson, both of whom were to play major roles in the fight to protect the California desert. But the most significant such discovery in Gaston's life was Lynne Foster, whom he met on a Desert Protective Council work party.

In 1984 Jim Dodson felt a pressing need for a detailed guidebook to the desert lands he cherished. He had no time to write it but urged Lynne to do so, agreeing to review the text for accuracy and otherwise help all he could. Jim and Lynne generated the outline of the book together. Then Jim sped off "to continue his commitment to overcommitment," as Lynne put it. For a couple of years Lyle drove Lynne everywhere, to places she knew casually and to others she had not seen, while she scribbled notes. Thus came into being *Adventuring in the California Desert*. Published in 1987, it is an essential volume for travelers who seek to explore distant corners of the desert. It is a mystery how Lynne Foster and Lyle Gaston managed to reach them all.

Years later Jim Dodson was to say there were two people, in particular, without whom he could never have become an effective desert advocate—Bill Holden and Lyle Gaston. "They were the ones" he said, "who taught us the single, most important thing of all—to get out and experience the desert."

"Wilderness is a vital part
of the American heritage.
From the days of
Daniel Boone
to the early Sierra crossings
by Jedediah Smith
and Kit Carson,
the tradition of wild,
undeveloped lands
runs strong in our blood."

—Norman Livermore, Jr.

FLPMA

A Promising New Wilderness Law Takes Shape

CHAPTER THREE

A remarkable and fortunate

series of events caused Congress to include provisions applicable *only* to the California desert in the Federal Land Policy and Management Act of 1976 (FLPMA). These provisions mandated a study of the desert's resources and preparation of a plan for its management by September 30, 1980. Included was authorization of essential funds for such a project. Miraculously, the funds provision grew from the original $28.6 million in Congressman Mathias's bill of 1971 to $40 million in FLPMA. Although no one could have guessed it at the time, the funding and completion of the California Desert Plan in 1980 was critical to the ultimate passage of a California Desert Protection Act.

The BLM Gets Authority to Study Wilderness

Another aspect of FLPMA that was critical to the future of the California desert was the first explicit requirement for the Bureau of Land Management to inventory lands possessing wilderness characteristics, defined in the Wilderness Act of 1964, and to recommend to Congress areas to be designated as wilderness.

How this came about is a subtle, complex and immensely important story.

The Federal Land Policy and Management Act grew out of the landmark report of the Public Land Law Review Commission, (PLLRC), established by Congressional action in 1964. The Commission took six years to complete its task, finally publishing its report entitled *One Third of the Nation's Land* in 1970.[8] Its first major recommendation was to reverse existing policy that the nation sell off its unappropriated public land. The report concluded that only public land that could "achieve maximum benefit for the general public in non-Federal ownership" should be sold, and added that most public lands wouldn't achieve such benefit if taken out of public ownership. Secondly, it recommended that all Federal land management agencies should engage in land use planning, which would recognize all of the values of the public lands and, where necessary, impose environmental controls on permitted uses.

The report's recommendations validated Russ Penny's desert initiatives of the late 1960s. Even though the BLM had been left out of the Wilderness Act, the Commission urged the BLM to inventory and review all its lands for wilderness characteristics and potential designation as wilderness. The report went ever further and implied that the BLM needed no additional authority to make wilderness *recommendations* on its own, although actual *designation* of land as wilderness was a matter solely for Congress. Thinking along these same lines, Penny had told directors of the Desert Protective Council in the late 1960s that he thought the BLM should propose areas in the California desert for designation as wilderness. He added that he hoped the Turtle Mountains in the eastern Mojave would be first on the list. He spoke too soon. When he broached this idea to his colleagues in the BLM's Washington office he was promptly turned down. More than likely, the bureaucrats in Foggy Bottom wondered what sort of a wild card they had on the West Coast.

The PLLRC report published in 1970 took six years to write, and it took another six years for its major recommendations to be embodied in law. Many finally realized that the BLM needed to be given a clear mission by Congress. An "organic act," as it came to be called, would specify management responsibilities and order land use inventory and planning processes. It would also provide for rule-making and enforcement authority. The act would incorporate or repeal literally hundreds of laws dealing with the public lands which, in the words of Representative John Saylor (Republican, Pennsylvania), "had accumulated like a tangled web of yarn for over a century."

In both Houses, bills to this end were introduced shortly before and immediately after publication of the PLLRC report in 1970.9 It was 1971, however, before the key bills that triggered serious committee work were introduced. Although these bills died at the close of the 93rd Congress in 1972, new bills were introduced in 1973, and this time the Senate moved the process forward, passing its bill in 1974. But the House failed to act and the

Senate bill died. Another new Congress opened, new bills were introduced in 1975, and both Houses passed their bills in 1976. FLPMA was at last near to adoption.

Throughout those years Congressional Committee work was in progress. On the issue of wilderness recommendations for BLM lands, it was clear that the implied authority noted in the PLL75RC report was not enough. It was important for Congress to give specific direction to the BLM for at least three reasons. First, the review of BLM lands for wilderness shouldn't be entirely at the discretion of the BLM, whose old-timers would be reluctant to act. Second, a deadline was needed for the review and the Secretary's recommendation to the President. Third, the process needed the political backing of both Houses of Congress. By 1974, in a meager response to the urgings of the Wilderness Society, the Senate included in its bill a short provision on wilderness inventory calling for identification of roadless areas with wilderness characteristics within five years. It omitted, however, both a deadline for recommendations to go to Congress and any provision for interim protection of those areas while the Department of Interior, the President and the Congress were reviewing the matter. The entire review process could, of course, take many years. The Senate Committee report implied that while this process was in progress, the committee did not want the BLM barred from considering and permitting new uses of roadless lands it had previously identified as potential wilderness! The House bills for a BLM organic act in the early 1970s contained nothing about wilderness.

Harry Crandell and the Wilderness Society Gain an Unusual Ally

Early in 1973 Harry Crandell, Director of Wilderness Review for the Wilderness Society, set up a meeting of the society's leaders with the new chair of the House Subcommittee on Public Lands, the respected Congressman John Melcher (Democrat, Montana). Crandell asked for Melcher's support for a wilderness review provision in the next House bill. "You don't need that," Crandell recalls Melcher saying. The Congressman told Crandell he envisioned a long series of hearings on the bill throughout the Western states, starting in August 1973. Crandell planned accordingly. First, he listed all key members of the society and others he knew who were active in different conservation organizations—more than 100 in all. Then he called each one, told them about the hearing schedule, and asked them to request to testify at the hearing closest to home. Crandell suggested that the testimony contain, in their own words, the message that without wilderness review provisions, they could not support the organic act.

Harry Crandell, organizer of the outpouring of public testimony that brought wilderness review of BLM lands into FLPMA.

Courtesy of Harry Crandell

Chairman Melcher was nothing if not conscientious. Hearings were held between August 1973 and April 11, 1975, in Montana, Colorado, Nevada, New Mexico, Oregon, Utah, California, and Washington, D.C.

Dozens wrote to the subcommittee and dozens of others asked to testify and did so. These included Bill Holden, Lyle Gaston, and Representatives Mathias and Pettis, authors of the pending House bills on the California desert that they wanted added to FLPMA. The Administration was unmoved. The Secretary of the Interior himself was deputized to come to a hearing and assert the Administration's position against granting wilderness review authority to the BLM. The BLM, he argued, already had in place a program to establish "primitive areas" on its lands. Apparently, the Administration feared that if wilderness review became a contentious issue, it might delay passage of FLPMA. By the close of his hearings, however, Chairman Melcher had been won over by the outpouring of citizen sentiment. He called Crandell, saying, "Harry, we're going to have a wilderness review provision in the bill. Will you help me draft something like the one [in the Wilderness Act] used by the Forest Service?"

Crandell immediately set to work with Charles Clusen, his friend in the Washington, D.C., office of the Sierra Club who had labored hard for the passage of FLPMA. Together, working with the subcommittee staff, they adapted key elements of the Wilderness Act to construct a single, compact section to be included in the House bill, incorporating its definition of "wilderness" by reference. The section differed significantly from the provision in the pending Senate bill by setting a 15-year deadline to complete both the wilderness review and the report of the Interior Secretary to the President, after which it directed the President to advise Congress of his recommendation within two years. During the wilderness review, all wilderness study areas (WSAs)— inventoried roadless areas 5,000 acres or larger with wilderness characteristics—should be managed by the BLM to protect them against damage that would preclude their later preservation as wilderness. The requirement was intended not only to ensure that WSAs would be cared for while awaiting the President's recommendations, but also that Congress would retain its option to create an unspoiled wilderness area out of a WSA with or without the recommendation of the Interior Secretary or the President.

With only minor changes, the House subcommittee, already familiar with the Wilderness Act from previously approved Forest Service wilderness bills, quickly approved this carefully crafted piece of legislative draftsmanship. The bill was backed by the full committee and passed the House in 1976. The appointed chair of the Conference Committee was none other than the wilderness review provision's new champion, John Melcher. He persuaded the committee to adopt the House version, not the weak provision in the Senate bill, before the Conference Report came to a vote. Thus FLPMA came into being.

BLM Begins Its First Wilderness Study Under Pressure of a Deadline

The wilderness review provision in FLPMA, Section 603, wasted no words and was less than a page in length.[10] Harry Crandell knew the Congressmen on the committee would find it easier to pass a provision that was as short as possible. The age-old conflict between brevity and clarity was once again settled in favor of brevity—they did what was necessary to get the statute enacted. After enactment, the Secretary of Interior laid the statute in the lap of the Solicitor of the Interior Department for his opinion on what it meant. The Solicitor labored two and a half years to finish his response. It was a 35-page legal opinion that bravely attempted to chart a course for BLM managers to follow when they

- Inventoried potential wilderness areas which possessed the necessary wilderness characteristics to become WSAs;

- determined the "suitability or unsuitability" of WSAs for designation as wilderness as the basis for a Presidential recommendation; and

- managed WSAs pending the President's recommendation to Congress and thereafter pending final Congressional action. [11]

The California BLM's Desert District decided it couldn't wait for the Solicitor's opinion. Under intense pressure to complete the comprehensive California Desert Plan mandated by FLPMA by the deadline of October 1, 1980, its first priority was to expand the existing Desert Plan staff, originally established on a shoestring by Russ Penny in 1968. Professional recreation planners, biologists, geologists, botanists, engineers, and other specialists were hired from the outside. Less specialized workers were hired on a temporary basis and all went to work on the Desert Plan. Under Section 603, the Interior Secretary had to make wilderness recommendations to the President by September 30, 1991, so the only statutory deadline for the wilderness review was almost 15 years away. Could not this wilderness business be postponed while the Desert Plan was put together? No other states rushed into their wilderness inventories— they were content to accomplish this task with deliberation, using permanent staff when they could spare the time. However, examination of California desert lands for wilderness characteristics was of a piece with the required study of their other characteristics and resources. This study had already begun under a tight deadline.

The only practical thing to do was to give the combined task to the new Desert Plan staff. The "inventory" and "study" phases of the wilderness review were completed with remarkable speed by the end of March 1979, listing 138 WSAs.[12] Now, the question was: What should be done with them?

Can Wilderness Study Areas (WSAs) Be Adequately Protected?

In December 1979, the BLM published "IMP," the Interim Management Policy and Guidelines for Lands Under Wilderness Review, following as best it could the legal analysis of the Interior Department Solicitor's February opinion. Until Congressional determination of their ultimate fate, WSAs under FLPMA were to be managed "so as not to impair the suitability of such areas for preservation as wilderness." This "nonimpairment standard" was a crucial element in the statute. There was an important statutory exception: Nonimpairment was "subject to the continuation of existing mining and grazing uses and mineral leasing in the manner and degree in which the same was being conducted" on the date of FLPMA's enactment. These became known as grandfathered uses. However, the statute also stated that the Secretary of the Interior "shall take any action required to prevent unnecessary or undue degradation" of, or "to afford environmental protection" to, *all* public lands, whether or not grandfathered uses of such lands were involved.

Finally, in interpreting the nonimpairment standard, it would be necessary to take into account another section of FLPMA, Section 701(h), which stated: "All actions of the Secretary concerned under the Act shall be subject to valid existing rights."

The Solicitor and the BLM declined to interpret the nonimpairment standard to mean that WSAs must be left in a completely primitive state. After all, the BLM's basic mission was to foster "multiple use" of its lands, and that must mean that various uses could be made of the WSAs during the "study phase" so long as they might be classified as "nonimpairing." The IMP established the following criteria for a "nonimpairing use":

- It must be temporary, and easily terminated if Congress should declare the area wilderness.

- It must "be capable of being reclaimed to a condition substantially unnoticeable in the WSA as a whole by the time the Secretary of the Interior is scheduled to send his recommendations on that area to the President.

- When the activity is ended, and after reclamation is complete, the area's wilderness value "must not have been degraded so far, compared to the area's values for other purposes, as to significantly constrain the Secretary's recommendation with respect to the area's suitability or nonsuitability for preservation as wilderness."[13]

The IMP did not attempt to define the statutory word "suitability." It would take an extended analysis to develop useful criteria to determine "suitability" for wilderness, including a means of ranking all of the values involved. No one has attempted it successfully.

As might be imagined, these provisions and other parts of the IMP, replete with the sort of language that gives lawyers a steady income, were a fountain of controversy in the years that followed. The IMP underwent at least one substantial revision and some of its provisions were amplified in separately published regulations. Many significant cases, law review articles and much Congressional testimony over the years commended or criticized the IMP and its implementation by the BLM. Suffice it to say, for the time being, a mandate for a wilderness review process had been given the BLM which was highly promising. For the *California* desert, by good fortune, this process acquired the same deadline (1980) as the California Desert Plan. Finally, thanks to thoughtful draftsmanship by Harry Crandell and Chuck Clusen and to Crandell's political skills, lands found to have wilderness characteristics *would* be protected, albeit imperfectly, until Congress acted. The hopes of the conservation community for the California desert took a long step forward.

"All men dream:
but not equally.
Those who dream by night
in the dusty recesses of their minds
wake in the day to find
that it was vanity:
but the dreamers of the day
are dangerous men,
for they may act their dream
with open eyes,
to make it possible."

—T. E. Lawrence

PETER AND
JOYCE BURK

The
Vision of
a Mojave
National
Park

CHAPTER FOUR

It was the evening

of the 4th of July, 1976. Peter and Joyce Burk were on one of their regular after-dinner walks through the residential area of their hometown, Barstow, California. "Joyce, we should do something to celebrate the Bicentennial," Burk commented to his wife. "What about a project right here in our own backyard? We might even go for broke, like proposing a national park in the Mojave Desert." Joyce Burk did not always agree with Peter's ideas. He liked to say that "ideas are the most important forces in history," and he was not one to keep his ideas and opinions to himself. But she liked this one. Both were idealists and America's Bicentennial had touched a patriotic nerve. Why shouldn't something big be proposed in its honor? Something like a major national park in the area that had enchanted both of them? Maybe someone had previously suggested a Mojave National Park, but neither of them thought so.

This story sounds almost too pat, but to those who know the Burks it rings true. All signs point to the fact that on that balmy desert evening on Independence Day, the idea of a Mojave National Park was born. It was to engulf their lives for the next 18 years.

Peter W. Burk was born in 1945 in Santa Barbara County but grew up in Redlands, California, under the shadow of Old Greyback—called Mt. San Gorgonio by the Spanish—largest mountain in southern California. He met Joyce Brady at the University of Redlands. A year after he graduated in 1967 *and* after Peter had found that Joyce truly enjoyed climbing Old Greyback with him, they were married. Joyce began her career as an elementary school teacher in nearby Rialto. Peter got his Master's degree in history at the University of California, Riverside, and in 1969 began teaching high school in San Bernardino. It took Burk a year to conclude that he was not cut out to be a teacher.

The Desert Beckons the Burks

In 1972 the Burks moved to Barstow, hub town of the Mojave Desert. Very tall, strong-voiced, unpolished, Peter has always had the appearance of a man thoroughly at home in rough country.

In Barstow, Peter was first a social worker for San Bernardino County and then tried other lines of work. In 1978 he found his ideal as librarian for Silver Valley High School in Yermo, a "desert mile" from Barstow. By this time Joyce was settled into her career at the Victorville branch of the San Bernardino County Library.

Conservation of wildlands—mountains and forest at first—had always been important to the Burks. In 1973 they both joined the Sierra Club's San Gorgonio Chapter and became active in its Mojave Group. Having discovered the desert around them, they found Barstow an ideal take-off point for exploration, joining desert study trips sponsored by the Desert Committee, trips organized by the Mojave Group, and other expeditions. More often than not they explored on their own. They soon discovered that a pie slice of the Mojave Desert, beginning east of Barstow and reaching almost to the border of Nevada between Highways I-15 and I-40, offered a treasure trove of natural wonders. By 1975 Burk was on the Executive Committee of the chapter. Later in the year he became chapter delegate to the club's Southern California Regional Conservation Committee, the SCRCC. Thus, in the early fall of 1976, he and Joyce knew where to find supporters for their new conception—the idea of a Mojave National Park. They outlined it on a single piece of paper with a rough-sketch map enclosing about 1.2 million acres.

Their Mojave Group was the first organization to sign up. A month later the San Gorgonio Chapter of the club endorsed the project. The next month the SCRCC resolved to support the proposal in principle and authorized creation of a Mojave National Park Task Force. An article on the proposal soon appeared in *Wilderness Record*, the periodical of the influential California Wilderness Coalition. It seemed to be an idea whose time had come. Why not organize a coalition for a Mojave National Park?

Citizens for Mojave National Park

While these first steps were being taken in Barstow, the Federal Land Policy Management Act (FLPMA) became law. It included special provisions mandating a California Desert Plan and authorized funds to complete the plan by a September 1980 deadline. As noted in Chapter Three, this was what Russ Penny of the BLM, Congressmen Mathias and Pettis, and Senator Cranston had all sought. Approached

Peter and Joyce Burk with Senator Cranston—the Burks were founders of "Citizens for Mojave National Park" in 1976.

Courtesy of Peter Burk

by Burk, Cranston said he considered the Mojave National Park idea premature until the Desert Plan was finished. The Desert Plan was going to take a while. But the idea of an organization devoted solely to a national park in the Mojave, without the distraction of any other conservation issues, appealed to Peter and Joyce. A new membership body, "Citizens for Mojave National Park," was formed in March 1977. It immediately began a publishing program which ultimately produced more than 30 booklets written by Burk, all dealing with aspects of the proposed park. The Desert Protective Council, along with other groups and individuals, provided early financial assistance.

Later in 1977 Burk asked several people to help him determine more specifically what the boundaries of the proposed national park should be. One of these was Lyle Gaston, then chair of the Desert Committee. Gaston was not especially taken with Burk's idea. He thought it might be better to take part of the East Mojave Desert and make it a separate section of Joshua Tree National Monument, thereby protecting it more swiftly since a national monument could be enlarged by Presidential action alone. But Burk wanted his opinion of the boundary for a new national park. Gaston took out an old Auto Club of Southern California map of San Bernardino County, spread it out on the hood of his Bronco, and started marking lines. Burk's main problem was what to do with the Lanfair Valley, a large desert valley east of the New York Mountains. Gaston said if you're going to have a park, it would be best to include that valley so as to eliminate the large "bite" which would otherwise be taken from the middle of the proposed park's eastern portion. Burk considered Gaston's suggestion and adopted it. That decision resulted in a 1.5 million-acre park proposal, larger than the 1.2 million-acre park originally sketched out by Burk. Its approximate boundary was identical to the one later adopted in the 1980 BLM California Desert Plan as the boundary of its East Mojave National Scenic Area and still later as the boundary of the proposed Mojave National Park in Senator Cranston's 1986 Senate bill. With only a few modest changes, it became the boundary of the new Mojave National Preserve in 1994.

Although put off by Senator Cranston for the time being, Burk overcame any shyness he might have felt in lobbying politicians by attending a March 1977 Sierra Club political action training workshop in Washington, D.C. Henceforth he passed up few opportunities to talk with members of Congress and their staffs about the proposed park. In the spring of 1978 he, Joyce, and two others persuaded San Bernardino Congressman George Brown (Democrat, California) to introduce a bill for the park in the House of Representatives. H.R. 4461 was a "bare bones" bill and no hearings were in prospect. However, it gave credibility to their efforts. A year later, in the new 98th Congress, Brown introduced the same bill a second time.

The BLM Rejects the Mojave Park Proposal Supported by Its Staff

The BLM Desert Plan staff, engaged in the complex of desert studies set in motion by the passage of FLPMA in 1976, became aware of the growing interest stimulated by the Burks in the idea of a Mojave National Park. So did the National Park Service. In September 1978, the BLM staff agreed to conduct a special study for the Park Service of lands in the desert that might possess national park quality. The conclusion of that study, transmitted by the BLM to the Park Service in June 1979, was that "the cultural and natural resource values of the East Mojave Study Area are so diverse and outstanding that the area readily qualifies for national park or monument status."14

This put the BLM in an uncomfortable position. If that conclusion were followed it would transfer 1.5 million acres of prime BLM turf to another agency, the Park Service, and there is nothing a governmental entity hates more than the loss of its turf. However, it could not be ignored. In a massive February 1980 "Draft of [Desert] Plan Alternatives and Environmental Impact Statement," the BLM listed the idea of a Mojave National Park as a "protection subalternative," whatever that might be, adding that an initial evaluation by the study staff showed the East Mojave area met all the criteria used by the Park Service to assess a potential new park. The Draft Environmental Impact Statement (EIS) stated, however, that "additional studies would be necessary to determine whether transfer of management would be feasible." In that sentence one could read the handwriting on the wall. Within the BLM, opinion quickly crystallized against the park idea despite many letters that had come in favoring the park alternative. Seven months after the February 1980 Draft EIS, a "Final Environmental Impact Statement and Proposed Plan" appeared. It rejected the park as part of the proposal Desert Plan and stated, in support of that determination, that the East Mojave "contains a wide spectrum of resources, including significant minerals, grazing lands and other socioeconomic values as well as superb scenery, cultural and natural values. This diversity…could be most effectively managed through a mix of Class L [limited] and Class C [controlled] lands" by the BLM, which could provide "the balance of protection and use prescribed by FLPMA." As adopted at the end of 1980, the final Desert Plan fails to mention that consideration had ever been given to a Mojave National Park. At the last moment, however, at the behest of the BLM and possibly in an attempt to leave the entire East Mojave as BLM turf while tossing a bone to the conservation community, Secretary of the Interior Cecil Andrus inserted in the plan a short statement designating the East Mojave a "National Scenic Area" and stating that a management philosophy for the area would be developed at some later date. The BLM giant won that round against the minuscule Citizens for Mojave National Park, but the Desert Plan staff's study, supporting a national park in the East Mojave, was destined to play an important role in the coming Desert Bill campaign.

In 1979, shortly before the Desert Plan was completed, Burk became chair of the SCRCC for a two-year term. Early in 1980 he appointed Jim Dodson, who also lived in the Mojave Desert, chair of the Desert Committee, replacing Lyle Gaston who had served for the previous six years. It was a significant move in the fight for desert parks and wilderness.

Burk had become thoroughly disillusioned with the BLM by the time the Desert Plan was completed. Not only had it summarily rejected his park proposal but it had omitted from its Desert Plan as "suitable" for wilderness designation such highlights of the East Mojave as the New York, Woods and Table Mountains, Cima Dome, Clark Mountain, and the Mid Hills. He tried unsuccessfully to organize a California Desert Alliance, headquartered in Barstow. But Citizens for Mojave National Park continued to thrive, sponsoring trips into the East Mojave, showing its East Mojave slide show to diverse groups, and submitting critical comments on BLM planning proposals. Booklets about the East Mojave continued to flow from Burk's pen. He will be heard from again.

" He believed
that even with
the worst possible forecast
for the future,
it is more fun to
take part in the battle
for what you believe in
than just to stand
on the sidelines
wringing your hands."

—Margaret Murie (writing about Olaus Murie)

JIM DODSON

The
Desert
Plan
and Its
Discontents

CHAPTER FIVE

James L. Dodson came

from a Navy family. His father, a Naval pilot, was stationed in Coronado, California, where Jim was born in the winter of 1943. Early in life he picked up his hunter-fisherman father's love of the outdoors. He recalls camping with his father in local state parks, including Anza-Borrego Desert State Park, largest in the nation, not far east of San Diego. He also hiked the local mountains with friends from Coronado Junior High.

James Dodson, early leader in developing broad public support and key strategist in passage of the Desert Bill.

Courtesy of Jim Dodson

Then the family moved all over, first to the East Coast, then to the South, while Jim was in high school. He chose Carleton College, graduated in 1965 with a major in government, and was offered a fellowship at Claremont Graduate School in California to pursue a Master's degree in International Relations. After a year in the complex of colleges in Claremont, sometimes referred to as the "Oxford of the West," he heard from a friend that his draft board in Virginia, where he had registered, was about to call him. The Vietnam War had begun. There would now be no chance to finish his Master's degree program. He elected to enlist in the Army, so back he went to Fort Dix and then Fort Belvoir, Virginia, having been selected for officer candidate school. Once more he was prevented from finishing the program in which he was enrolled, this time by a serious leg injury. After the leg healed, he completed his commitment to the armed services as the regimental photographer and returned to California, this time to Riverside.

While looking for a job in the winter of 1969–70, he joined the Sierra Club in order to take its Basic Mountaineering Course. In the spring of 1970 he was accepted as a trainee in financial management at Edwards Air Force Base in the western Mojave

Desert. There he met and married Jo Ann Hickerson, who hailed from northern Arizona. They settled near the air base in Lancaster, California, where they raised their two daughters and where they still live. Jim was then, and is now, a member of the Republican party.

The year 1971 found Jim and Jo Ann on a hike in the Red Rock Canyon country, a complex of desert canyons some 25 miles north of the town of Mojave at the intersection of the Garlock and Sierra Nevada earthquake faults. The spectacular colors of these canyons, products of centuries of wind and water erosion, are unsurpassed in the California desert and have lured tourists and film companies for many decades. In the '50s and '60s the canyons also became a mecca for motorcyclists. Jim and Jo Ann had to jump out of the way several times that day to avoid being run down. For the first time, Jim stopped and took a look at what this activity was doing to the natural scene as well as to the natural quiet of the area. They were both offended.

Dodson discovered a citizens' group in the town of Mojave, the Red Rock Canyon Citizens Committee, composed largely of local business people and ranchers who had banded together to try to protect the canyon area. Among its members were Vickie Arajo of Bakersfield, spark plug of the project; Lansing Warren, a rancher/biologist from Delano; and Joe Fontaine, long a Sierra Club leader and an expert on the southern Sierra. The Red Rock Canyon country was, in large part, a checkerboard of BLM land and old homesteads purchased by the state. In 1928, Frederick Law Olmsted, the famous landscape architect, made a survey of California to determine outstanding locations for state parks. (Without Olmsted and the survey, Anza-Borrego Desert State Park would not be what it is today.) At that time he selected Red Rock Canyon as a prime state park candidate. The Citizens Committee developed suggested boundaries for a proposed Red Rock Canyon State Park and had lobbied the State Parks Commission to take action—so far without success. By this time Dodson was thoroughly in love with the desert and he joined the group with enthusiasm.

Dodson sensed that the Sierra Club would be a leading force for desert protection and, with Joe Fontaine's sponsorship, became more active. By 1972 he was chair of the SCRCC Off-Road Vehicle Committee, using his spare time to explore the desert and examine the extent of damage done by uncontrolled ORV play. The Red Rock Canyon area had seen its share of this. A club of 4-wheelers from Ridgecrest held a large, annual rally at "Nightmare Gulch," a spectacular part of the area held by the BLM. The BLM was favorably disposed to this activity and not inclined to give up any of its land for a state park. In 1973, however, Dodson and his friends persuaded the State Parks Commission to designate the portion of the canyon area held by the state as a State Recreation Area.

This set in motion a study of routes in the recreation area that might be open to riders and routes that should be closed to vehicles to allow those who wished to visit the canyons on foot to do so in peace. The same year saw Dodson elected to the Executive Committee of the Sierra Club's Angeles Chapter. He was by now a recognized desert study trip leader. He was in the sights of the old-timers on the Desert Committee. He had found his space.

Detour to Japan

Suddenly, an opportunity came up that Dodson did not dare to miss. Accompanied by Jo Ann and their first daughter, Eleanor, he left for Japan in April 1975 on a tour of duty as Budget Officer for 475 Air Base Wing and Advisory Budget Officer for the Fifth Air Force. For almost three years he was away from the United States. These were important years for the desert—years during which FLPMA was finally enacted, Peter and Joyce Burk had their inspiration for a Mojave National Park and began to develop support, and the BLM's expanded Desert Plan staff was recruited and went to work. Dodson kept in touch with his Sierra Club friends. He had anticipated the family's return to the desert and had arranged with one of these friends to store his 4-wheel drive Scout in the latter's desert chicken barn. By April 1978, he and Jo Ann and two little girls were on the plane for home.

"We decided to grab you as soon as we could—we need to talk," said Bill Holden to Jim Dodson as Jim stepped off the plane at John Wayne Airport in Orange County. Dodson had called Bill from San Francisco asking, if possible, to be met at the airport.

Bill and Andy McClure were there. Both were old friends who, with their wives, had gone camping with Jim and Jo Ann in the days when the desert study trips, first organized by Holden in 1971, were in full swing.

Dodson had been vaguely aware of the passage of FLPMA and the beginning of a major BLM effort to develop a California Desert Plan. Holden and McClure resolved to get Jim into it without delay.

First, they took him to McClure's home to brief him on the status of desert planning and the crucial fact that a desert wilderness inventory was already well under way. Then Holden and McClure got down to business. "As you know," said Bill, "Lyle [Gaston] took over the Desert Committee before you left the country. It's still functioning but there's going to be a helluva lot to do. DPC [the Desert Protective Council] has no desert committee. It needs a desert committee chair—someone to be a spokesman in the coming months. We want you to do it."

Bill Holden was then Treasurer of DPC. Whether or not he had sought specific authority to offer the "Desert Chair" position to Dodson is unclear, but he had no doubt that it would be welcomed by DPC.

Dodson agreed to take it on. For the next 17 years, apart from his full-time job as Budget Officer for Edwards Air Force Base, the California desert was to be the main focus of his life.

Taking an Inventory of Desert Wilderness

It was high time. A small wilderness inventory field team had already been hired and placed under Robert Badaracco, head recreation planner for the Desert Plan staff. John Sering, a former student of Badaracco at the University of Utah, led the team. Sering and his colleagues had already poured over auto club and U.S. Geological Survey topographic maps to make a "dry lab" survey, as they called it, of desert areas that appeared from the maps to be over 5,000 acres in size and roadless. These were the primary rough-cut criteria for wilderness under FLPMA.

They were now ready to go into the field in teams of two (though Sering usually worked alone) for the "wet lab" survey to ascertain how well the areas assigned to each team met the criteria of the Wilderness Act:

- areas "where earth and its community of life are untrammeled by man, where man himself is a visitor who does not remain"

- areas "retaining primeval character and influence, without permanent improvements or human habitation, which is protected and managed so as to preserve their natural condition"

- areas which "generally appear to have been affected primarily by forces of nature, with the imprint of man substantially unnoticeable"

- areas which have "outstanding opportunities for solitude or a primitive and unconfined type of recreation"

- areas which "may also contain ecological, geological, or other features of scientific, educational, scenic or historical value"[15]

It is said that a camel is a horse that was designed by a committee. Perhaps it was such a committee that developed a definition of "wilderness" in 1964, when the Wilderness Act was adopted. Apparently several draftsmen produced a definition of "wilderness" and, being unable to agree, stuffed bits of each concept into the statute. Which elements of the resulting definition were absolutes? Which were relative—modified by adverbs such as "primarily," "generally," or "substantially"? Which ranked higher on the scale of values—opportunity for solitude? scientific value? scenic value? geological features? There were *no* established guidelines.

It was a tall order for the field teams to tackle but there was no time to lose. A stark deadline for completion of the entire Desert Plan (September 30, 1980) loomed, and preliminary decisions had to be reached long before that date. Fortunately, they could count on a relatively clear definition to determine whether an area was "roadless." The key Congressional Committee report on the wilderness provisions of FLPMA, issued by the House Interior Committee in May 1976, stated:

> *The word "roadless" refers to the absence of roads which have been improved and maintained by mechanical means to insure relatively regular and continuous use. A way maintained solely by the passage of vehicles does not constitute a road.*[16]

By the time Jim Dodson stepped off the plane from Japan on that spring day in 1978, the members of the field team had already taken their first forays into the desert. A "Preliminary Inventory Map," based solely on existing printed maps, had just been published. Seventeen public workshops were held in the first three months of the inventory process to obtain comments on what the team was doing and what should be examined more carefully. Between workshops there were few interruptions and no one counted the hours. Much of the fieldwork had to be done during the hot summer months. Team leader Sering recalls that the two-man groups worked for two days in the field, sleeping out. They then met by prearrangement at a motel in a desert town, had a short swim if possible, showered, shaved, discussed what they'd found over supper and into the evening, and returned to the desert and their sleeping bags for two more days. Occasionally they would sit down together somewhere for several days to write up reports of what they had found. Meanwhile, dozens of Sierra Club desert study trips were taking place, examining special areas and collecting data on wilderness characteristics to submit to the Desert Plan staff at all levels. As Jim Dodson became more involved, he organized much of this.

An "Interim Inventory Map," prepared by professionals using field team data, was in print and distributed by August 1, 1978. A comment period, more public workshops, and more field trips followed. The field teams went over their reports with the BLM line staff—including State BLM Director Edward (Ed) Hastey or Assistant Director James Ruch and often with the two desert District Managers, Gerry Hillier of Riverside and Lon Boll of Bakersfield.

By and large, Sering recalls that the line staff at this stage deferred to the judgments reached by the field teams as to which areas met the criteria of the Wilderness Act. Only in the California desert was this the case, since elsewhere in the country, the wilderness reviews mandated by FLPMA did not have to be completed as swiftly.

By October of 1978, when Sering transferred to Colorado, the inventory was largely finished with 138 areas, aggregating 5.7 million acres, "determined to possess wilderness values meeting the criteria of the Wilderness Act." It remained to edit the information in the study team's reports into final descriptive narratives about each of these areas and publish them in a booklet along with a final map, all of which was accomplished by March 1979.[17] These were the Wilderness Study Areas (or WSAs) which, under FLPMA, were to be protected by the BLM from "impairment" until Congress acted to determine their ultimate destiny as wilderness or nonwilderness. So far, so good. The conservation community was not unhappy with the wilderness inventory and it was to prove an immensely valuable source of detailed information when those charged with drafting the Desert Protection Act went to work.

During the period between the spring of '78 (when he returned from Japan) and the spring of '79, Jim Dodson became increasingly active. At first his task was to stimulate input to the wilderness inventory from the conservation community. His role rapidly evolved into something far larger—that of melding, insofar as possible, ideas and drafts prepared by various desert conservationists (and their organizations) into comprehensive joint submissions. This would maximize the effectiveness of the conservation community's input in the several upcoming hearings on the Desert Plan.

How Can a Plan Be Designed to Comply with the Law?

The projected Desert Plan was becoming increasingly complex. In the early '70s, before FLPMA, the small BLM Desert Planning staff had decided to plan separately for each major desert area that shared roughly the same ecological characteristics. This, they believed, made sense because there were major differences between southern, northern, eastern and western areas of the desert. In fact, the California desert included the great bulk of the Mojave Desert system together with parts of two other well-recognized desert systems, the Sonora and Great Basin. Each system had relatively distinct weather patterns, vegetation, wildlife, opportunities for recreation, and accessibility. Before FLPMA was adopted in 1976, rough drafts of plans had been prepared for the Yuha Desert in the far south and for the Red Mountain and El Paso Mountain areas; work was already under way on an East Mojave plan. But the greatly enlarged post-FLPMA staff, following a tumultuous first year trying to determine how to tackle its task, decided on a different approach. FLPMA had laid down a daunting mandate: The Desert Plan must provide for administration of California desert lands "within the framework of a program of multiple use *and* sustained yield *and* maintenance of environmental quality." The statutory definition of "multiple use" was full of contradictory elements. It read:

> *The term "multiple use" means the management of the public lands and their various resource values so that they are utilized in the combination that will best meet the present and future needs of the American people; making the most judicious use of the land for all of these resources; to the use of some land for less than all of the resources; a combination of balanced and diverse resource uses that takes into account the long-term needs of future generations for renewable and nonrenewable resources, including, but not limited to, recreation, range, timber, minerals, watershed, wildlife and fish, and natural scenic, scientific and historical values; and harmonious and coordinated management of the various resources without permanent impairment of the productivity of the land and the quality of the environment with consideration being given to the relative values of the resources and not necessarily to the combination of uses that will give the greatest economic return or the greatest unit output.*[18]

It is perhaps understandable that the *Los Angeles Times* was once provoked to refer to multiple use as a "hybrid, self-conflicting concept."[19]

"Sustained yield" was defined about as one would expect. "Environmental quality" was left undefined, but the statute contained three findings:

- The California desert environment was "a total ecosystem that is extremely fragile, easily scarred and slowly healed,"

- The California desert "environment and its resources, including certain rare and endangered species of wildlife, plants, and fishes and numerous archaeological and historic sites, are seriously threatened by air pollution…and pressures of increased use, particularly recreational use…," and,

- Use of desert resources should be managed "to conserve these resources for future generations" but shall "include the use, where appropriate, of off-road recreational vehicles."[20]

How were all these requirements to be fulfilled when they were expressed almost entirely in terms that required subjective judgment? The Desert Plan staff faced a problem of staggering complexity. Whatever it did in order to accommodate the statutory mandate was bound to be controversial.

The staff finally decided to attempt a single plan for the entire desert. It would subdivide the desert into areas believed to be appropriate for differing levels of "use." (Ultimately 108 such areas, of all sizes and shapes, were selected.) There would be four levels of use (designated "multiple use classes" [MUCs]), "intensive" (Class I), "moderate" (Class M), "limited" (Class L) and "controlled" (Class C). On top of this first mosaic, irrespective of the "class" involved, would be superimposed a panoply of Areas of Critical Environmental Concern (ACECs), of National Natural Landmark Areas, of National Historic Landmarks, of Recreation Vehicle Open

Areas, of Research Natural Areas, and, finally, of Wilderness Study Areas (WSAs). The "controlled" class would consist only of those WSAs deemed suitable in the judgment of the BLM management to be recommended to Congress for designation as wilderness.[21]

It would be necessary to develop guidelines to specify the types of uses to be permitted in each MUC or multiple use class. To facilitate this, studies were projected of each of the resources of the desert lands as the Desert Plan staff conceived them. Initially, there were to be four categories of desert resources, called "plan elements": livestock grazing, utility corridors, motor vehicle recreation, and miscellaneous recreation. Soon, however, persuaded by its specialist members, the staff added cultural resources, Native American concerns, wildlife, wild horses and burros, geology-energy-minerals, and land tenure adjustment elements. Surprisingly, the staff had still forgotten about plant life. This was ultimately added much later.

All was new. And on top of this, the agency's lawyers in Washington advised that an EIS would have to be prepared under the law before the Plan could be made effective. To assist people in understanding the issues, the EIS would be required to present several alternative plans differing from each other in opportunity for consumptive uses versus the degree of environmental protection afforded. Neither the BLM nor, it was believed, any other land agency had ever tried to produce an EIS on a plan such as this.

What Do the *People* Want for the Desert?

As Bob Badaracco put it in subsequent Congressional testimony, "It was becoming clear [in the planning process] that the voices of special interests were loud, clear and heard. It was not clear that the general public was being heard."[22] Badaracco had joined the Desert Plan staff in 1974. At his suggestion, a statewide public opinion survey was conducted for the BLM by the respected Mervin Field organization in November 1975 to obtain data on attitudes toward the California desert. The results of the poll were surprising. Participants were asked to select the three issues regarding the California desert they believed should have top priority. The composite result was as follows: *Number one:* "more protection of desert wildlife and ecology;" *two:* "more protection of areas of historical importance;" and *three*: "less development of all kinds." Near the bottom of the ranking were *eight*: "more roads and sightseeing places;" *nine*: "more development of mineral resources;" and *ten*: "more places for off-road vehicle use."

As might be expected, interest groups such as miners and off-roaders reacted with shock, insisting that the poll had been rigged or poorly done. The BLM sent the poll and information on the methodologies employed to three universities for independent review and got unanimous response that the survey was fair and proper.

When the expanded Desert Plan staff got to work it was deemed important to conduct a new poll in order to test the validity of the 1975 statewide survey as well as the constancy of the views expressed by the public. Again, the Field Organization was retained and questions were somewhat revised to satisfy the critics. The results, in 1977, indicated even stronger sentiment for protection of the desert. This raised the objection that the scope of the poll was too narrow—a nationwide survey was needed to get an accurate view. So Badaracco got permission to conduct a nationwide poll, this time using the Gallup Organization. The results of the Gallup Poll were published in January 1978. Six hundred twenty-five interviews were conducted and once again, and by a wider margin than ever, *number one* on the wish list of the respondents (85% of them) was to "protect desert wildlife and ecology." Following this, in terms of progressively lower "net scores," were *two*: "protect scenery and natural character;" *three*: "protect areas of historical importance;" *four*: "control recreation and other public use;" *five*: "educational programs;" *six*: "campgrounds;" *seven*: "energy development;" *eight*: "amusement parks;" *nine*: "roads;" *ten*: "places for off-road vehicles;" *eleven*: "mining;" and *twelve*: "commercial development."

The only objection left to be voiced on the validity of the polling results was that they didn't specifically record what people who actually resided in the desert wished. So a fourth poll was ordered, this time from Stanford Research Institute International, and limited to desert residents. Some members of the BLM study and line staffs thought that this poll would find strong support for consumptive activities, since local desert economies were thought to be highly dependent on such activities. But again, the survey results were remarkably consistent. Fifty-eight percent of those polled wanted more desert protection, exceeding by 27% those who desired more energy development and by 60% those who wanted more mining. Desert activities most widely disliked by desert residents were found to be those involving motorcycles, dune buggies and four-wheel drive vehicles, and indiscriminate use of guns for target shooting and hunting. Strikingly similar results were obtained by a Field Institute poll taken in 1988, long after adoption of the Desert Plan.

A more formal sort of public input to the planning process was also needed in order to comply with the law. A citizens' "advisory committee," each member of which was chosen to represent a special interest, had been appointed as required by FLPMA and began in 1977 to hold a series of meetings on the plan elements. The public was invited to these meetings; they took the form of seminars where several experts, both from the staff and outside, would offer their views and could be questioned by public participants. While this elicited a certain amount of ad-hoc public comment, Jim Dodson quickly reached the conclusion that participation in Advisory Committee meetings, although interesting, would have little impact on the planning process. It would be essential to send the Desert Plan staff detailed written materials with carefully documented comments in order for the conservation community to have a solid public record of its submissions.

Until more was known about the shape and substance of the several alternative plans that would be proposed, it was difficult to frame specific comments. Not until mid-1979 did the Desert Plan staff finally decide how it would attempt to prepare the necessary EIS.

The decision was to offer the Advisory Committee and the public three alternative plans:

- "A Use Alternative plan" which would emphasize consumptive activities throughout the desert plus a great expansion of ecologically damaging vehicle recreation and would perforce result in an abundance of Class I areas but few Class L or Class C areas;

- "A Conservation Alternative plan" which would be the reverse of the first alternative;

- "A Balanced Alternative plan" which would consist of a compromise of sorts between the other two.

Did the Plan Process Allow Useful Public Input?

A draft preview of the EIS was finally published in December 1979, less than a year before the statutory deadline for adoption of the Desert Plan. It was intended to give sufficient information on the scope and content of the forthcoming Draft EIS, which would include the several plan alternatives, so that people could prepare to comment on that document, expected to be published within a very short time. It was not very helpful. Little could be done in the way of careful analysis until February 1980 when the massive Draft EIS came through the mail to many hundreds of interested parties, calling for written comments within 90 days and scheduling hearings on its proposals during the intervening period.

This formidable document was 14 inches high and 436 pages long, not including 42 maps. Some members of the public commented that it was too complex to comprehend, certainly within the time allowed. Wes Chambers, a very senior member of the Desert Plan staff who wrote a history of the planning process, said: "A case could be made that in order to meet legal requirements the draft document was made unreadable to the general public. It is most conceivable that very few actually read the document."[23]

Nor was the Desert Plan staff any happier than the public with the Draft EIS. Most of the scientists and other professionals on staff would be leaving when the Desert Plan was finished, and their influence swiftly waned. Some had become increasingly concerned with what were perceived to be political decisions made to balance out the allocation of desert lands between mining, grazing, ORV activity, and conserving desert resources. They felt that the excellent resource data that they had accumulated was, at least in part, being ignored. The failure to include wild plant life of the desert as a significant resource element was noted. Others were offended by what was felt to be a strong bias in Sacramento and in Washington toward consumptive uses of the desert and by the rejection of Desert Plan staff recommendations such as including the East Mojave and Saline Valley in the National Park System.

Struggling to solve the problems it was facing with the Draft EIS, the BLM commissioned the American Arbitration Association (AAA) to determine the reactions of various interest groups, assess their most serious concerns, and advise the BLM what it should do. The AAA reported that grazers and miners both believed they could live well with the Balanced Alternative plan. As for the conservation community, the AAA report said that it almost unanimously rejected the Balanced Alternative plan as meeting neither the statutory language nor the intent of FLPMA, and many who were actively involved felt frustrated by the planning decisions taken to date. Many were unsure they wanted to participate further. The AAA's suggestions were of questionable value—they included such vague proposals as establishing more credible procedures for incorporating public input into the final plan.[24]

A particularly critical part of the Draft EIS pertained to the 138 WSAs that met the criteria of the Wilderness Act established the previous year. In the Draft EIS, the BLM for the first time set forth a crude ranking of the WSAs, classifying them as outstanding, good, fair, or poor. This was based on a set of standards which seemed remarkably obscure to the conservation community— standards such as nearness to population centers (in what way this quality was pertinent was not disclosed), scenery (determined by whom?), manageability (undefined), adjacent wilderness (why was this a criterion?), and accessibility. As best one could make out, the least accessible WSAs were ranked highest. Such standards appeared to focus largely on questionable human factors to the neglect of careful analysis of the intrinsic wilderness values offered by the WSAs.

Apparently following this rating scheme, a selection was made of those WSAs that the BLM would recommend as "suitable" for wilderness designation, depending on which of the three plan alternatives was used. In the Protection Alternative plan, 5.2 million acres of WSAs would be deemed "suitable;" in the Balanced Alternative plan, 1.8 million acres; and in the Use Alternative plan, only .6 million acres—essentially only a few mountaintops and one desert valley, the Saline.

Were these "*realistic* alternatives, *reasonably* available," as required by the case law interpreting the National Environmental Policy Act that was the statutory basis for preparation of the EIS? Did they present three *real* choices to the public? The conservation community most emphatically believed they did not, and that the planning process had been badly skewed, if not thoroughly subverted by an institutional bias within the BLM in favor of consumptive uses. Apparently the polls taken during the planning process had been consigned to the dust bin.

A month before the Draft EIS came out, Jim Dodson had been appointed chair of the Sierra Club's Desert Committee. He plunged into the task of organizing the Sierra Club's comments on the Draft EIS. These would incorporate the views of leading members of other conservation groups in order to present a united viewpoint, if possible. Many in the conservation community credit Dodson with an uncommon ability to grasp a nettle such as this one. Someone had to grasp it. Dodson gathered input from highly experienced desert hands, among them Harriet Allen of the Desert Protective Council; Charles (Chuck) Bell of the High Desert Legal Defense Fund; Ike Eastvold, the great petroglyph expert; Russell (Russ) Shay, Linda Wade, and Pamela Brodie of the Sierra Club staff; Patricia (Patty) Hedge of the Wilderness Society; Johanna Wald of the Natural Resources Defense Council; Lyle Gaston, Robert Webb, Professor Freeman Allen of Pomona College, and his own wife, Jo Ann Dodson.

The resulting memorandum was largely put together in the privacy of an unheated cabin behind Chuck Bell's house in Lucerne Valley by Jim, Jo Ann (who did most of the typing), Lyle, Chuck, Ike, and a couple of bottles of Wild Turkey. In size, it was appropriate to the document it criticized. Its 112 pages, not counting appendices, included generic comments on the Draft EIS, comments on each of the "plan elements," on the ranking of the WSAs, on the selection of ACECs, and on implementation. It concluded that there were serious flaws in the structure of the Draft EIS pervading all of the alternative plans, particularly the Use Alternative. The very proposal of this alternative, as written, made no sense whatever. It would directly contravene the mandate of FLPMA that the framework of the ultimate California Desert Plan must be consistent with "sustained yield and the maintenance of environmental quality." Therefore, merely the proposal of such an alternative was a violation of law and actively misleading. In fact, said the memorandum, the statement in the Draft EIS that its Use Alternative would meet all minimum environmental protection standards legally required was not only erroneous but was contradicted by the Draft's own environmental analysis of that alternative. That analysis indicated that the Use Alternative violated the Clean Air Act, the Native American Religious Freedom Act, the Antiquities Act, the Endangered Species Act, and a host of other Federal laws and policies. *If* the Balanced Alternative was intended to find a balance point between the Use and Protection alternatives when the Use Alternative was so far off the chart in one direction that it violated numerous laws, this would inevitably lead to a fatal imbalance favoring consumptive uses of desert resources.

Possibly the most pointed critique of the Draft EIS had to do with its treatment of wilderness and its failure to give any supporting data for ratings of WSAs. The Sierra Club memorandum notes, for example, that for some unaccountable reason, eight of the WSAs rated "outstanding" were *not* recommended for wilderness even in the Balanced Alternative! Other "outstanding" areas were radically reduced in size. No realistic or reasonable set of choices was presented by the recommendation as "suitable" under the three alternatives of 10%, 30% and 90%, respectively, of the total potential wilderness encompassed by the WSAs. No area-specific information was given, hence a meaningful discussion of other possibly more realistic levels (such as 50% to 75%) was effectively blocked.

Many other organizations submitted critical comments on the Draft EIS, including various chapters of the Audubon Society, the California Native Plant Society, Citizens for a Mojave National Park, a group of graduate biology students at the University of California, Berkeley, working under Professor Robert Stebbins, and the President's Council on Environmental Quality. The Council's April 23, 1980, letter to the BLM identified a range of major deficiencies, particularly "failure to present the decision maker and the public with a reasonable range of alternatives." It stressed that to be within the law, specifically, the National Environmental Policy Act (NEPA), such a range "must include an alternative premised on the sustained yield and long-term maintenance of extremely fragile desert soils, vegetation, wildlife resources, and historical, cultural and aesthetic values," while also allowing those multiple uses which are compatible with the foregoing. This, it said, the Draft EIS had failed to do. The Council on Environmental Quality pointedly noted the failure of the draft to disclose any basis for reducing the 240 ACECs identified by the Desert Plan staff to only 50 in each of the three plan alternatives!

The BLM Tries Again

The Sierra Club memorandum also concluded that the failure of the Draft EIS to include a plan alternative identified as "preferred" or "recommended" by the BLM had so confused the public as to make it essential that such an alternative be prepared and submitted. Apparently the BLM agreed. In September 1980, it published what amounted to an amendment of the Draft EIS which although it was entitled "Final" EIS, repeated the same distribution of multiple use class lands among each of the three original alternative plans and then submitted a fourth alternative, designated the "Proposed Plan." This was the previously missing "preferred" plan that the BLM now expected to adopt. The statutory deadline for such adoption had already passed. Nothing was done to revise the original plan alternatives, considered by many commentators to have been fatally flawed. The new Proposed Plan was, not surprisingly, close to the Balanced Alternative plan, with adjustments reflecting a very modest response to some of the comments of the conservation community.

The so-called Final EIS for the first time added "vegetation" as deserving the dignity of recognition as a resource element of the Desert Plan. On the other hand, the Proposed Plan permitted commercial harvesting of native plants and other native vegetation, by permit, even on Class L lands and expressly permitted two organized competitive motorcycle events to be routed through Class L lands on cross-country routes to be designated by the BLM. Such activities were thought by the conservation community to be totally inconsistent with the Class L guidelines in the Proposed Plan. One WSA, the core of the South Algodones Dunes, well away from the areas of those dunes used extensively for dune buggy recreation, continued to be classified as a WSA in Class L, but (amazingly) the Proposed Plan opened it to ORV free play! The BLM told surprised conservationists, "We couldn't manage it and, besides, it's only lightly used." Finally, the total acreage allotted to ORV free play was increased from 289,000 acres in the Balanced Alternative to 485,000 acres in the Proposed Plan. Under the BLM's own analysis, its preference—the Proposed Plan—was far from balanced!

A new set of hearings was scheduled with limited time allowed for comments. Many organizations and their members, as individuals, commented once again. Once again, Jim Dodson managed the preparation of the most comprehensive comments sent to the Bureau. While the Sierra Club's comments noted some specific improvements in the Proposed Plan over the Draft EIS, they concluded that all of the major structural flaws pointed out in previous comments still applied. The Proposed Plan could neither achieve "sustained yield" nor "maintenance of environmental quality"—two principal requirements for the Plan specified in FLPMA. Careful analysis of decisions embodied in the Proposed Plan showed that continued deterioration of many of the desert's natural resource values would inevitably follow its implementation. The BLM had failed to acknowledge this and the public had a right to know it before a true, Final EIS was approved.

The treatment of WSAs in the Proposed Plan caused particular dissatisfaction. As noted previously, even the BLM's own ranking system for WSAs gave very high marks to a sizable number which were nevertheless labeled "unsuitable." It appeared to many that the BLM had determined it would not, for political reasons, designate more than approximately one-third of the WSAs as "suitable" regardless of the quality of those left out by this approach. The principal justification offered by the BLM, in rationales for its nonwilderness recommendations seemed to be that the highest and best future use of the "unsuitable" WSAs would be for ORV recreation, mining, or both, rather than for preservation of their wilderness values. But the Proposed Plan had already added almost 200,000 acres to the areas set aside for ORV "free play"! How could this possibly square with the results of the four polls the BLM itself had commissioned, all of which showed without a shadow of doubt that protection of desert ecosystems was considered *by the public* of far greater importance than mining or ORV activities?

While the foregoing comments were being prepared in detail, Dodson made one more effort—he wrote an extensive guide for Sierra Club publications to assist those who would comment on particular points in the Proposed Plan by way of individual letters. It was hard to anticipate that further comments could result in any changes in the Proposed Plan, however; time simply did not permit the agency to review with care the ideas submitted in another round of comments. The Desert Plan staff had been working for too many months at forced draft pace, and it was burned out. Public frustration was also evident: In one public hearing on the so-called Final EIS a citizen wheeled in a cart containing not just that document but all the other documents he had received over the four-year life of the planning project—an entire wheelbarrow load! He dumped them all on the floor in front of the Advisory Committee, announcing that he didn't feel the effort to submit further comments was worth his time.

Will Time Run Out for the Desert Plan?

The conservation community, disappointed and discouraged as it was with the emerging Desert plan, took stock. Some wished to seek a court decision to invalidate the plan on the basis that the alternatives it posed to the public failed to meet the requirements of either FLPMA or the National Environmental Policy Act. It was learned that prominent ORV organizations also were planning to attack the plan in court. Ronald Reagan had just been elected President and his appointee to head the Interior Department was James Watt, well-known as the outspoken head of the Mountain States Legal Foundation, which specialized in litigating against conservation measures that might impact business interests. What sort of a Desert Plan, if any, would come out of this new Interior Department if the plan on which so many had worked so long was not approved?

By mid-November, cooler heads in the conservation community had reached the conclusion that the forthcoming plan, with all its flaws, was the best they could hope to get for the foreseeable future. The plan included a mechanism for consideration of amendments at annual intervals. It was possible that sound criticisms might result in favorable changes if pursued with diligence and scientific support.

Jim Dodson was of this opinion. Moreover, the Citizens Advisory Committee which had worked hard overseeing the planning process for almost four years was not anxious to see its efforts come to naught. Back to Washington went Clayton Record, a Supervisor of Riverside County and former chair of the Advisory Committee, and his committee colleague Frank Devore, an official of San Diego Gas and Electric Company, both well-known Republicans. Their message to the new Administration was: We've worked very hard on this and under no circumstances should it have to be done over again. The Secretary of the Interior should now adopt the plan, and the Administration should implement its adoption as soon as possible after it takes office. Also back to Washington went Jim Dodson, representing the Sierra Club and the Desert Protective Council.

His message on their behalf was much the same as that of the Advisory Committee representatives.

Nevertheless, when Secretary Cecil Andrus signed it on December 19, 1980, the Plan held several surprises.[25] Largest of these was the designation of the east Mojave region as a "National Scenic Area," whatever that might signify, with plans for the area to be adopted in the indeterminate future. It appeared that one or more comments received by the BLM on the Proposed Plan in October 1980 had suggested such a move as a substitute for transferring jurisdiction over the East Mojave to the National Park Service. Conservationists were not happy with the surprise inclusion in the Final Plan of three competitive ORV race courses in the desert—one from the Johnson Valley to near Parker on the Colorado River, one called the "Parker 400," and one from the Stoddard Valley ORV play area to the Johnson Valley ORV play area. But, at least the Barstow-Vegas race had not been added. All were eventually eliminated by the BLM. The Final Plan closed the Coyote Dry Lake ORV open area but established play areas at Mammoth Wash, at the Olancha Dunes, and at the dunes in Rice Valley, even though the last two of these were wilderness study areas. Reminded of this by Dodson, the best the Department spokesman could say was, "Oh, it won't hurt them." It would take scientific testimony in later hearings on desert legislation to demonstrate the harm done to largely nocturnal small animals and to many plants by off-road vehicle play on what appear at first glance to be rather barren sand dunes.

The Plan Goes Through; Attacks on it Fail

In March 1981, Secretary Watt finally announced that the Plan would be implemented. Only then was it ordered printed in final form to be distributed to the public in June 1981.

As expected, the American Motorcyclist Association (AMA), the National Outdoor Association (NOA) and the County of Inyo filed suit in Federal court in Los Angeles against Secretary Watt to enjoin implementation of the plan.[26] So did Louis McKey, a motorcyclist whom we shall later meet as "the Phantom Duck of the Desert," the California Mining Association, the California

Native Plant Society, the Desert Tortoise Council, the San Bernardino Valley Audubon Society and the Wilderness Society. Even the Sierra Club, through its San Gorgonio Chapter, joined the fray, limiting its objection to the Johnson Valley to Parker motorcycle race. Ten temporary restraining orders were sought and all were denied. At this point all of the plaintiffs withdrew their suits except the AMA, the NOA and Inyo County. The Sierra Club and California Native Plant Society, after first officially withdrawing their suits, intervened in the case on behalf of Secretary Watt, and with an amicus brief opposing the three remaining plaintiffs who were seeking preliminary injunctions against implementation of the entire plan. It is said that politics makes strange bedfellows, and stranger ones would be hard to find!

It was late in 1981 before Federal Judge A. Wallace Tashima ruled against the remaining plaintiffs. In a lengthy opinion, he concluded that the Final Plan involved violations of both FLPMA and the BLM's own Planning Regulations. The judge specifically mentioned the BLM's failure to designate a "Preferred Alternative" plan at the Draft EIS stage and the failure of the BLM to publish for examination and comment any of the material changes unexpectedly made in the Final Plan. In his words, there was a "strong likelihood that the plaintiffs would prevail on the merits at trial." But he denied the preliminary injunction, holding that the plaintiffs had failed to prove they would suffer irreparable harm from implementation of the Final Plan before their case could be tried, as required for injunctive relief. All three organizations appealed this ruling and, in 1983, the Ninth Circuit Court of Appeals affirmed the Federal District Court decision.[27] Although they were then free to do so, the plaintiffs never sought to take the case to trial. By 1983 they may have decided the California Desert Plan was working very much in their favor.

Jim Dodson's skills in bringing people together, organizing persuasive data and arguing the conservation case had not been able to prevent a primarily use-oriented agency from bringing into being a seriously flawed Desert Plan. But as time passed, his vigorous voice for the desert would inspire many whose support would be needed to carry the day for the Desert Protection Act of the future.

Red Rock Canyon Takes a Step Forward

Dodson had gone to Japan in 1975 just after Red Rock Canyon, his first love in the desert, was made a State Recreation Area. He did not forget the canyon during his years in Japan. Soon after he returned, he became chairman of the Red Rock Canyon Citizens Committee and learned that in his absence his old friend Vickie Arajo, the former spark plug of the committee, had been appointed to the State Parks Commission. She told Dodson that if the committee would come in with plenty of data strongly showing why the area should be designated a State Park, she thought it could be done.

Working with Victor Maris, ranger in charge of the State Recreation Area, Dodson put the case together, including a suggested set of boundaries, and it was presented to the commission. Vickie Arajo was right. In 1980 Red Rock Canyon State Park was formally dedicated. It was still a patchwork of state and BLM lands, and it was necessary to agree with the BLM on days when motorcyclists could use certain trails, with alternate days for hikers. The BLM, under pressure from the ORV community, still resisted appeals to transfer any of its Red Rock Canyon sections to the State Parks Department. Apparently forgotten was the era of goodwill in the late 1930s when the then Secretary of Interior, Ray Lyman Wilbur, supported legislation to transfer 200,000 acres of Federal public land to the State of California. The subsequent transfer of yet *another* 300,000 acres made possible today's Anza-Borrego Desert State Park, the largest state park in the nation.

The final chapter of the Red Rock Canyon story is a happy one. In last-minute negotiations with Senator Cranston in 1985, Dodson asked that enlargement of Red Rock Canyon State Park be made part of the California Desert Protection Act, with appropriate BLM lands transferred for this purpose to the State Parks Department. It was done. Some time after introduction of the

Desert Bill, the BLM did transfer to the State Park lands that the Park wanted in the west and south, but held it onto the wild and scenic northeast (including "Nightmare Gulch," favorite of ORV enthusiasts) until the Desert Bill was passed. Today the State Park incorporates this magnificent northeast canyon country. Its highlight is the historic "Last Chance Canyon," through which a party of '49ers, lost in the far reaches of the desert, made their way following their escape from Death Valley. Looking southward from the mouth of the canyon, their hopes rose that they might at last reach civilization at the little town of Los Angeles.

" I have always
admired the ability
to bite off more
than one can chew,
and then to chew it."

—William de Mille

JUDY
ANDERSON
AND
FRIENDS

Getting
The Act
Together

CHAPTER SIX

Old Desert Hands Assess the Situation

A bunch of old desert hands met to discuss their favorite part of the world and its problems on the night of April 24, 1981, in Riverside, California. It was five months since the outgoing Carter Administration in Washington had adopted the California Desert Plan; it had not yet been published by the new Administration but Secretary of Interior James Watt had indicated he would permit it to be implemented. He had let it be known, however, that he would immediately seek from Congress authority for the early release, to the usual multiple uses, of all WSAs that had not been recommended in the Desert Plan as "suitable" for wilderness designation.[28] Such a release would apply to roughly two-thirds of the desert land which the BLM itself had found both roadless *and* possessing the wilderness characteristics specified by the Wilderness Act.

Congressional approval would be required for Watt's contemplated action. Under the Federal Land Policy Management Act (FLPMA), *all* WSAs, whether or not recommended as "suitable," were to be managed under FLPMA's "nonimpairment" standard until Congress decided on their designation, or nondesignation, as wilderness. Terry Sopher, BLM Issues Specialist for the Wilderness Society, voiced the concern of the conservation community, warning that the contemplated action would release lands for multiple use that have high wilderness potential—"their wilderness characteristics will be ruined before Congress has a chance to examine them."

Sopher's Wilderness Society colleague Larry Moss was at the Riverside meeting. So were Bill Holden, Harriet Allen (mainstay of the Desert Protective Council), Jim Dodson, and Judy Anderson, all volunteers in the cause of desert conservation. Anderson had recently chaired the Sierra Club's Angeles Chapter.

Moss had been a career conservationist since 1971 when he became Southern California Representative of the Sierra Club. In 1974 he was promoted to National Conservation Director of the club; later, he had five bureaucratic years as Secretary of the California Department of Resources. In 1980 he joined the senior staff of the Wilderness Society in Washington, D.C. He was an expert on the Washington scene.

Anderson had worked on some of the maps which were part of the California Wilderness Bill for Forest Service lands, introduced in Congress in the 1970s but not destined to become law until 1984. It was quite clear that a similar bill would be needed for *desert* wilderness in California. Not surprisingly, Jim Dodson, chair of the Sierra Club's Desert Committee, had already asked Anderson if, assuming such a project went forward, she'd be willing to take charge of the mapmaking. She had said she would. Now, she was hearing Larry Moss tell the assembled group that this might have to take place quickly. He referred to what Secretary Watt was reported to have said about the early release to multiple use of allegedly "non-suitable" WSAs. She also knew that Dodson and others had in mind many boundary changes in the WSAs already recommended as "suitable" in the Desert Plan. It was likely that attention would now focus on the BLM "nonsuitables" which the conservation community considered outstanding wilderness candidates—some of which had, in fact, been labeled "outstanding" in the BLM's own rating scheme.

A shiver ran down her spine. She thought, "These guys have no idea what a job it is to make those maps." She knew this from hard experience, although she was as yet only half trained in mapmaking. She could see many months of work ahead. The task actually stretched into many years, and her role would grow substantially as the time passed. Well before even the preliminary mapping had been completed four years later, Anderson was, by acclamation, elected chair of the California Desert Protection League, the coalition of all the organizations backing the California Desert Protection Act

A Lady from Dark Forests Comes to the Desert

Judith Ann Anderson was born in 1942 in Tomahawk, Wisconsin, youngest of a family of two brothers and two sisters. She was so much the youngest that she was flower girl in her older brother's wedding. Her father, a soft drink distributor, was part owner of a hunting camp in Wisconsin's backwoods, a family cottage on a forest reservoir nearer home, and some timberland outside town. Much of Judy's free time was spent walking the woods and swamps by herself, crossing lakes, fishing (mostly with wet flies and grubs, she says) for trout, pan fish, muskies and walleyes. Later she roamed the trails on horseback. She recalls the joys of wild berry picking—blackberries, blueberries, raspberries, chokecherries, occasionally cranberries. Her beloved father died with his boots on at the hunting camp in 1970, marooned there by a violent storm.

Judith Anderson led the mapping of the desert for the Desert Bill and chaired the California Desert Protection League.

Courtesy of the Colby Library, Sierra Club

Second in her high school class, she was awarded a tuition-free scholarship to Wisconsin State College in Plattville. There she graduated with a degree in mathematics and chemistry in 1964. She gained practical experience managing a crew of volunteers as editor of the college newspaper. For two years she taught high school math at Lake Geneva, Wisconsin, spending summers back in Plattville in miscellaneous courses that might lead to a Master's degree. Research for a course entitled "Contemporary Issues in American Politics," led her to *Time and the River Flowing*, a Sierra Club coffee-table book in the college bookstore, full of magnificent photographs of the West. She bought the book and decided this was where she, someday, had to go. By sheer chance she found a membership application for the Sierra Club inside the cover of the book and would have sent it in except, in those days, it required a member to vouch for the applicant. She didn't know one. Years elapsed before she finally found the necessary member to sign her membership application.

A decision to seek that coveted Master's degree in mathematics led her to the University of Kansas where she was offered the chance to teach half-time and study the other half. A summer's holiday gave her a chance to explore the West with campus roommates, traveling through western national parks, then north-westward along the western coast, and finally back to the Midwest across Canada. Hiking on a mountain was something new to her. So was crossing the California desert in mid-July, an experience she admits she both feared and hated.

In 1969 the Master's degree she was about to receive provided little help in landing a college teaching position. Too many frustrated and unemployed PhD's were floating around at the time. But a recruiter from the Los Angeles Unified School District turned up at the University of Kansas and offered her a job at Franklin High School in the Highland Park district of Los Angeles. She has remained on the math faculty of Franklin High School to this day. Administrative positions would have meant more money, prestige, and longer hours, but by the time they came along she rejected them. She had found her second career in conservation.

In the early '70s she became a summer volunteer in the office of the Sierra Club's Angeles Chapter. Membership on the Executive Committee of the Chapter was not long in coming. She found the high altitudes of the Sierra uncomfortable; closer to home was the California desert. Hope Peter, a fellow teacher at Franklin High, finally persuaded Judy to come with her to the desert. "That first trip brought home to me," she says, "what a great place the desert is, full of wonders and surprises."

The desert would have to wait, except for the pleasure of joining a number of the desert study trips led by Bill Holden, Lyle Gaston, Jim Dodson, and others to explore and gain firsthand knowledge of as much of the desert as she could. On the front burner was the California Coastal Initiative, in which she became heavily involved, and the California Nuclear Initiative in which she gained valuable political experience including a stint on the staff of a firm of professional campaign consultants. The Alaska Lands Act campaign followed. Then the California Wilderness Act, for which she was an apprentice mapmaker of wilderness areas. By this time she had risen to chair the largest chapter in the Sierra Club; however, it seemed to her that she was always coming late into conservation campaigns that others had organized and were leading. At last, in 1981, it appeared that a major campaign for the desert was about to begin. This was new, she was delighted, and she threw herself into it.

Maps, Glorious Maps

Anderson's earliest adventures with maps had led to a further venture in higher education. She had been collecting maps from an early age. In the spring of 1980, eager to develop mapmaking skills, she signed up with the Extension Division of UCLA for a college course in drafting and when it was finished, for a longer-range evening program looking toward a certificate in Landscape Architecture. She had finished the second quarter of this course when desert mapping got underway in 1981. First priority was reserved for important areas the BLM had left by the wayside as "unsuitable," such as the New York Mountains, Clark Mountain and the Lower Saline Valley. Second priority lay with mapping expanded boundaries for "suitable" wilderness, such as the Kingston Range. The BLM had left out of the Kingston Mountains WSA, the rich, gently sloping desert land flanking the steeply rising mountains and even the lower slopes of the mountains themselves. Beyond this there were third and fourth priorities.

In order to get the benefit of work done by the BLM Desert Plan staff in establishing WSAs, Anderson took tracing paper to the BLM's Desert District headquarters in Riverside where some, at least, of the large scale WSA maps were located and could be traced. Others she had to find in the BLM's El Centro, Needles, Barstow and Ridgecrest offices. Some had unaccountably disappeared. This was a start, as far as it went. Fortunately, in the early summer of 1981, Susan Berger, a practicing landscape architect with an advanced degree, looked in at the Angeles Chapter office and Judy persuaded her to help. She knew precisely how the best maps should be made. It was decided that *each* wilderness area deserved its own large, detailed map with all the important information on its face, reflecting the seriousness of the conservation proposals being made. To demonstrate that there were no orphan wilderness areas, all area maps would get equivalent first-class treatment. It was a tall order, but Susan's expertise was quickly recognized as a godsend. She became a major factor in preparing the Desert Protection Act for introduction in Congress.

Anderson had a special talent for persuading people to work with her, people who, like her, held daytime jobs and had to join her in the evenings. Starting in the summer of 1981 she pulled together a group of volunteers. They met every Wednesday evening for supper, which usually consisted of soup or chili. The earliest "regulars" were Annette Tarsky (who hosted a good many of the meetings), Bill Jones, Susan Berger, and Anderson herself. Drafting tables were set up as mapmaking workstations. Base sheets were prepared, including the name of the area, a small "location map," a "key" and a topographic map of the area in which the wilderness lay (usually composed of parts of several USGS 15-minutes series topographic sheets cut and pasted together). Sent to the blueprint shop, the base sheet was transformed into a semitransparent vellum copy on which could be drawn the proposed boundary, the ownership data, boundary roads, trails and other information. Until 1984 the mapmakers had to use press-on lettering for all this. At last, the Angeles Chapter bought them a Kroy lettering machine. Judy had meanwhile been working to amass a file on people with special expertise on given portions of the desert or particular potential wilderness areas. Such experts were asked to come over and make suggestions and corrections. Then back went the corrected vellum copy to the blueprint shop for multiple copies. Blueprinting was a major expense. Judy and others scrounged for contributions from individuals and friendly organizations such as Sierra Club groups, chapters, the club's regional conservation committee, which used its own budget liberally, and the ever-helpful Desert Protective Council.

Secretary Watt discovered during mid-1981 that there was only weak support in Congress for his bid to obtain authorization for a massive early release of WSAs from interim protection. It appeared at first that he had given up the idea. In the fall of 1981, however, he announced that he now had a legal opinion stating that the President, on motion of the Interior Department, could release for immediate development all WSAs he, Watt, considered "unsuitable" without any approval from Congress. It was found that the so-called legal opinion was no more than a memorandum to Secretary Watt prepared at his request by the Associate Solicitor of the Department. Nevertheless, in November 1981, lawyers from the Earthjustice Legal Defense Fund prepared a scholarly 30-page petition to the Secretary demanding his compliance with FLPMA and refuting all aspects of the Associate Solicitor's memorandum. It's unknown whether or not this had the desired effect, but the Secretary attempted nothing further along this line.

The first FLPMA-mandated amendment cycle for the California Desert Plan began in the fall of 1981 with publication of a preliminary set of amendments proposed by the BLM and others. Both proposed and final amendments dealt with relatively noncontroversial matters. Was Watt's pressure on the BLM diminishing? Although it seemed so in the fall of 1981, the year 1982 would tell a different story.

James Watt, Secretary of the Interior when the Desert Bill was conceived by California volunteers; he had a hand in the conception!

Courtesy of Department of Interior

The Great Disillusionment

It quickly became apparent that Secretary Watt's agenda did not include backing away from his commitment to push commercial development of the desert. In the spring of 1982, without notice to the public, the BLM was instructed to immediately process its entire backlog of applications for oil, gas, and geothermal lease rights in the desert and to proceed to lease anything left over. A total of 3 million acres, including many WSAs and ACECs, were affected. There had been no previous environmental assessment, in the Desert Plan process or otherwise, of the impact this would have on other desert resources, nor was any such assessment proposed. On its face, this appeared to be inconsistent with the BLM's own regulations for the protection of WSAs and ACECs. The conservation organizations learned about it through the back door from Agency personnel. So did the

Commanding Officer of Edwards Air Force Basein the Mojave. His home was on BLM land. Apparently, the BLM had not bothered to determine the present use of the proposed leased lands. The officer was not amused.

The Sierra Club and other conservation organizations quickly appealed to the Interior Board of Land Appeals, requesting that leases that had been granted involving any ACECs be revoked. The appeal also asked the Board to overturn a particularly egregious action—the BLM's proposal to lease for geothermal energy development 6,400 acres of the WSA that had been given highest BLM rating for wilderness values. This was Saline Valley, northwest of Death Valley National Monument. The first such appeal was denied because the leases had already been issued. According to the best available information, only a few exploratory drillings occurred, no production permits were issued, and the leases have by now expired.

Before a second appeal could be heard, Secretary Watt backtracked and declared a moratorium on any more leasing in WSAs. This was not enough. Continuation of such a voluntary moratorium would depend on the Secretary's mood. Congress helped out early the next year with a leasing ban. The ban was attached as a "rider" to the Interior Department Appropriations bill, a lawmaking procedure that the conservation community was later to deplore when it was used against them.

Still, the Secretary of Interior was not discouraged. The 1982 Desert Plan Amendment cycle was at hand. In early September 1982 the amendments proposed to be adopted by the BLM were published in a thick volume, subject to a 60-day comment period. It is an understatement to say they shocked the conservation community. Apparently, the BLM would gladly dance to Secretary Watt's tune.

Among the many proposed amendments which would substantially diminish protection of the desert were the following:

1. Remove from EMNSA (the East Mojave National Scenic Area established by the Desert Plan) *all* of the area north of Highway I-15 containing Clark Mountain,

highest in the Mojave Desert, and its surroundings, as well as the Ivanpah Mountains and Mescal Range south of the highway, a reduction of 140,000 acres or almost 10% in the Scenic Area.

2. Reopen the Barstow-Vegas motorcycle race that had not been permitted since the last environmentally disastrous race was run in 1974.

3. Modify the Panamint Dunes WSA (closed to all vehicle entry under the Desert Plan) to open the northern portion to ORV free play.

4. Shift 240,000 acres of WSA lands recommended by the Desert Plan as "suitable" for wilderness designation to "nonsuitable." This included all of the Sheephole Valley and Hunter Mountain areas, parts of Saline Valley and the Bighorn Mountains, much of the Resting Springs Range and Greenwater Valley, part of the Kelso Dunes and the Nopah Range. It reduced the net recommended wilderness area from 2.1 million acres to less than 1.9 million acres.

5. Revise the Desert Plan's motor vehicle use standards for "limited" vehicle access to define an "existing route of travel," over which vehicle travel is permitted until further notice even in Class L (limited use) areas, to mean a route established before December 1980 (changed from December 31, 1978) with a width of *at least two feet* (!) showing surface evidence of prior vehicle use. Revise the rule limiting vehicle use in Class L areas from "approved routes of travel— carefully chosen" to any existing route of travel unless closed after review and opportunity for public comment—the same standard as that chosen for Class M areas.

6. Further weaken the already weak distinction between Class L (limited use) and Class M lands to increase the availability of Class L areas for intrusive

uses, such as mining and the siting of communications structures. The conservation community wondered whether any real significance would be left under BLM management policies for a so-called "limited use" category.

7. Eliminate two key criteria previously used in determining the carrying capacity of grazing allotments: the distance of forage from water and the degree of slope of the terrain. The BLM concluded they were not applicable to California desert grazing. They most certainly were, according to experts in the conservation community, who believed the change to be a sure invitation to overgraze.

All of the significant amendments to the plan proposed by the Sierra Club, the Audubon Society, the Desert Protective Council, and the California Native Plant Society were rejected; these included, among others, expanding the boundaries of several WSAs recommended by the BLM as "suitable" (Saline Valley, Inyo Mountains, Chuckwalla Mountains) and placing in Class C (equivalent to a "suitable" recommendation) the Woods and New York Mountains WSAs.

Judy Anderson had submitted four recommended amendments with extensive supporting data. Two were not even considered by the BLM, which later asserted they had been lost, and the remaining two were rejected. Anderson and others did support three minor proposed amendments dealing with the ACEC program. These added one new ACEC, relocated another, and expanded a third to cover an area of high archaeological value. In two cases, WSAs of minimum size, the 5,000-acre Black Mountain WSA and the 4,000-acre Morongo WSA, were shifted from "non-suitable" to "suitable" for wilderness designation.

To the conservation community, the changes in the Desert Plan proposed in 1982, and in large measure put into effect by the BLM's final decision of May 1983, illustrated a willingness by the BLM to remove for flimsy or totally inadequate reasons many of the protections afforded by the original Desert Plan. The justification offered for opening the Panamint Dunes to ORVs, proposed by Inyo County, was that this "would increase opportunities for this kind of recreation in Inyo County" with no response given to the many comments which had been received predicting serious adverse impacts from this decision.[29] Through a long and laborious process, this amendment was appealed to the Interior Board of Land Appeals by the Wilderness Society, the California Native Plant Society, the Desert Protective Council, the Sierra Club and the Timbisha Shoshone Indian Tribe, all represented by the Earthjustice Legal Defense Fund. It was 1986 before the board finally issued a unanimous ruling against the BLM stating that the BLM's own record contained little if any evidence to support its amendment.[30]

The final decision to reduce the size of EMNSA was limited to 47,000 acres, eliminating the Mountain Pass rare earth mine north of I-15 plus a sizable area of the Ivanpah and Mescal Mountains south of that highway which contained rare earth mining claims. No adequate explanation was given as to why almost 10% of EMNSA (over 140,000 acres) was originally proposed to be deleted.

The huge proposed shift in WSA lands from "suitable" to "nonsuitable" (240,000 acres) was particularly galling. It was principally justified on the ground that potential for mining or geothermal development or, in some instances, prior ORV use, trumped wilderness as the highest and best use for these areas. It had been tentatively determined less than three years before, using the geological and mineralogical data accumulated over four years of work by specialists on the Desert Plan staff, that wilderness was the highest and best use of these WSAs. This determination was subject to the results of mineral surveys to be made by the U.S. Geological Survey and the Bureau of Mines in order to comply with FLPMA. At the time of the 1982 amendments, such surveys (of the WSAs in question) had not yet been completed. What the amendments proposed to do was to terminate, with little or no new basis for doing so, the orderly evaluation of these WSAs for Congressional recommendation. In fact, because the BLM was asking the Geological Survey/Bureau of Mines to study *only* those WSAs it now considered "suitable" and omit all others, this plan amendment would prevent any serious future Congressional evaluation of the validity of the BLM's principal reason for crossing these WSAs off its recommended list.

Justification for reopening the annual Barstow-Vegas race was that "there is a great desire on the part of the off-road vehicle community to add this course to the plan." Most of the course had already been used in the past, the BLM stated and "although there would be unavoidable adverse impacts on a number of resources directly on the race course" these would be less than the impacts that caused cancellation of the race from 1975 through 1982. The reasons given were that entrants would be limited to 1,200 (three times the number allowed on any other race permitted by the BLM) and better controls were promised.[31]

Desert thunder—start of the famous Barstow-Vegas race across the Mojave Desert.

Totally disregarded in the decision to reopen the race was the fact that of more than 800 comments received from the public on the Draft Environmental Impact Report, only a few supported the event. As specifically noted in the final BLM report on the amendments,[32] the vast majority of commentators urged protection of the desert and denounced an amendment which would authorize a "use" not permitted since the Desert Plan's adoption in Class C or Class L areas. A large percentage of the designated racecourse ran through Class L land, supposedly so designated "to protect sensitive natural, scenic, archaeological and cultural values" in the language of the plan. Also disregarded were comments of the U.S. Fish and Wildlife Service, County of San Bernardino Planning Department, Federal Environmental Protection Agency and State Resources Agency, all of which urged rejection of the proposed course designation.

Challenge Fails to Stop the Barstow–Vegas Race

In *Sierra Club v. Clark*, the Sierra Club, Desert Protective Council, and California Native Plant Society, represented as plaintiffs by attorney Michael Sherwood and legal assistant Deborah Reames of Earthjustice Legal Defense Fund, challenged the action by the BLM allowing the reopening of the Barstow–Vegas race. Federal District Court Judge A. Wallace Tashima denied the plaintiff's emergency motion to halt the 1983 race. He left for trial the issue of long-term adverse impacts of the race and whether those impacts were sufficient to violate the "nonimpairment" standard established by FLPMA for WSAs, one of which the racecourse crossed.[33] He specifically invited resource experts to monitor the race and submit their testimony at the trial.

The 1983 race involved not only the course itself but a 1,600-acre core for the mass start of the race and three 8-acre "pits" along the course where racers refueled and spectators parked and congregated. Many miles of the course designated by the 1982 Plan Amendment were off-road, and the course traversed about 9 miles of the Soda Mountains WSA where there had been no prior track. Under the amended plan, the course was not only to be used, under permit, for the annual November mass–start race, but also for an unlimited number of other kinds of competitive and noncompetitive ORV events along all or portions of the course.

The BLM's EIS prepared for the race predicted "minimal impacts." Later, the BLM's own evaluation report documented substantial disorganization along the route and serious permit violations from start to finish. Other race monitors, as requested by Judge Tashima, submitted extensive reports to the court. Although the BLM evaluation stated "no damage occurred except for the visual element of the tracks," nine experts testified that the BLM's evaluation had no scientific basis.[34] All but one of these experts had PhDs in the biological and geological sciences. They testified that the BLM's improper monitoring techniques had grossly understated the damage done to desert plant and wildlife resources.

Dr. Robert Curry, a prominent expert on soils and land reclamation, noted that vehicles impact *desert* soils, in contrast to soils in other areas, by breaking up and pulverizing the protective crusts that form over hundreds of years. These crusts are a necessary protection against wind and water erosion. He testified:

> *Contrary to BLM's assertions, the 1983 race caused severe and long-lasting damage to surface and subsurface soils and vegetation. A highly visible course track is now indelibly impressed through the [Soda Mountains] WSA. Vegetation cannot and will not become re-established in the overcompacted soils barring major changes in climate and long passage of geologic time.... If future races are allowed to be run, the damage will become even greater and more widespread as the course widens and more and more vehicles stray off the course onto undisturbed areas.*

Another scientist, Dr. Howard Wilshire, examined a 1.2-mile stretch of the course and found 869 perennial plants destroyed or seriously damaged. Numerous observers of the route testified that the race produced a highly visible scar throughout the Soda Mountains WSA—in effect, it created a road, from 8 to 18 feet in width, where none had previously existed.

The plaintiffs finally argued that the EIS produced by the BLM violated the National Environmental Policy Act (NEPA), which requires presentation and analysis of a reasonable range of alternatives to the proposed action. Although the BLM did address one alternative to designating the course, its only discussion of that alternative, which was simply to take "no action," was superficial. The BLM rejected this alternative solely on the ground that without the new course, annual illegal "protest rides" would continue to occur in the area, presumably inflicting damage. No explanation was given as to why the BLM could not or would not enforce its own regulations and stop the illegal use, and why no other alternative (such as using one or more other courses already designated in the Desert Plan) was considered.

On October 31, 1984, the District Court rejected all of these arguments and held for the Interior Secretary.[35] It appeared that the judge had almost totally disregarded the evidence of the plaintiff's resource experts whom he had invited to monitor the race and submit evidence. He simply referred to the BLM's IMP, the agency's Interim Management Policy for WSAs. Under the IMP, the nonimpairment standard for WSAs is not violated if an admittedly damaging impact is "capable of being reclaimed to a condition of being substantially unnoticeable in the wilderness study area…as a whole." The Federal defendants had stressed that the Soda Mountain WSA was a large area. In the court's view (the judge having visited the area prior to the race but not after it was run), the road which had been cut through the Soda Mountain WSA, even though no attempt was made to reclaim it, was nevertheless "substantially unnoticeable *in the area as a whole.* The judge did not address the question of whether this provision of the BLM's IMP properly carried out the intent of the FLPMA's nonimpairment standard.

Plaintiffs appealed. It was October 1985 before the Ninth Circuit Court of Appeals issued its opinion affirming the District Court's decision. The Appeals Court, like the District Court, was sympathetic to the problem confronting the BLM. Congress had stated in FLPMA that ORV use of the desert, damaging as it may be, was to be allowed on BLM land "where appropriate." BLM was stuck with a difficult balancing act, required by law. It had developed a substantial number of mitigating measures for the race. It did not have a large staff of scientists and engineers. Only if the District Court had abused its discretion through failing to find the BLM's interpretation of its own regulations both "arbitrary and capricious," could the appellate court reverse. This it was not prepared to do.[36]

It was a solid win for the BLM and for off-road vehicle enthusiasts, and it raised serious doubts as to whether ORV racing in the desert could ever be ended. But, as Yogi Berra said, "it ain't over till it's over." Seven years later, under renewed pressure from the conservation community, the BLM terminated the race on its own motion.

The "Watt Drop"

Almost immediately after the conservation community had responded to the Draft EIS on the proposed 1982 Desert Plan amendments, Secretary Watt tried a new tack. On December 30, 1982, he published an order shortly to become known as the "Watt Drop."[37] The Secretary's order was in three parts:

1. Remove from WSA status any lands in which the U.S. did not own the subsurface mineral rights (split-estate lands).

2. Drop all WSAs amounting to less than 5,000 acres on the ground that they should never have been considered for WSA status in the first place.

3. Drop from WSA status any BLM area larger than 5,000 acres found to have wilderness characteristics only in association with contiguous wilderness or wilderness candidate areas administered by another agency, such as the Forest Service.

It appeared that only number 3—the "in association with" drop— significantly affected WSAs in the California desert, principally parts of the Santa Rosa and Orocopia Mountains WSAs.

Quickly Larry Silver of the Earthjustice Legal Defense Fund and several of his colleagues, representing the Wilderness and Audubon Societies, the Natural Resources Defense Council, the Environmental Defense Fund, the National Wildlife Federation, and the Sierra Club, challenged the validity of Secretary Watt's order in Federal court. Federal Judge Lawrence Karlton issued a preliminary injunction against any activities in the areas in question, not previously permitted in wilderness areas and the case settled down to a long round of briefing and argument. Finally, in 1985 the court held that the Secretary had failed to follow the law as to split estates, had failed to exercise any proper discretion as to areas under 5,000 acres,[38] and the parties stipulated that the "in association with" areas would all be put back into the WSA inventory for further examination as to their suitability. The effect of this order was to return to their former status over two million areas of candidate wilderness lands nationwide. No appeal was taken. The Watt Drop, after a vast amount of legal wrangling and a 40-page court opinion, was in the last analysis a drop in the bucket in its impact on the California desert. It demonstrated, however, the fervent desire of the Secretary of Interior to roll back such protection as the desert had at the time.

The Marks of Failure of The Desert Plan

It was the combination of the efforts of the Interior Department to rush the release of two-thirds of desert WSAs for consumptive uses, contrary to the intent of Congress as expressed in FLPMA, the BLM's leasing frenzy of 1982, the "Watt drop," and *particularly* the experience of the 1982 Desert Plan Amendment cycle, that persuaded conservation organizations large and small that the Desert Plan under BLM management had failed. It simply could no longer be relied on for protection of the resources they cared about. The Plan seemed to have no stability. Attempt after attempt was made to weaken it, and all had to be fought with enormous expenditures of energy and time. Almost all of the conservation-minded specialists who had been on the Desert Plan staff during the study that preceded the Plan had been terminated or transferred elsewhere. It would be necessary to resort to legislation to protect the desert.

It was the favorite tactic of those opposed to the proposed legislation to attack its supporters by complaining that their legislative effort was a "breach of faith" with the process by which the Desert Plan had been developed and in which the conservation community had participated. Nothing could be further from the truth. As demonstrated in these pages, it was not the Desert Plan itself that led to the legislative effort of the conservation community. It was the *failure* of that Plan, caused by the actions, and failures to act, of the Department of Interior and its agency, the BLM.

Another opposition argument, used time and again, was that adoption of legislation for desert protection would amount to wasting the $8 million the opponents claimed the government spent to develop the Desert Plan. To the contrary, little was wasted; most of that money was spent to study and describe a wealth of desert resources, to identify where these were found and in what proportions, to determine what areas were roadless and otherwise qualified as potential wilderness, to prepare maps and descriptions, to complete an inventory of WSAs, and otherwise to examine the desert scientifically. This wealth of information was a foundation for the Desert Bill; in particular, it was used extensively in careful selection of areas for park additions and wilderness designation. Its data and studies also guided and would continue to guide the BLM in managing the 6.5 million acres of BLM land in the California desert (excluding new BLM wilderness lands) not affected by the Bill.

What Can We Agree to Do?

It was inevitable that the cause of desert protection would be taken up primarily by Californians. Many men and women had spent prolonged effort over the years to awaken in others an appreciation of the California desert's beauty and vulnerability. Some of them now began to talk openly about the legislation they believed to be essential. Judy Anderson and Jim Dodson found themselves in agreement on a key issue: there should be no rush to judgment on the legislation. Patience was required to be sure as many persons and organizations as possible were united on the best approach.

Anderson observed, "We went to different conservation groups, asking them which areas of the desert they felt most needed protection." Serious consultations also began in late 1983 with senior staff members of the major conservation organizations, both in California and in Washington, D.C., particularly the Wilderness Society and the Sierra Club. The wrap-up California wilderness bill dealing with Forest Service land (following passage of a series of much smaller forest wilderness bills) was being negotiated between California's two Senators, Pete Wilson and Alan Cranston. Wilson believed Cranston's bill should be substantially reduced in size and the negotiations were at a delicate stage. It was agreed that this legislation took priority over desert legislation. The "California Wilderness Act," as it was called, was passed in September 1984 with Senators Wilson and Cranston roughly splitting the difference in acreage between their opposing positions, apparently the only way a compromise could be reached. This left to advocates of that bill the agonizing task of deciding which areas to sacrifice in order to reach the stipulated aggregate acreage limit—not the most sensible way to craft legislation of a peculiarly site-sensitive character.

When the Desert Plan was under development by the BLM, the Southern Californians on the Desert Committee had strongly urged that it include a Mojave National Park. This had remained almost an obsession with the somewhat prickly Peter Burk. Those with practical political experience in Washington were cautious. Was it asking too much to combine a national park proposal with a bill for wilderness? Would the one detract from the appeal of the other? Did they not have somewhat different constituencies? Could adequate grass roots support for both be found throughout the country? Should they really be considered in separate bills? Wouldn't the inclusion of a proposed new park in the bill bring on the powerful opposition of the National Rifle Association, endangering the rest of the bill, since the National Park Service and the National Parks and Conservation Association would not hear of a new national park that permitted hunting?

Jim Dodson toyed for a time with the idea of enshrining a modified California Desert Plan in legislation. It had been demonstrated that the current Desert Plan was shaky at best—it could seemingly be changed, its protective features weakened, without the consent of Congress and despite the strongest public objections. How could this be avoided? The more this legislative notion was analyzed, however, the more it was realized that such legislation would be far too complex and would open up a hundred issues for controversy. Not everything—in fact, not a great deal—could be put into a successful statute.

Fairly quickly the desert volunteers concluded that there should be a single bill, and that it must be as simple as possible, limited to the key objectives: Designate the needed wilderness *and* establish a new national park, if that should prove feasible.

Meanwhile, Judy Anderson and her crew continued working on maps of wilderness areas which were sure to be necessary for the prospective legislation, calling on an increasing number of volunteers to provide her with data from personal knowledge regarding boundaries. Jim Dodson, as Desert Committee chair, continued prior committee efforts to increase the size of the knowledgeable desert constituency with more desert study trips. Citizens for Mojave National Park and several chapters of the Sierra Club scheduled similar trips. Early in 1984 Judy Anderson and others decided to raise the visibility of the East Mojave area by organizing a weeklong trip at Easter time. Well over 50 vehicles signed up, many from northern California and out of state. BLM staff personnel from Needles were invited; Joe Fontaine, President of the Sierra Club, was there. Judy recalls that it was windy and "beastly cold" in their camp in the Lanfair Valley. Jim Dodson got the assignment of renting a port-a-potty and hauling it out and back in a trailer attached to his desert vehicle. On the return trip it almost capsized in the wind on the highway and had to be left in a small town in the desert to pick up on another day. On one frigid night when the wind was blowing fiercely, people would not even come out of their shelters for the campfire! Mabel Barnes, a famous desert explorer, declared it the coldest she had ever been in the desert in more than 30 years of camping. Nevertheless, a successful trail construction project was undertaken and there were many hikes to points of interest.

The next year the trip's organizers, undismayed by the bitter weather they had encountered the first time, did it again, camping for a week in a spot slightly more sheltered from the wind near Granite Cove in the Mojave. In the following year the affair reached the exalted status of a "national outing" of the Sierra Club, becoming so popular it had to be conducted in two sections. Anderson was the assistant leader on the first of these national outings and in charge, as she learned much too late, of all camp kitchen equipment. Despite this, by some means everyone was fed and, many hikes were led on the peaks and through the canyons. Judy got a friend named Elden Hughes to come on the final weekend with his guitar to lead campfire singing. He continued to do this in following years as he undertook an important role in the fight for desert parks and wilderness.

Senator Cranston Offers Help

In October 1984, barely a month after the California Wilderness Act (Forest Service) was enacted, a number of conservationists met with Senator Cranston in his Washington, D.C., office. He had been instrumental in gaining its passage and they congratulated him. His question to them was, "What's your priority now?" All replied: a bill for the California desert.

Later that same month Katherine Files (later Katherine Lacey, henceforth referred to as "Kathy" Lacey), the Senator's Assistant for Environmental Affairs, came home to California to take a look at the desert. Gerry Hillier, Director of the BLM's Desert District, which now included the entire California desert, was only too glad to give her and her friend Patty Hedge, California Director of the Wilderness Society staff, the BLM's promotional guided tour of EMNSA. On the way back to Los Angeles, Lacey and Hedge stopped for breakfast with the Burks in Barstow. Early in the game, Peter Burk had asked the Senator to support a Mojave National Park and had met and talked with Lacey on several occasions.

Peter recalls a two-hour discussion. Finally, Lacey said there were two alternatives. "We can sponsor a Mojave National Park bill which will take ten years," she said. "Or, we can sponsor a somewhat more environmentally protective but practical EMNSA bill that would pass Congress and not be opposed by the Administration." Without a moment's hesitation, Burk replied, "We need a Mojave National Park."

Did Kathy Lacey possess psychic powers? Ten years? In actuality, ten years and seven days elapsed between the date of her prediction and the day the California Desert Protection Act was signed into law, including the Mojave National Preserve to be managed by the National Park Service.

In Los Angeles on the same trip, Lacey met with Debbie Sease, Sierra Club Public Lands Director from Washington, D.C. (who was visiting California), Judy Anderson and other Southern Californians. Inquiring about local views, Debbie found strong sentiment for a large desert wilderness bill and somewhat more guarded sentiment for a Mojave National Park. Noncommittal, she returned to Washington. Within a week, she sent back word to the effect that, as Anderson recalls, "we should ask for what we want" and that she'd like to have it quickly.

Now the pressure was on. National staff leaders of the Sierra Club and Wilderness Society were not yet prepared to go for a national park. In November, Terry Sopher, BLM Issues Director of the Wilderness Society in Washington, D.C., asked Patty Hedge, who had just been through EMNSA with the BLM, to go with him to the desert, and stopped to meet the Burks. Sopher indicated to Peter Burk that he was not yet ready for legislation to establish a Mojave National Park but that the society was considering it. Sease was not ready, either, and it was vital to bring both on board. Sopher was not even fully persuaded about projected wilderness areas which Anderson and her cohorts had been working on. He had once been Wilderness Director of the BLM. Jim Dodson, in particular, bent his efforts to persuade both of them to the view held by the Californians.

In January 1984, the evening map-drafting sessions had moved to the Sierra Club's Los Angeles office. By now, anyone who walked into the office and could read a map was recruited to help. Anderson recalls that Barbara Reber, George Ostertag, Betsy Reifsnider, Ron Jones, and Linda Wade were regulars. Jim Dodson and others were occasional volunteers. Ostertag, who was at the time working during the day for an oil company, learned to be one of the most skilled of mapmakers. With special equipment at his disposal in his off-hours, he photographed all the original maps with a nondistorting camera so that clear presentations of maps with a slide projector could be made, if needed. When the mapping was approaching completion in 1985, Ostertag and his wife retired to Oregon where he began writing guidebooks containing elegant maps, including one describing California's state parks.

By late 1984 the mapmakers had finished mapping two million acres of wilderness but there was still a very long way to go. They had been at it steadily for four years! Before 1984 came to an end, they cranked up their meeting schedule to twice a week.

The idea of including Death Valley and Joshua Tree National Monuments in the proposed bill soon came to be espoused by the California volunteers. Many thousands of people were acquainted with these historic national monuments and would support a bill that recognized their park quality. Burk stressed his idea of a Mojave National Park as the "flagship" of the bill. It would, in his view, give the other parks and the proposed wilderness areas a better chance to pull through. In the final analysis, the Mojave National Park proposal became the lightning rod of controversy, taking some of the heat off the Death Valley and Joshua Tree park proposals and the many wilderness areas included in the bill.

Four critical meetings now took place in quick succession. The first, in Senator Cranston's Washington office with Kathy Lacey on December 2, 1984, involved staff officers of three conservation organizations:

- Three representatives of the Sierra Club—Bruce Hamilton, Debbie Sease and Robert Hattoy, its Southern California Field Representative

- Terry Sopher and Patty Hedge of the Wilderness Society

- Jim Eaton, Executive Director of the California Wilderness Coalition

All were under pressure from the California volunteers to support a bill that would include three national parks plus wilderness. Some admitted to each other that they were not quite prepared for this. It was not yet clear where Senator Cranston stood. Lacey pressed for decision and action. She wanted a bill ready for introduction no later than March 1985.

The second meeting was organized by the California volunteers, assisted by Bob Hattoy, to bring everyone under the same tent, if possible, to plan the preparation of the bill for submission to Cranston, and to develop the elements of a campaign strategy. It was held at the home of Mabel Barnes, Grande Dame of the Desert, in Los Angeles and lasted all afternoon on December 9. Twenty-five persons were present, including Sease and Sopher from the East Coast. An important individual attending was Douglas Scott, Conservation Director (in effect, second-in-command) of the Sierra Club, who had spent several years in Washington, D.C., as chief Sierra Club lobbyist for the Alaska Lands Act. Scott said that in his opinion the best strategy would be to push for a single bill, discarding any idea of separate, or partial and successive bills, although he was not yet sure what its precise content should be. This strategy had worked well in the Alaska campaign. Dodson, Anderson, and Burk were thoroughly in accord and glad to have Scott's authoritative word on the best way to approach Congress. Coordination of events, a media plan, meetings with the Superintendents of Death Valley and Joshua Tree Monuments, lobbying and letter writing campaigns were discussed. A steering committee representing all the organizations present was established and its next meeting scheduled in mid-December. Doug Scott's enthusiasm had been kindled. He even prepared detailed minutes of the meeting. (Thank you, Doug—such complete documentation was rare!)

The California Desert Protection League Is Born

There followed the second meeting of the steering committee on December 17, 1984. On December 9, when it first met, that committee had consisted of seven people, representing six conservation organizations. By December 17 its membership had increased to 28. The Committee's objective was to grow into an active coalition of all organizations, large and small, which would support the legislation. A name was chosen: The California Desert Protection League (CDPL). By common consent, Judy Anderson became its chair and remained so throughout the entire campaign led by CDPL. By the time the Desert Bill was first up for debate in the House of Representatives, CDPL represented 120 conservation organizations, all of which had thrown their support behind its passage.

It was high time to pin Senator Cranston down to specific terms. The Sierra Club set up a meeting with the Senator in Washington early in January 1985. Dr. Edgar Wayburn, a good friend of the Senator and Sierra Club Vice-President for National Parks and Protected Areas, was present. For many years Dr. Wayburn had been a renowned leader of the conservation movement and president of the Sierra Club during several separate terms. Also present were leading club staff members Carl Pope, Russ Shay, Debbie Sease, and Bob Hattoy, as well as key volunteers from California: former Angeles Chapter chair Sally Reid, club board member Michele Perrault, and Jim Dodson. With the Senator were Roy Greenaway, his administrative assistant, and Kathy Lacey.

Cranston cautiously suggested moving a part of the program first, to be followed by another bill a year later. To Dodson's relief, Wayburn immediately took issue with this idea, stressing that in his experience one gets the same opposition to a small proposal as to a big one, and assuring the Senator that a major bill for the California desert would constitute a magnificent project for him to sponsor. When the meeting was over, Greenaway took Wayburn aside to say: "I think you've persuaded the Senator to go for an omnibus bill. And you don't need to persuade me." It was Roy's job to think politically. In his view the Senator needed to author something visionary and highly significant for his home state before his next re-election campaign.

Wayburn had a kindred spirit in Jim Dodson, who would be on the firing line of the campaign. As Wayburn later wrote to Jim: "We can help the Senator achieve his desire to be known as a leading conservationist in Congress...It is our job to see that he takes on a proper-sized project...an omnibus proposal."

Desert Legislation Takes Shape

Meetings of the CDPL were now occurring frequently; everyone was welcome to come and many organizations were represented by several persons. It was during this period that Judy Anderson's talents were particularly needed. She was a driving force in pulling the new coalition together. As one admirer put it, "She is not soft but never threatening, never 'in your face,' always perfectly honest." Everyone credits her with a vast store of common sense and remarkable organizational skills. All were essential at this moment when open controversy could sidetrack the developing consensus.

By February it was agreed that it was highly desirable to expand the boundaries of Death Valley and Joshua Tree, as well as transforming them into parks, both to highlight the significance of those well-known treasures of the public lands and to bring under park protection their critical bordering areas. For example, Saline Valley and the Eureka Dunes, bordering Death Valley, were at the very top of the BLM's list as meriting protection. These areas, the Owlshead Mountains to the south and the Greenwater Range to the east, also included in the Park's expansion, were all part of the north Mojave Desert ecosystem. Rick Anderson, Superintendent of Joshua Tree, urged several additions to his national monument and various boundary adjustments for easier administration. Joshua Tree had an unsatisfactory southern boundary. The Eagle Mountains had earlier been removed from the monument because of a now abandoned mine; to the east, half the magnificent Coxcomb Mountains had somehow been left out of the monument.

Here were new mapping requirements for Judy Anderson and her crew. Needed were both the additional maps and, if possible, adequate descriptions of the features of all proposed protected areas. This would inevitably stretch Kathy Lacey's original timetable for a March 1985 introduction; with great effort it might be managed by early to mid-summer. As important as maps themselves were, experience with the California wilderness bill had shown that where there was little available information about an area it would fall out of the bill. Anderson therefore spent much of the spring of 1985 preparing narratives to go with all of the maps. She extracted information from the BLM's Desert Wilderness Inventory of March 1979, from Appendix III of the Desert Plan, from all other written references she could find, and from the panel of experts she had located.

Among others, George Barnes wrote up the areas around Death Valley, both park additions and wilderness. Robert Barnes knew the Sierra shoulder. Cary Meister from the Yuma Audubon Society took on the areas along the Colorado River. Jim Dodson developed the expansion of Red Rock Canyon State Park and covered parts of the western Mojave, Peter Burk parts of the Eastern Mojave, Ronald and Mary Ann Henry reviewed the Sacatar Trail area and areas along the Argus Range, Lyle Gaston the areas around Joshua Tree and many others throughout the desert. Anderson herself camped in the Dead Mountains with a draft map in her pack that needed revision. Critical data came in from Michael Prather, June Lanning, Harriet Allen, Joe Fontaine, and others. As they were ready, Anderson sent her drafts to Stanley (Stan) Haye, a retired County Assessor in Independence, California, who was a lifelong desert explorer and an expert on the northern Mojave. He read them, compared boundary descriptions with his full set of maps, added information from his own knowledge, and rewrote parts of Anderson's narratives to make them entirely consistent with each other. The resulting text, sent to Senator Cranston, came to two volumes or four computer disks, along with the maps, it was the heart and soul of the Desert Bill.

By the March 17 CDPL meeting, final boundaries for Death Valley National Park had been agreed to. Joshua Tree's final boundaries quickly followed. In late spring, Bob Barnes and Joe

Fontaine finished mapping desert wilderness in the southern Sierra Nevada Mountains. On June 6 Doug Scott decided to take a last look at the East Mojave to see if he could satisfy himself that the case for a Mojave National Park could be sold to other conservation organizations and to skeptical Congressional environmental staffers whose views would be influential. He and Bob Hattoy rented a plane and covered the ground, after which they met with Peter and Joyce Burk in Barstow. "I'm a friendly skeptic," Doug said. "Try to convince me." There followed a long afternoon of argument with Doug playing devil's advocate. Finally, Doug recalls looking squarely at Peter and saying, "Has anyone of importance [presumably not including Sierra Club and Wilderness Society types] said this should be a national park?" Silence. Then Joyce spoke up: "You know, the BLM itself said it." Doug's jaw dropped. Peter exclaimed: "Oh, that's right!" He rummaged in his papers to find the June 1979 report of the BLM's Desert Plan staff study made for the National Park Service of desert areas that possessed national park quality. Following a detailed analysis, the report said: "It is the conclusion of the Desert Plan staff that cultural and natural resource values of the East Mojave Study Area are so diverse and outstanding that the area readily qualifies for national park or monument status."[39]

Apparently no one else had a copy of this crucial piece of paper! Scott adjured Burk not to make any copies for the time being, except one for him. "At last, we have the icing for the cake," he thought to himself. "We'll want to make good use of this at the right time." He then said to Burk, "I'm convinced. You're right. We'll go for it all." This key report later reached Kathy Lacey and, possibly a bit prematurely, was used by her in preparing the press release to accompany introduction of the Desert Bill in February 1986.

Scott now drafted the findings and policy statements for the bill, many of which were used in the legislation that was ultimately enacted. Judy Anderson's finished maps and map narratives were added and the package was delivered to Kathy Lacey. It was early fall and the first session of the 99th Congress was about to end. The structure of the bill and its essential legal language remained for Lacey to draft. Inevitably, introduction of the bill would have to wait until the next year. In Washington, statutory protection for the Desert Lily Sanctuary and designation of Andreas and Murray Canyons in the San Jacinto Mountains south of Palm Springs as a "National Historic Site," which would preclude a threatened development in the mouths of these "Indian Canyons," were added to the bill. (Subsequently, in June 1988, a successful California bond initiative proposition provided funds for the State Department of Parks and Recreation to acquire the threatened land, and the "Indian Canyons" provision was dropped from the Desert Bill.)

California Congressman Richard Lehman. His House subcommittee led the way to the first favorable Congressional action on the Desert Bill.

Courtesy of Richard Lehman

Otherwise, Lacey was discreet about what was happening to the draft bill in the Senator's office. Those who for years had shouldered most of the planning were nervous. It was learned that Jim Eaton, Executive Director of the California Wilderness Coalition, had invited the Senator to come to the Coalition's fall conference in Visalia, California, on October 25–26, and that he had accepted. Bob Barnes of the Audubon Society, who had organized the conference, arranged a meeting for the bill's proponents on the first evening. Doug Scott informed the meeting that he was now reasonably sure of a positive stance on Mojave National Park by major national conservation organizations, including particularly the National Parks and Conservation Association and the Wilderness Society. At a second meeting on the next day those who had labored on the legislative package were assured that the Senator would soon introduce it. Finally, following his arrival, Senator Cranston, in a major speech before the conference, said that he was ready to introduce his Desert Bill. Democratic Representative Rick Lehman, whose district crossed the Sierra into the northern desert of Inyo County, also spoke encouragingly but in more general terms, saying that the California desert was a legislative priority of his. Applause and cheers!

A Bill at Last

Arrangements could finally be made for a press conference to celebrate the introduction of S. 2061, "the California Desert Protection Act" with Senator Cranston present in person along with celebrants from sponsoring organizations. This took place in Los Angeles on February 7, 1986. By this time, the CDPL had 21 organizational sponsors.

And what sort of an act was it that was now revealed to the public?

- A new national park of 1.5 million acres would be established with almost the same boundaries as those of the existing East Mojave National Scenic Area.

- Death Valley and Joshua Tree National Monuments would be made national parks and enlarged: Death Valley from 2.1 to 3.3 million acres and Joshua Tree from 550,000 to 800,000 acres.

- In the rest of the desert, wilderness areas would be created totaling something over 4 million acres and remain under the management of the BLM.

Senator Alan Cranston, sponsor and Senate spokesman for his Desert Bill through four successive Congresses.

Courtesy of Eldon Hughes

- Within the new Mojave National Park, within the expanded Death Valley National Park and in the additions to Joshua Tree, roughly another 4 million acres would be protected as wilderness.

113

That was the essence of the Desert Bill. It contained three minor provisions:

1. Enlarge Red Rock Canyon State Park by including the canyons to the east,

2. Give statutory protection to the existing Desert Lily Sanctuary, and

3. Make the two Indian Canyons near Palm Springs a "National Historic Site."

Opponents said it was a "desert closure act." But was it? As later study would show, its cost was minor. It reflected no change in the policies governing management of the existing national monument areas which, under National Park Service rules, had always been managed as if they were national parks. Only a change of title was involved, together with upgraded status in the public mind. The BLM lost jurisdiction over the land allocated to the Mojave National Park and the additions made to Death Valley and Joshua Tree. But it retained jurisdiction over the millions of acres of designated wilderness outside the parks (85 separate areas) and over approximately 6.5 million acres of its land not affected at all by the bill. This amounted to three-quarters of the California desert land previously managed by the BLM. As for the new wilderness areas remaining under the BLM, almost the only changes to be made in their management would be

- No further use of motor vehicles within the wilderness boundaries, and

- No future non-mineral commercial developments,

- No new mining claims were to be filed after the Act was passed and

- All existing valid mining claims and valid mineral leases, as well as all existing hard rock mines were grandfathered.

- All existing grazing could continue,

- Rockhounds were not restricted, and

- Hunting could continue as before.

In the Mojave National Park and the additions made to the two existing national monuments, the restrictions were somewhat stronger:

- Commercial development, rockhounding, and hunting were prohibited. (Hunting was subsequently permitted in the Mojave National Preserve, as well as grazing without a cutoff date, by the Desert Bill as enacted.)

- Grazing was limited to the life of existing leases.

- All mining claims determined to be valid, all mineral leases, and all existing mines were grandfathered.

- It was expected that the Park Service would not handle mining operation plans as cavalierly as had sometimes been the case with the BLM.

The bill was especially sensitive to access needs. Many wilderness area boundaries included "cherry stem" boundary adjustments to permit vehicular access into the heart of the protected area. Only 1,500 miles of unmaintained routes and not a single mile of road would be closed by the designation of wilderness. Some 32,500 miles of roads and routes of travel would remain open. In 85% of all wilderness areas there would be no location more than three miles from an open road or route of vehicle travel, and none of the remaining 15% would be more than ten miles from such a road or route.

None of the "open areas" already set aside for ORV play by the BLM in the Desert Plan as of the time the act was introduced would be closed except for two sand dune areas already designated as WSAs. That left 14 open areas equaling over 450,000 acres plus an estimated 300,000 acres of private lands lying within, or adjacent to these areas, available to the ORV community for free play.

The act had been drafted with special care to avoid conflict with existing consumptive uses of the desert. No mines producing any of the four major minerals (borates, rare earths, sodium sulfate and soda ash) for which the California desert is an important provider existed then, or exist today, within the areas protected by the act. *None* of 14 minerals labeled "strategic" by the Federal Office of Technology Assessment are found, to the knowledge of mining experts, in the areas protected by the act.

For all of the reasons mentioned, would the bill as introduced be deemed a moderate proposal that would not be too hard to enact? Please don't hold your breath.

...What tongue shall tell
the majesty of it,
the external strength of it,
the poetry of its widespread chaos,
the sublimity of its lonely desolation.
And who shall paint
the splendor of its light;
and from the rising up of the sun
to the going down of the moon
over the iron mountains,
the glory of its wondrous coloring.

—John C. Van Dyke in *The Desert*

ELDEN
HUGHES

Reaching for the Brass Ring

CHAPTER SEVEN

"Someone We Should Get to Know"

It was a cold, cloudless night in November 1983 far above Saline Valley, and the stars were flashing in the desert sky. Trip leaders Jim Dodson and Judy Anderson were at last able to relax by the fire and take stock. Everyone had made it up the road to Hunter Mountain. They looked over their group. It was distinguished by the presence of Mabel Barnes, widow of a highly regarded professor of Physics at UCLA, and herself head of the Department of Mathematics at Occidental College. She and her husband had come to California from Iowa in 1947 and had become passionate lovers of the desert, devoted rockhounds, and influential mentors of younger leaders like Dodson and their own son, George Barnes. There was also someone new at the fire, a bulky fellow with a beard, named Elden Hughes. Judy noticed that he had brought with him a copy of the 1980 California Desert Plan.

Had a copy of the Desert Plan? Brought it with him to the desert? Judy and Jim had recently tangled with the BLM over its damaging 1982–83 amendments to that plan issued just six months previously. Judy recalls thinking, "This is someone we should get to know." Her thought proved prophetic.

Elden Hughes was born in 1931, in Whittier, California. Both his father and mother came originally from Modoc County where his father's forebears had run cattle since the middle of the last century. World War I interrupted his father's apprenticeship on the family cattle ranch and, in the 1920s, the family moved south to Whittier, where his father went into the construction business. By the time Hughes was 13, his family had had enough of town life and they bought a cattle ranch not far away.

It was "earn your own way" in the Hughes family. Elden soon found it possible to make enough money raising hogs to buy an old car and, by the time he was in the 10th grade, began a lifetime of exploring and hunting in California's wild places.

He managed to pay his way through Whittier College, where he graduated in 1953, raising hogs on the family ranch and, in the summers, unloading boxcars filled with iron pipe. Everything interested him; he majored in four different subjects—business administration, economics, history, and geology. Perhaps this would account for the fact that his outdoor life as an adult centered around four quite different interests: spelunking, river-running, archaeology, and, at the last, the desert.

After briefly taking advantage of a scholarship for graduate study at Vanderbilt University, Hughes spent eight years working with his father in the wholesale plumbing supply business. It was tough to compete against larger companies equipped with computer systems to control inventory and perform other tasks. After it became possible to sell the family business, he went to work for Warner Information Systems, a Los Angeles computer service company, convinced of the advantages to small businesses of the computer technology he was able to install to serve their needs. He became the company's executive vice president.

By the mid-1970s he had three sons, was divorced, and was ready to rediscover the joys of exploring he'd found as a youth. He joined the Sierra Club and the Pacific Coast Archaeological Society. As vice president of the society in the '70s, he joined or led digs and exploring trips throughout the great petroglyph storehouse of the Mojave Desert. Soon he was also leading river, caving, and desert outings for the Orange County Sierra Singles, a section of the Sierra Club's Angeles Chapter. His first date with his future wife, Patty Carpenter was on a "singles" trip to Pinnacle Cave in Nevada in 1977. Through the early '80s both served the singles, she as conservation chair and he as the section chair. He went on to be elected a member of the Executive Committee of the Angeles Chapter and, in 1985, was urged by Jim Dodson to run for chapter chair, a position he held in the years '86–'88.

At first, the rivers held him captive. Canoeing with Patty was a favorite sport. Beginning in 1980, both worked in the successful campaign to obtain "wild and scenic" designation for an important stretch of the Tuolumne River. Two thousand letters from the Orange County Sierra Singles helped to bring Senator Wilson around, and the Tuolumne bill passed in 1984. It was a stunning example of the grass roots in action, a vital and almost unique feature of the Sierra Club's effectiveness. Hughes was a leader in the club's successful 1985–87 "three rivers campaign" to protect portions of the Kings, Merced, and Kern Rivers as wild and scenic; again, the Orange County Sierra Singles played a key role, sending thousands of letters to Senators and members of Congress. The Kern River Act finally passed the Congress in 1987. By now the campaign for the California Desert Bill was well underway, and, as Jim Dodson and Judy Anderson had hoped, Hughes was prepared to join that campaign as soon as he could.

Pictures Speak for the Desert

Jim Dodson, who had planned the February 1986 press conference in Los Angeles on the introduction of the Desert Bill, asked Hughes to attend as the new chair of the Sierra Club's Angeles Chapter. A serious amateur photographer, Elden asked if a few large blowups of good desert pictures, which he had on his office walls, would be useful. Jim too had been an avid photographer for years and brought along a number of his own. All their photographs received attention and praise from the media present at the conference.

This stuck in Elden's mind. He was beginning to attend meetings of the CDPL (California Desert Protection League) but the work of chairing the largest Sierra Club chapter, with its broad range of issues, took all the time he could spare. By mid-1987, as his term was coming to an end, someone raised the question: "What are we doing about pictures of the wilderness areas in the bill?" Elden volunteered to undertake that project and raised several thousand dollars to pay the cost. The task exceeded his predictions, taking more than two years.

A single, detailed map of the entire desert was needed for the project. Hughes put it together by taking the excellent Auto Club of Southern California maps of the desert counties, shrinking some by copying techniques until all were of equivalent scale, fitting them together and drawing the projected wilderness area boundaries on them. Here was one map that Judy Anderson did not have to make. Its duplicates guided volunteer photographers to areas needing to be photographed, demonstrated the network of roads which would continue to exist if the Desert Bill passed and which made access by vehicle to all parts of the desert possible. In future years it proved useful to Congressional staff personnel working on the Desert Bill. Versions of the map were overlain with cattle and sheep grazing allotment boundaries and tortoise habitat areas to enable them to be visualized at a glance. Hughes recalls talking to the environmental assistant to Congressman Leon Panetta (Democrat, California, and later White House Chief of Staff), who told him the Congressman was dubious about the Desert Bill. It was "just too big." Hughes spread out the composite map showing all of the proposed wilderness areas and asked her to pick out any three at random and he would tell her what was there and why their resources deserved protection. That week Congressman Panetta became a co-sponsor of the bill.

Hughes and his wife Patty conceived the idea that they might somehow find time to explore with their cameras, at least briefly, *all* of the wilderness areas included in S. 2061, the Senate version of the Desert Bill in its first Congress. They devoted almost every weekend to their project when no significant meetings or other trips were scheduled. They traveled in Hughes's aging 1969 Blazer. The vehicle was usually up to the challenge, but not always. In August 1988 the Cady Mountains WSA, east of Barstow, was on their agenda. They approached it by driving up the wash that drains the area. It was hot and they had run the air conditioner, a recent retrofit. No one had suggested that a bigger alternator was required. When they stopped at sunset to take pictures in Hidden Valley, the Blazer decided to call it a day.

As experienced desert rats, they had plenty of water (a 5-gallon bottle) and adequate food. Someone just might come by in the next week or two. But they were impatient. On foot in the desert, one travels best at night. Doubled plastic garbage bags over the shoulder held a gallon of water for each of them. After about 15 miles, dawn came and found them approaching several houses. They managed to locate one without a large, mean dog. On the phone, the Auto Club said, "Where, did you say?

We can't get you out of *there*." But a new battery and a ride back to the Blazer in a tow truck saved the day.

The final product of the photography project consisted of four sets of a three-volume "Wilderness Picture Book" including 400 pictures, the best of about 8,000 desert photographs Elden and Patty had collected, plus textual descriptions of all 116 candidate wilderness areas. Elden and 31 other photographers contributed to the project. The photographs were invaluable for lobbying and were shown on more than one occasion in television broadcasts. Many were included in *Time's Island* by T.H. Watkins, published by Peregrine Smith Books in 1989. Watkins, long-time editor of *Wilderness Magazine*, selected ten photographs taken by Elden and four by Jim Dodson. Senator Dianne Feinstein (Democrat, California) used super-size computer enlargements of some of the photographs on the Senate floor in 1992 when she introduced the final Desert Bill.

Long before the Wilderness Picture Book was conceived, others had put together slide shows to reach people who knew little of the desert's magnificence. Early in the 1980s when a wilderness bill for the state of Nevada was before Congress, Judy Anderson had purchased her own audiovisual equipment to present a sophisticated Nevada wilderness slide show to meetings of Sierra Club groups and sections in southern California. Her snarl of equipment and electrical cords became the mainstay for the first California desert slide show put together in the mid-1980s. Anderson, Jim Dodson, and Lynne Foster gathered the slides and Foster, then hard at work on *Adventuring in the California Desert*, wrote the script. None of them could spare the time to take the show around. Jeffrey (Jeff) Widen took up the challenge when he became Southern California Field Representative of the Sierra Club early in 1987. He presented the show to just short of one hundred programs and letter-writing sessions around southern California until the equipment literally wore out. It had proven itself the educational workhorse for the Desert Bill.

Later in the 1980s, Victoria (Vicky) Hoover, half-time staff assistant in San Francisco to Dr. Edgar Wayburn, the "Grey

Eminence" of the Sierra Club, independently determined that northern California needed a desert slide show. She put one together using slides principally taken by Eric Wilson, one of her frequent desert trip companions, and by members of Desert Survivors, headquartered in Oakland. She took this show to many Sierra Club chapters in the northern part of the state, to Audubon chapters through Bob Barnes, "Mr. Audubon" in that part of the state, and to any other organization that wished to schedule it in a program.

Finally, someone was bound to think of video. About the time the Desert Plan was adopted in 1980, a series of short film segments entitled "The Desert's Broken Silence" were shown on public television. A few people recalled it as an excellent piece of work, but it had disappeared. The introduction of the Desert Bill provoked arch-conservative California State Senator H.L. Richardson (Republican) to produce in 1987 a half-hour video entitled "The Desert Lockout," starring actor Roy Rogers, self-proclaimed "King of the Cowboys." Richardson was quoted as saying he had decided to produce this video because the one he had produced a year earlier for the campaign to unseat California Supreme Court Chief Justice Rose Bird had proven so successful.[40] This was another pure attack vehicle. Richardson asserted that if the Desert Bill were passed "our desert will be padlocked," that the cost of the bill would run into hundreds of millions of dollars, that those families who camp "would have to restructure their lives," and that many people would lose their jobs all absurd inaccuracies. It was hardly a vehicle for public television stations. Whether it was ever shown on commercial TV is doubtful; however, hundreds of copies were distributed around the country, and it was sent to all members of Congress.

No one could accurately assess the impact of the Roy Rogers video, but it certainly wouldn't hurt to have one that presented the case for desert protection with sufficient impartiality that it could be used as an educational film on public TV. Such a project had already begun in southern California, with test desert footage shot from a helicopter, when it was discovered that two distinguished scientists, both strong partisans of desert protection, had joined Douglas Prose, a young independent producer in the San Francisco Bay area, with the same objective. They were Dr. Robert Stebbins, Professor Emeritus of Zoology at the University of California, Berkeley, author of *A Field Guide to Western Reptiles and Amphibians* and many scientific papers, and Dr. Howard Wilshire of the U.S. Geological Service, another prolific author of scientific papers. The three of them were ready to go to work but had no money. Volunteers in southern California raised the money (independently of the major conservation organizations) and Wilshire and Stebbins became the stars of *Desert Under Siege*, a half-hour film released in 1991. It was distributed free to member organizations of the CDPL, offered to schools and public television stations throughout the country, and shown by stations from San Francisco to Washington, D.C. The film won for Prose, its producer, awards for "best coverage of an endangered species" and "best use of video" at the International Wildlife Film Festival held in Missoula, Montana, in 1992.

Someone in the San Francisco-based California Academy of Sciences saw the film and asked its producer, Doug Prose, if he could put together a 5-minute version to be a part of an exhibit entitled "The Vanishing Desert—California's Threatened Habitat," then being organized. Prose had excess footage and it was easy to do. "The Vanishing Desert" on videotape was available to all comers in the Academy's exhibit room. It was enthralling, colorful, fast-moving.

"We anticipated a strong reaction" says Linda Kulik,[41] chair of the Academy's Exhibits Department, although the exhibit had tried to present a balanced view. She was right. Major objectors were the ORV groups, their publications, and the American Motorcyclist Association. The AMA demanded changes. The Academy refused; in its view; such changes would have compromised scientific integrity. The April 1991 issue of *In Gear* told its readers, "If you can't see the exhibit, at least write a letter to [the Academy] and tell them what a biased, politically misrepresented exhibit they have promoted." A phone campaign against the desert exhibit generated up to a dozen calls a day for several weeks. At least 90% of the callers, says Kulik, had not seen the exhibit. They were invited to come and view it, and a majority of those who did thought it not as bad as they'd been led to believe. All of the Academy's trustees received packets of material from the objectors as part of an unsuccessful effort to close down the exhibit. It was kept open for its scheduled six-month run.

Some letters received by the Academy chastised it for not taking a *stronger* advocacy position! Kulik was pleased by one letter which observed: "It's very easy to avoid presenting information that makes it necessary for us critically to examine the consequences of our ways of life."[41]

Finding Common Ground at the Old Kelso Depot

In the midst of the struggle for desert parks and wilderness, the threat of demolition of the historic Kelso Depot presented a cause that unified miners, off-roaders, the BLM, railroaders, San Bernardino County, and conservationists. It was a unique phenomenon.

The old Kelso Depot. Friends and foes of the Mojave National Park joined forces to save it, and it may someday be a visitor center in the Mojave Preserve.

Courtesy of Elden Hughes

The depot had been constructed in 1924, and stood across the tracks from the hamlet of Kelso in the center of the East Mojave National Scenic Area. It was a handsome two-story Spanish-style building with wide, arched arcades and tile roofs, surrounded by a green lawn and many trees, for Kelso was a desert oasis. The station was one of a string of passenger depots and freight offices along the line of the San Pedro, Los Angeles and Salt Lake Railroad, later a part of the Union Pacific. Its heyday came in the early years of World War II when military trains arrived as often as several times an hour. Iron ore dug from the nearby Vulcan Mine during the war was shipped from Kelso to the Kaiser Steel Works in Fontana, largest of its kind west of the Mississippi. Some 2,000 people, employees of the railroad and of the mine with their families, populated the town of Kelso. Part of the main floor of the depot was devoted to the "beanery," which operated 24 hours a day, feeding train crews first and passengers second. Upstairs, 18 small sleeping rooms and a single bathroom served employees, all male it is believed, who lay over temporarily. These were the last days of steam; springs at Kelso supplied boiler water, and up to a dozen "helper" locomotives, kept in an old-fashioned "round house," assisted the trains up the steep grade from Kelso at 2,126 feet to Cima, 18 miles away but over 2,000 feet higher. Alas, by the end of the war the diesel locomotive was king and there was no more need for Kelso. It quickly shrank, the passenger trains no longer stopped there en route to Las Vegas, and by June 1985 the Union Pacific had determined to demolish the depot as it had so many others in California.

Before they became heavily involved in the nascent campaign for the Desert Bill, Elden Hughes and Patty Carpenter had fallen in love with the old Kelso Depot, which was now quite dilapidated inside. When they heard about its upcoming demolition, they decided to do what they could to help develop support for its preservation. Peter Burk charmingly tells the entire story in one of the best of his many booklets on the Mojave Desert, *The Kelso Depot Story*. It was Patty's game plan. With help from Elden, she persuaded Amtrak to provide a special train for an outing that brought 40 people to the desert, many of them from the Orange County Sierra Singles, to publicize the effort to save the depot. The "Desert Wind" left Union Station in Los Angeles at 9 a.m. on April 19, 1986. Train crews were switched from the Santa Fe to the Union Pacific at Yermo, the train passed through Afton Canyon at twilight, negotiated the Devil's Playground, and reached Kelso at 8 p.m. It was the first passenger train to stop at Kelso in more than 20 years.

The whole town of Kelso turned out to welcome the travelers. "O.B." O'Brien, a member of one of the remaining 25 families in Kelso and a lover of the old depot, had prepared a nearby campsite and railroaders' dinner of salad, steak, beans, bread, and steaming coffee. Patty brought railroaders' caps for everyone. O.B. had built a stage for a program, MC'd by Patty, which included old railroad songs dug up by Elden to be sung lustily by the crowd. Highlight of the evening was a playlet in which the actors testified before the members of the Board of Directors of the railroad, played by the entire audience, to tell why they wanted the old depot saved. Speaking extempore and playing themselves were the BLM's District Manager, several old timers from the town, and railroad men who had been stationed there. Inspired, some of the Kelso youngsters hopped onto the stage to tell why they, too, wanted to keep the old depot. Peter recalls one little girl who said, "So I can get ice cream there in the summer again." No way to top that one, so the Board of Directors shut off debate and cast a unanimous vote "FOR."

As Peter Burk puts it, when Ev Hayes, the BLM's Needles Resource Area Manager, and Gerry Hillier, the BLM's Desert District Manager, learned of the demolition decision, they reached California Congressman Jerry Lewis. His district contained the depot. Just before the bulldozers were ready to go, the Chairman of the Board of the Union Pacific Railroad received a letter from the Congressman saying

> To destroy the building, or even to consider moving it
> from its original site, would be a tragedy…I'm sure
> you share my belief that the beauty of [the East Mojave]
> is enhanced and enriched by such historical edifices

*and sites as the Kelso Train Depot. Its preservation
is worthy of your organization's fullest and most
positive consideration.*

The bulldozers were sent away. It was an act of chivalrous courtesy for Burk to say it, and he did: Ev Hayes, Gerry Hillier, and Congressman Lewis were "the three heroes who saved the Kelso Depot from demolition." The *San Bernardino Sun* helped out with a supportive editorial.

Now, there was no time to lose. The railroad wanted a plan and the conservators had to form an organization to act. Joining in its formation were Burk, Hayes, Hillier, ORV leader Marie Brashear, San Bernardino County planner and old desert hand Charles Bell, and Kelso resident and writer Robert Asmus. Necessary repairs were assessed. Money was needed and a nonprofit corporation, the Kelso Depot Fund, was projected. Marie Brashear was its first president, Peter Burk its treasurer. In 1986 Patty Carpenter became president, Burk remained treasurer, Elden Hughes joined the board, and attorneys working on a *pro bono* basis completed the incorporation and obtained the tax exemption. All were agreed on the objective: to restore the building as a visitor center and museum to be managed by whatever agency—the BLM or National Park Service—ultimately was given responsibility for this part of the desert.

The Union Pacific agreed conditionally to lease the depot to the Kelso Depot Fund, but the fund was never able to raise enough money to pay for the insurance required by the railroad. The fund had quarterly meetings and worked to keep the project alive. It held special cleanup days, repainted the depot, replaced the irrigation system, cared for the tall palm tress brought from another desert, and built up a membership of 500 people. Finally the railroad was persuaded to sell the land and building to the BLM.

On November 21, 1992, all who had played a part in the effort could put on their railroad hats and celebrate the final transfer of title to the old Kelso Depot. Bob Asmus was gone. Ev Hayes had transferred to Reno, Nevada. Henri Bisson had succeeded Gerry

Hillier, though it was Gerry who finally made the deal with the Union Pacific. Elden and Patty Hughes, and Peter and Joyce Burk were there to celebrate the ups and downs, the fits and starts, and finally the success of their years of work to preserve an historic and picturesque desert landmark.

Waging a War of Words

"You'll need a press kit," someone said as plans were laid for the press conference to introduce the Desert Bill in 1986. Jim Dodson took on the task. With assistance from Bob Hattoy and others of the Sierra Club staff in Los Angeles, he produced a series of separately printed miniature essays including *Why Protect the California desert? Desert Plants and Animals, Human History in the Desert, Geology, Wilderness Areas, Mojave National Park, Death Valley* and *Joshua Tree National Parks, Red Rock Canyon State Park, Supporting Organizations,* plus a map. The essays focused on the positive benefits of the legislation and criticized no one.

As the first published statement about the legislation, this series was a truly gentle beginning if a "war of words" was in store. The BLM responded within a week, assuring the members of its Desert District Advisory Council that it would oppose this bill. However, its overview of the bill was relatively mild in tone as well as factual. Its main thrust was that the Desert Plan was working well.

In June the bill's sponsors published a memo of questions and answers concerning the bill, also mild in tone. Was the debate going to be polite and decorous?

Not so. A strident opposition was mobilizing under the banner of "California Desert Coalition," including ORV groups and their suppliers, a lesser number of mining and grazing interests, associations of public land inholders, and gun enthusiasts. The Coalition was a serious organization. It soon hired a staff, and in the final months of 1994 it engaged a prestigious lobbying firm. Mouthpieces of the Coalition included *Cycle News* (a weekly), *ATV News, the American Motorcyclist, Dirt Bike, In Gear, Dirt Rider, the Firing Line, People for the West, Off Road, Four Wheeling, The Blue Ribbon Coalition Magazine,* and the *National Inholders Association*

News. Under the headline "Cranston Opponents Blast S. 2061," *Cycle News* reported in June 1986: "According to the California Desert Coalition, the [Desert Bill] would eliminate most recreational and business activities in the desert, including hunting, camping, rockhounding, sightseeing, photography, mining, grazing and back country exploring."

After quoting that statement in his article in the November/December 1986 issue of *Sierra*, Jim Dodson laconically concluded: "Not a word of this is true." However, by that time news had reached sponsors of the Desert Bill that members of the California Congressional delegation had been bombarded by hundreds of postcards and letters expressing violent opposition to the bill. Could supporters of the bill have been left behind at the

Courtesy of *Copley News Service*, Ken Alexander

starting blocks? They reacted by organizing a Desert Protection Act Seminar at the end of June 1986 to stimulate a letter-writing campaign and gave wide distribution to Jim's article and one by Senator Cranston in the same issue of *Sierra*.

Next to be heard from was the Wilderness Society. In July 1986, Norbert (Nobby) Riedy, Jr., was sent by the Society to southern California as its point man to help with the Desert Bill campaign. It was a mission he'd been preparing for most of his life. He was soon out in the desert to examine the BLM's performance under the Plan. Over the next eight years he was destined to play an increasingly critical role representing the Wilderness Society in the fight for the Desert Bill, culminating in the agonizing vigil of the last few days in October 1994.

An unassuming man of slight build and youthful aspect, in 1993 Nobby surprised those who did not know him well by climbing Aconcagua in the Andes, highest mountain in the Western Hemisphere at 22,800 feet, and then during the descent, remaining far behind his companions at night in a storm to assist a climber who was in trouble.

Nobby grew up in North Carolina, graduating in 1981 from Marlborough College. On trips to New England mountains and to the barrier islands offshore Georgia, he cultivated an early interest in field biology. Following graduate work in environmental studies at the Yale School of Forestry, he was for a time an aide to Congressman James Clarke (Democrat) of North Carolina. He joined the Wilderness Society staff in 1985 to work on BLM issues under Terry Sopher, helping to organize the testimony for Representative John Seiberling's 1985 oversight hearings on the BLM wilderness program. It was no surprise when the society decided to send Nobby out to Los Angeles shortly after the Desert Bill was introduced. He welcomed the chance to work in the approaching campaign.

Two months later Patty Schifferle replaced Patty Hedge as the society's Regional Director for California and Nevada. Quick on her feet with the press and highly quotable, she soon became an important contact person for media interested in the Desert Bill. Together, Riedy and Schifferle wrote *Failure in the Desert*, a pamphlet published in October 1986. It straightforwardly charged that in some 16 or more instances, the Desert Plan as amended in 1983, and the BLM's management under that plan, had grievously failed to protect significant desert resources.

The California State office of the BLM under Director Ed Hastey now joined the battle in earnest. In December 1986, it responded that the Wilderness Society's report was "misleading" and "an affront to the American public."[42] This only provoked Riedy (and the society) to produce, two years later, an expanded and more detailed *Failure in the Desert*, complete with extensive supporting data and footnotes. To this, the BLM never responded in detail.

The election in the fall of 1986 did not involve a presidential contest. However, it saw many a crucial battle, none more immediately important to proponents of the Desert Bill than that between Senator Cranston and his Republican opponent, Ed Zschau, a Congressman from the Silicon Valley, personable, intelligent, and very well financed. It was close to the most costly Senate race in the country's history, with over $25 million spent by the two candidates before Election Day.[43] Cranston won re-election by a narrow margin, the Desert Bill was reintroduced in the new 100th Congress, and the war of words continued.

A 33-point attack on the bill was circulated by opposition organizations, now joined by the High Desert Multiple Use Coalition from Ridgecrest. The Wilderness Society circulated a response called *Point/Counterpoint,* which labeled 17 of the 33 opposition statements flatly false, two true, and provided explanations deflecting the rest. In July 1987 an extensive *Briefing Book* on the bill analyzing all of its key issues was ready for publication, prepared by the Sierra Club, Wilderness Society, and National Parks and Conservation Association for the CDPL. Jim Dodson and Judy Anderson were major contributors, with Dodson editing and polishing and Nobby, by now back in Washington, working on production of the book with Debbie Sease of the Sierra Club staff.

Back came the California State office of the BLM in the fall of 1987 with an extensive effort to refute the *Briefing Book.* Another Wilderness Society *Point/Counterpoint* came out the next year, followed by a BLM response more testy in tone than ever. Meanwhile, pungent booklets and revisions of prior booklets continued to flow from the pen of Peter Burk, published by Citizens for Mojave National Park and focusing on alleged BLM mismanagement in areas such as grazing, mining, and hunting.

This sort of debate between opponents has its limits and, in fact, it tailed off toward the end. In 1989 the CDPL published a largely positive short booklet of 20 pages entitled *Decision for the Desert* about what the act would accomplish. It was largely written by Dodson, Hughes, and Riedy, edited by Vicky Hoover, and contained black and white photographs. The BLM's extended response, *Desert*

Conservation, A Management Showcase, was also less negative in tone, touting its accomplishments under the existing Desert Plan on coated paper illustrated with extensive *color* photography. It was alleged in a leak from the BLM staff that funds for publication and distribution of tens of thousands of this "showcase" booklet had come not from some newly discovered budget surplus but from monies intended for management of desert wilderness study areas.

Long before this, however, the proponents of the Desert Bill had come to realize that their effectiveness in reaching the media would be more critical to the success of the bill than debates in print with the BLM and its allies. Apart from articles in conservation magazines, it was slow going at first. Not until the spring of 1987 did substantial articles about the battle for the Desert Bill appear in several major California newspapers, including the *Los Angeles Herald-Examiner* and *San Francisco Chronicle.* The *Los Angeles Times, Fresno Bee, Sacramento Bee* and *Oakland Tribune* had by then printed editorials supporting the bill. In January 1988, after a six-month investigation by a team of its reporters and editors, the *San Bernardino Sun* published a lengthy, five-part series on "The California Desert— Refuge at Risk." It had special credibility as the product of the largest newspaper in the state's largest desert county.

The *Sun* gave more coverage, in lines of print, to the concerns of desert ranchers, miners, and ORV enthusiasts than to those of conservation proponents. However, it raised serious questions about the BLM's stewardship of the desert and about the publicity campaign being mounted by that agency against the pending Desert Bill. The *Sun's* closing editorial showed some sympathy for lonely miners and strong sympathy for the two families in the area projected for Mojave National Park which stood to lose at a future date their long-held grazing leases. It urged that they be allowed to remain on the land until the deaths of the current leaseholders. (In the final bill, grazing was permitted to continue in perpetuity.) Otherwise, the *Sun* was favorable to the Desert Bill, concluding, in a final editorial on January 21, 1988, that opposition claims that the desert was resilient and did not need legislative protection were "false." It was clear to the *Sun's* team of journalists that the BLM had faltered on the job and would always be subject to political influence. In recent years, they concluded, "protection had taken a back seat." As to the complaints of the off-roaders, the *Sun* said: "The truth is, off-roaders who obey the rules would hardly notice if the Cranston bill were passed."[44]

The prestigious *Los Angeles Times* published a four-part series in the spring of 1989, beginning May 21 and continuing in the ensuing three days, focusing on the problem of managing public lands under the BLM's statutory mandate and under the provisions of the antiquated 1872 General Mining Law. The *Times* cited many examples to support its conclusion that "when preservation policies come into conflict with production, the BLM rules in favor of politically potent 'consumptive users' over other groups." It quoted conservation supporters who agreed that "in many instances, BLM's failure to do an adequate job can be traced to lack of staff and funding" but cited other evidence that the Bureau had deliberately downgraded wildlife and resource management programs and failed to request needed funding for them. According to the *Times*, a Congressional committee, after reviewing the BLM's 1989 budget proposal, became alarmed with what it termed the agency's "skewed priorities" and recommended that Congress add $17 million to the agency's budget request. The money was added.

Could this sort of media attention to the Desert Bill campaign be maintained? It was perhaps too much to hope for more major series on the desert put together by large newspapers like the *Sun* and the *Times*. However, shorter articles on the campaign, which gave proponents an opportunity to be quoted along with the opposition and thus stimulate public interest, would be invaluable in keeping the issue alive. Such articles—and editorials if they could be provided—gave an opportunity for "letters to the editor," which was another way to reach the public. Prominent among the bill's supporters who wrote effective letters to the editor when they had the chance were Jim Dodson, Peter Burk, Patty Schifferle, Nobby Riedy, Judy Anderson, Elden Hughes, Stan Haye, and Nick Ervin of San Diego.

Early on, Peter Burk had become known to many California reporters and had frequently been quoted. The *Sun's* series included a profile on Burk; the story of a lonely figure in a desert town pursuing his dream of a Mojave National Park amid hostile neighbors captured the interest of reporters far and near. It was certainly true that life in Barstow in 1988 wasn't easy for the Burks with the city council against them and a hotbed of other local residents taking verbal potshots at them. The *Sun* quoted Barstow resident Howard Dare, President of the United Mining Councils of America, on the subject of Burk: "I think he's actually against our form of government, that's what I think."[45] Jim Dodson, Judy Anderson and Patty Schifferle were less colorful, but they also became well known to the press for the depth of their knowledge of the desert and their ability to comment forcefully and clearly.

Toward the end of 1987, Elden Hughes began to capture the interest of the media. Here was a fellow with a full beard (anything but Shakespearean), a beer belly, and the powerful shoulders and arms of a wrestler under his usual T-shirt. One would have guessed he spent his spare time astride his Harley with his pals of the Desert Vipers Motorcycle Club. But on closer examination, the T-shirt gave him away. It pictured a petroglyph.

The press—in fact, almost everyone—loves a paradox. Here, they found a conservationist who looked every inch a Hell's Angel. If that wasn't enough, he was executive vice president of a successful computer service corporation in the big city of Los Angeles yet did not appear to have a button-down shirt or a dark suit to his name. In addition, he was knowledgeable, quotable, pleasant to be with, and willing to go to great lengths to show members of the press what the Desert Bill was intended to protect. Soon he was drawing reporters as a lamp draws moths. His hours at his job were flexible and he was easier to reach than Dodson and Anderson, both of whom who had demanding full-time jobs. In fact, he soon began to taper off his own business activity and early in 1990 decided to retire permanently to devote all his energies to the fight for the desert.

Hughes gradually came to be a primary spokesman for the Desert Bill on the West Coast. In the climax year of 1994, his log shows him initiating or responding to nearly 350 media contacts. From 1989 onward he was often asked to appear in radio and television interviews, programs, and debates on issues involved in the bill. An example was an interview for the "Today Show" on May 25, 1989. The backdrop for that interview pictured a group of large motor homes at a desert rendezvous, complete with elaborate dune buggies and dirt bikes climbing the nearby hills. The spokesman for the opposition, using popular opposition rhetoric, asserted: "People who want to close up the desert to recreation are an elite group," to which Hughes responded: "Can someone who drives a $60,000 RV pulling a $10,000 dune buggy call *me* an elitist?" Not shown was Elden's own desert vehicle, a twenty-year old Chevy Blazer.

The conservation proponents in the war of words showed sophistication in their dealings with the press, treating it with respect and offers of help. Their facts were reliable. Lawrence "Larry" Freilich, who succeeded Jeff Widen on the staff of the Sierra Club's southern California field office, never ceased sending facts and ideas to editorial boards throughout the state. Even so, the harvest reaped from editorials in California newspapers was unexpectedly fruitful. The strong support of the *San Bernardino Sun* and the *Los Angeles Times*, the two papers which had devoted the greatest amount of expensive staff time to their own investigations, took the form of editorial after favorable editorial. Of course, there were papers which took an opposite view—the *Antelope Valley Press, Victorville Daily Press, Orange County Register* and *Wall Street Journal* to name a few. A few other papers elected to stay on the sidelines. However, all of the major city newspapers in California lent repeated and powerful support, including the conservative *San Diego Union-Tribune*, the *San Francisco Chronicle*, the McClatchy newspapers in Sacramento and Fresno, the *Oakland Tribune*, and the *Los Angeles Herald-Examiner* before its demise. Smaller supportive newspapers included the *Times-Tribune* (Palo Alto), the *Star News* (Pasadena), the *Marin Independent Journal*, the *San Jose Mercury-News*, the *Whittier Daily News*, the *Palm Springs Desert Sun*, the *Riverside Press-Enterprise*, the *San Gabriel Valley Tribune* and, in a particularly courageous gesture, given the strong sentiment against the bill expressed by the Inyo County Board of Supervisors and other local organizations, the *Inyo Register*, "Eastern Sierra's Home Newspaper Since 1870." Lone Pine teacher and unfaltering supporter Mike Prather deserves credit for this breakthrough. Finally, a few major papers from across the country reached out to support the Desert Bill, among them the *Detroit Free Press*, the *Louisville Currier-Journal*, and *USA Today*. To say that the extent and constancy of media support through the years helped to keep alive the spirit of the conservation community would be an understatement.

It was not solely the arguments put forward by proponents of the Desert Bill that accounted for the solidity of press support. Several independent voices delivered highly critical appraisals of the BLM's management of California desert lands. The first of these was a report prepared by the U.S. General Accounting Office (GAO) in June 1989 entitled "Planned Wildlife Protection and Enhancement Objectives not Achieved." The GAO concluded that the BLM had not only failed to follow the specific program for wildlife set forth in the Desert Plan but, in many areas of the desert, had resolved in favor of consumptive uses whenever conflicts arose between such uses and wildlife interests. Page 4 of the report stated, "the BLM has not demonstrated the willingness to take actions necessary to protect wildlife interests."

Below are a few of the more specific findings of the GAO:

- The Desert Plan required that a large number of wildlife management plans be developed for areas with abundant wildlife, rare or unique habitat or sensitivity to conflicting uses. More than eight years after the plan was issued, nearly one-half of these plans had not been developed. It was certainly true, as the report pointed out, that the BLM had never received the level of funding it estimated was required to carry out the plan; in fact, the shortfall had been so severe that even highly significant tasks could not be performed.

- Even when plans had been developed, they were implemented for the most part only partially or not at all. Those plans that were completed stressed 349 specific action items to protect wildlife. Work on only 33% of these had been completed, 21% had been partially completed and work on 46% had not started. (Some plans, the report noted, had been implemented successfully.)

- Monitoring the wildlife impacts of permitted uses of the desert, essential to achievement of the objective of the Desert Plan, had rarely been performed. Thus, the report stated, the BLM was not in a position to know the extent of such impacts so that corrective action, if needed, might have been taken.

- Some monitoring data was available, however, to illustrate the conclusions of the report. For example, data existed which showed that desert tortoise populations had decreased generally by 50% since 1979.

The report resulted in news articles in a number of California papers and an editorial in the *Sacramento Bee* that analyzed the report. The *Bee* concluded that, although the BLM had been consistently denied the funds and staff it needed to do a competent job, the funding it had received for desert preservation "has been spent on helping out miners, ranchers, motorcycle riders and other so-called consumptive users rather than trying to compensate for the damage they do."[46]

The second report, dated March 1991, was an audit report by the Inspector General of the Department of the Interior based on visits to ten California BLM resource areas. In the desert, the resource areas visited were Barstow, Palm Springs, and Ridgecrest. The overall assessment which the Inspector General conveyed to the Secretary of Interior by letter dated April 17, 1991, was that the California BLM "had not taken the necessary actions to effectively manage Federal lands and protect their resources."

There were three management functions of the Desert District resource areas that received critical assessment in the report. One of these was control of vehicle routes in the Barstow and Ridgecrest Resource Areas. The report observed that public lands in these areas had been degraded through a proliferation of unapproved and undesirable vehicle routes. It was stated that local Bureau personnel in the resource areas estimated that 600 miles of unapproved vehicle routes had been created *annually* in the two areas and further estimated that 3,500 miles of such routes would require reclamation at an estimated cost of $875,000. It was estimated that 15,000-18,000 miles of routes required effective closure. The problem was clearly immense, the question of signing routes open or closed was unsolved, and additional funding and staffing was needed to complete the designation and signing of routes open or closed in the desert. The report, at page 16, concluded, "unless those resources are provided, the Bureau will be unable effectively to manage off-road vehicle use in the California desert."

The performance of all three Desert District resource areas was faulted by the Report when it came to the second management function, reclamation of lands disturbed by mining activity. The BLM's own regulations implementing FLPMA require mining claimants to reclaim lands disturbed by mining operations. Ridgecrest, Barstow, and Palm Springs Resource Area personnel reported they were aware of unperformed reclamation needed on *hundreds* of mining claims at an estimated cost of over *one million* dollars. "With limited exceptions," the report said (on page 9), "these Resource Areas had not pursued the needed reclamation with mining operators."

All three resource areas were again criticized by the report for failure to comply with laws which required locating, evaluating, and managing cultural resources on public lands. The report said (on page 20) that progress made in recent years to inventory cultural resources "had been minimal" and that without such a strategy to identify and locate cultural sites, the resource area offices "not only violate existing mandates but cannot adequately manage and protect existing cultural resources." Artifacts legitimately removed from BLM lands are government property and the law requires the Bureau to be accountable for them—to know they are properly safeguarded in museums or otherwise. But there were no inventories of artifacts removed from lands in the three Desert District resource areas visited. (The Bureau later agreed to implement an inventory and accounting strategy.) As to all three functions in which the Bureau's performance was criticized by the report, stress was laid on misallocation of available funds in the Bureau's own budgeting process, with too little allocated to the functions in question.

Showing off The Baby

The war of words over the Desert Bill may have been inevitable. More enjoyable aspects of the campaign for the Desert Bill were trips to the desert to "show off the baby."

Desert study trips and later annual Sierra Club "national outings" had served the vital function of introducing the desert to potential supporters. Now, the baby needed to be shown to those who could more directly influence the legislative process—

California Senator (later Governor) Pete Wilson: originally neutral on the Desert Bill, he finally shifted to hard opposition.

Courtesy of U.S. Senate Historical Office

legislators, their staffs, and the media. Judy Anderson, Peter Burk, Jim Dodson, Elden Hughes, Nobby Riedy, Patty Schifferle, and other dedicated volunteers and staff members of organizations which had joined the CDPL were ready for action, prepared by their own vivid desert experiences to play a vital part in this aspect of the campaign.

Pete Wilson, California's junior Senator, would clearly be critical to the future of the Desert Bill, up or down. Even before the bill was first introduced in early 1986, its proponents had been anxious to invite his support. The first opportunity came in August 1985 when the Senator's environmental aide, James Burroughs, accepted an invitation to visit the California desert, never having been there before. It was midsummer, but the chance could not be missed. A stellar team was assembled—Judy Anderson, Jim Dodson, and Joe Fontaine from the Sierra Club, Doug Kari from Desert Survivors, Harriet Allen from Desert Protective Council, plus a volunteer pilot, Mike Henstra from the Kern Plateau Association with his plane. The group met with Burroughs in Lancaster, across the mountains from Los Angeles, for an evening of wide-ranging discussion. Early the next morning the plane took off with the discussions continuing as it flew northward, circled the Trona Pinnacles WSA, and crossed the mountains into Death Valley. Edwin L. (Ed) Rothfuss, the Monument Superintendent, gave an overview of monument operations and problems. In the air again, the party circled the Eureka Dunes, made several passes over Saline Valley, and pinpointed Darwin Falls—all areas intended to be made part of Death Valley National Park. Returning southward, the flight circled the off-road play area at Dove Springs and then Red Rock Canyon, already a state park, to be enlarged by the Desert Bill. It had been an exhausting day. "Come and see me when you have some maps." was Burroughs's parting comment.

A little more than one year later, with the desert cooled down and Congress adjourned, Pete Wilson accepted an invitation to take a similar flying visit. A date in November 1986 was fixed. Dodson, Anderson, and Bob Hattoy took him aloft over the Mojave. Schifferle and Carpenter were on the ground when the plane landed to give him a quick tour of the magnificent proposed wilderness area of the Whipple Mountains, jutting up against the Colorado River—the only place in California where a few giant saguaro cacti grow on steep mountain slopes. Back in Palm Springs, Joan Taylor, long a mainstay of the Sierra Club and the Desert Protective Council, entertained the Senator and his guides at a reception. Wilson had received first-class treatment. He had duly "admired the baby" but was otherwise noncommittal.

The need was felt to have more precise data as to the impact of the Desert Bill on access to desert areas. What roads and lesser, unmaintained dirt routes, often referred to as "ways," would remain open after passage of the Desert Bill? Nobby Riedy of the Wilderness Society, recently arrived in California, conducted an examination of BLM files and determined that approximately 34,000 miles of paved and unpaved roads and ways currently existed inside the California Desert Conservation Area, a figure never subsequently challenged. This figure did not include some thousands of miles of desert washes that would in all likelihood remain open to vehicles. Riedy and Judy Anderson then sat on her living room floor for almost two days, matching the data he had obtained with Judy's maps of the wilderness areas included in the Desert Bill. Using a measuring device adjusted for the scale of each map, they calculated that approximately 1,500 miles of roads and ways would need to be closed in order to preserve critical wilderness boundaries. The 32,500 miles of roads and ways not affected would circle the earth one and one quarter times! A later BLM calculation, subject to question, put the mileage to be closed at 2,500 miles. Anderson subsequently determined that 85% of the land area of all wilderness areas provided in the bill would lie within three miles of an open road or way and none of the remaining 15% would be more than ten miles from such a road or way (except for one part of the Saline Valley WSA which lay 11 miles from a road or way). These figures were later used extensively to counter the tiresome bromide of the opposition that the bill "locked out" of the desert the many members of the public who enjoyed recreational opportunities there.

Jim Burroughs, Wilson's environmental aide, was duly informed.

In January 1987, when the Desert Bill was reintroduced in the Senate and introduced by Congressman Mel Levine for the first time in the House, the media was again briefed at a Los Angeles press conference. Senator Cranston was present but Congressman Levine had been unable to leave Washington. Cranston now asked his son Kim, a young Los Angeles lawyer, to organize a new support group for the Desert Bill. Kim went to the Senator's friends and supporters, recruiting a membership that included notable Hollywood people. He hired as chief of staff Melinda Bittan, who had previously worked for the Senator. The "Committee for California Desert National Parks" made its debut at a press conference in April 1987, represented there by Kim and Melinda and by actress Morgan Fairchild, star of "Falcon Crest," actress-producer Shelley Duvall, and songwriter Billy Steinberg. Stalwart advocates like Ed Wayburn, Jim Dodson, Judy Anderson, Patty Schifferle and others were present and, of course, the Senator. Immediately following the conference, all but Wayburn accompanied the Senator, with reporters and photographers, on a tour of the proposed additions to Death Valley National Park-to-be. They crossed the Inyo Mountains to Eureka Valley, and camped beside the Eureka Dunes, where Morgan Fairchild displayed her talents as a camp cook. The trip concluded in Death Valley with a meeting joined by Superintendent Ed Rothfuss.

This trip paid a dividend when Senator Dale Bumpers (Democrat, Arkansas), chair of the Senate Subcommittee on Public Lands, National Parks and Forests, proposed to hold the first hearing on the Desert Bill in July 1987. He did this at the request of its author and his Senate colleague. Cranston recalls Bumpers saying, "Yes, I'll take up your bill, but you could do better if you'd get Morgan Fairchild to come back and lobby me." She must have been flattered by the suggestion of the veteran Arkansas Senator, for that is exactly what she did, testifying with eloquence and verve. Jim Dodson remembers standing with Shelley Duvall and Morgan Fairchild outside the hearing room. Washington was suffering from a typical heat wave and the air conditioning was on the fritz. Duvall wiped the sweat from her face, but Fairchild seemed totally cool and relaxed.

Arkansas Senator Dale Bumpers— forceful friend of the Desert Bill throughout its long journey in Congress.

Courtesy of Office of Senator Bumpers

"How do you keep cool in this heat, Miss Fairchild?" asked Dodson. "Oh," she said without a moment's hesitation, "it's a special knack one develops when one acquires great fondness for the desert."

A second Senatorial trip in the spring of 1987 followed swiftly, this time taking in the proposed wilderness of the Mecca Hills and centering on the proposed Joshua Tree National

Park. Organizers were Bittan, Hattoy and Jeff Widen, and participants included Shelley Duvall and Bill (Billy) Steinberg. En route up a gentle slope in the Mecca Hills, the cavalcade came to a stop while an entire herd of desert bighorn sheep crossed the track. Most desert travelers have never seen a bighorn—and here was Senator Cranston enjoying a whole herd! An onlooker was heard to mutter, "I'll bet those Sierra Clubbers penned them up and turned them loose at just the right moment." In camp at sunset inside the monument, the noted biologist Professor Robert Stebbins gave the Senator a private lesson on how to mimic a pygmy owl's hoot. Almost all the onlookers were doubled up.

Senator Cranston's next trip to the desert came in November 1987. This time there was substantial press interest and Bittan gathered some 24 participants. Elden Hughes (whose wife Patty Carpenter was in charge of the food) led them to high points of the proposed Mojave National Park. The tour included Piute Canyon, Wild Horse Mesa, Mitchell Caverns, Kelso Dunes, Granite Cove, and the startling "Rebirth Rocks," site of ancient Indian sacred ceremonials.

Finally, in the spring of 1988, Congressman Mel Levine by then the sponsor of the Desert Bill in the House, was ready for a tour of a part of the desert that he'd never seen, although he'd been several times as a youngster to Death Valley. This was Saline Valley, a WSA adjacent to and intended to become part of the proposed Death Valley National Park. Joining him were his son Adam, his aide Betsy Ford, Senator Cranston, Cranston's son Kim, Melinda Bittan, Congressman Anthony Beilenson (Democrat, California), one of the bill's most devoted supporters, actor Ed Begley, Jr., and once again Professor Stebbins of the University of California, along with other supporters and many members of the press. At each stop on the way to Saline Valley, shouting, sign-carrying opponents of the Desert Bill who wanted to get at the Senator dogged the cavalcade. He often talked to them at length, giving the accompanying press the benefit of several impromptu debates. On occasion, the talk rose to the level of the merits of the legislation.

Next morning, the professor led the group on a walk up Hunter Canyon in the Inyo Mountains west of Saline Valley. An endangered, lungless salamander *(Batrachoseps campi)* no longer existed anywhere except possibly in three canyons on the eastern slopes of the Inyos. Stebbins had never seen it in Hunter Canyon although he'd looked for it there again and again. In a tiny pool at the foot of a waterfall in the canyon, not really expecting anything, Stebbins reached beneath the surface and quickly brought out Mr. Salamander to be admired by all.

A showing (of sorts) that provided a bit of relief from the serious work of campaigning occurred in the late 1980s. The Marine Corps wanted to build an access road between two parts of its training area north of the town of Twentynine Palms. To avoid a range of mountains, the road would have to cross part of the Cleghorn Lakes WSA, a proposed wilderness area in the Desert Bill. The base commander was prepared to go to Congress on the subject but his environmental adviser knew Jim Dodson and decided to try negotiation. In a pair of helicopters he took up Dodson, Judy Anderson, Bob Hattoy, and Doug Scott, conservation director and second in command at the Sierra Club, wanting to show them the proposed route and possible alternatives. The 'copters landed on one of the off-white, dry desert playas from which the proposed wilderness area took its name. To everyone's vast amusement Scott, who had lived everywhere but southern California, looked around and asked, "*Where* are the lakes?"

Scott's question became a campaign anecdote no one could forget. In the event, agreement was reached that the pending Desert Bill would be amended to permit the Interior Secretary, on the Corps' application, to grant a designated road corridor. No such application has yet been made.

Now the baby was out of the basket and the showings became more frequent. Secretary of Interior Donald Hodel was taken on tour by the BLM. Representing conservation interests on the BLM's Desert District Advisory Council, Elden Hughes was entitled to take part. Elden and his wife Patty volunteered to supply the food for the group's lunch at the Kelso Depot. They listened to a speech by the Secretary in which he compared the National Park Service most unfavorably to the BLM. He had long since announced his and the Administration's strident opposition to the Desert Bill.

Magazine writers or news hawks who wanted material for a story could almost always get Jim Dodson or Judy Anderson to guide them on weekends. Elden Hughes was often available as a guide both on weekends and in midweek—almost always so after his retirement early in 1990. Jeff Widen of the Sierra Club's field office traveled incessantly, either to gatherings of organizations with his slide show or out to the desert with the media. Any representative of the media or environmental aide in Congress who missed a chance to stuff down a rare steak and baked potato cooked on a camp stove under the canopy of desert stars had only himself or herself to blame.

The Littlest Lobbyists

In October 1989, Hughes was in Washington, D.C., on a trip to testify and lobby for the Desert Bill. The previous day had not been highly successful even though he had talked with Kathy Lacey and Betsy Ford, the environmental aides on the staffs of Senator Cranston and Congressman Levine, and with a number of environmental aides to other members of Congress. Congress was so busy that even the environmental aides, much less the members themselves, had been unable to give him much time. As he paused for breakfast, glancing at the front page of the *Washington Post*, his eye landed on the pathetic photograph of a cormorant, its beak so twisted that it could barely eat, much less catch a fish. The accompanying article referred to the growing pollution of Lake Erie's waters which was poisoning both fish and waterbird life.

Thoughts swiftly ran through his mind. This was the major newspaper of the city where members of Congress lived and worked much of the year. Not only that, this was the front page of that newspaper. The article would not have reached the front page but for the compelling photograph of the bird whose life was endangered. It was the picture that had drawn his attention to the article. Then the idea struck: *We* have an animal in *our* desert—an animal that has just been given emergency listing as a threatened species—one that might be just as compelling as a deformed bird!

Back in California he called Kristin Berry, the BLM's Desert District Research scientist specializing in the desert tortoise. Dr. Berry had collected the data that led to its emergency listing. How could Elden and his wife adopt a pair of tortoises? It was illegal to take tortoises in the wild. Once a tortoise has lived in captivity and could have acquired a respiratory infection, it should not be returned to the wild where it could infect others. Such is the appeal of this peaceful and intelligent reptile that at one time the number of pet tortoises in southern California was informally estimated to equal or even exceed the number left in the wild.

Dr. Berry knew someone who had four adult tortoises and wanted to find a new home for them without breaking up the family. By great good fortune one was a male and the rest females. It being wintertime, all were hibernating and aside from waking them for transport to their new home, all were allowed to continue in deep sleep until they awoke in March. By July "Mr. Bebee" had been attentive to the ladies, and one of them laid five eggs which were quickly installed in an incubator. Seventy days later five, healthy hatchlings broke out of their shells, miniature duplicates of an adult tortoise, a little smaller than a silver dollar, complete with all the wrinkles of an adult but with colorful shells not yet dulled by the desert sun. A sizable 50" x 50" plastic vivarium

Elden Hughes and Patty Carpenter with Mr. Bebee, sire of "the littlest lobbyists" for the Desert Bill.

Courtesy of San Gabriel Valley Newspapers

constructed by Elden's neighbor was their home. They were kept warm, given plenty of exercise, and fed a balanced diet of raw vegetables. They thrived. Swiftly the tortoises became Patty's babies. They were given names and unceasingly pampered.

Soon they were five months old, and it was time for their debut. Patty and Elden planned a trip around the country to generate "home state" letters to key Senators on the Senate Energy Committee. Appointments were scheduled and the station wagon was packed.

First stop was Albuquerque, New Mexico, for a scheduled general meeting of the Albuquerque Sierra Club group. Everyone had a chance to hold the babies—Bandit, Scotty, Troublemaker, Peewee, and Sonny. Elden presented a slide show on the desert. Result: more than 50 individual letters written that evening to New Mexico's Senators Jeff Bingaman (Democrat) and Pete Dominici (Republican), with more to be written later.

The baby tortoises then met the *Albuquerque Tribune*. The editorial writer to whom Elden and Patty had an introduction was not interested in writing an editorial about the California desert. As they were leaving, a sports and outdoors writer looked up from his desk and asked, "What do you have there?" Seeing the tortoises, he commandeered a table in an empty conference room and got a photographer. The tortoises were having their picture taken when the writer asked, "Do they bite?" "Of course not!" Patty said. He held his finger out in front of six-month-old Sonny and sure enough, Sonny bit it! It must have looked much like the carrot Sonny was used to eating. The resulting article and pictures were picked up by the wire services and appeared in papers around the country, including the *San Francisco Chronicle*.

Other Albuquerque meetings included the staff of the *Albuquerque New Mexican* and the Special Projects Staff Assistant to Senator Bingaman. More slide shows, tortoises held, questions asked. And so it went. Highlights of the remainder of the trip included: Alabama (*Birmingham News, Birmingham Post-Herald* and ABC-TV "Public Comment"), Georgia (*Atlanta Constitution* and *Gannett Daily News*), Kentucky (*Lexington Herald-Leader* and Channel 36—four whole minutes!), Frankfort, Kentucky (the *Frankfort State Journal*—front-page picture story next day), Louisville, Kentucky (half-hour radio interview, two school visits carried by separate TV channels and the *Louisville Courier-Journal* with picture story the next day), Cumberland, Maryland (*Cumberland Times-News* picture story, coverage on WHAG-TV and radio interview), and Washington, D.C. (press briefing covered by CBS, which taped the briefing and put out two national feeds that ran in other states).

On their next trip they flew east to Washington, D.C. on the redeye, bringing with them Elden's briefcase and Patty's five babies in a 10" x 12" plastic box with see-through top and sides, plenty of exercise room, and air vents.

"You can't take pets into the passenger compartment," said the guard. "They have to be in the baggage compartment." Patty, outraged, looked him squarely in the eye and shot back, "They aren't pets, they're lobbyists."

After a brief argument, Hughes paid an additional $80 and the tortoises came with them onto the plane. Later, to mollify his wife, he wrote a letter to the president of U.S. Air commenting on the "misunderstanding" by the airline's employee and asking for return of the $80. He got it.

Before leaving Washington to take the babies home, Patty, a native of Maryland, called at the office of Maryland's Senator Barbara Mikulski (Democrat) and met with her chief of staff. Later that day Senator Cranston's office received a call from an aide to Mikulski who said "five little tortoises came to see Senator Mikulski and she wants to co-sponsor the California Desert Protection Act." This was special, indeed—the first co-sponsorship by a Senator whom Cranston had not directly asked to become a co-sponsor.

Over the years, Patty and Elden took a total of nine lobby trips with the baby tortoises. They tallied 70,000 miles for Scotty before they stopped counting. Congressional guards and staff recognized and welcomed the little lobbyists. The *Los Angeles Times* assigned a writer and photographer to spend a day with them in the Senate halls, writing a feature story about it. One man stopped Patty in an upper hall of the Longworth House Office Building. Patty let him hold a tortoise while Elden told him briefly about the Desert Bill. As he turned to leave he said, "You've got my vote." Looking through pictures in the *Congressional Directory* they discovered that they had been talking to Congressman Robert Torricelli (Democrat, New Jersey). Shortly thereafter a call was received in Congressman Mel Levine's office, and Torricelli became a co-sponsor.

Much could be told about the mishaps and frustrations of Washington lobbying, both for and against the Desert Bill. Only Elden Hughes and Patty Carpenter had the baby tortoises to help them gain entry into those offices on Capitol Hill. For many others who volunteered to help the lobbying effort, it was useful to participate in a "lobby week" in Washington. These were usually but not always timed to coincide with a hearing on the Desert Bill. Training was critical. The earliest training events were held in the Bellevue Hotel, hardly a fancy establishment. During "role-playing" sessions, Debbie Sease, the Sierra Club's Director of Public Lands (now its Legislative Director), Terry Sopher of the Wilderness Society, and other old-timers played the differing types of Senators and Representatives likely to be encountered—the glad-hander, the brash "Sorry, but I have to leave for an appointment," the patronizing opponent, the truly interested legislator, and their staffs. Bob Hattoy could play them all. Afterwards, home base for the volunteer lobbyists from which they could make appointments was upstairs in the old Sierra Club offices with no furniture except a few folding chairs, a few phones, no air-conditioning and one bare lightbulb.

When the offices moved to a new location, also within walking distance of the Houses of Congress, Debbie had a conference room for the training meetings and also a large basement with many available telephones plus the volunteer lobbyists' other needs—coffee, pencils, sweet rolls, phone directories, and more coffee. It was relative luxury. Debbie was a fount of information on where legislators stood and which of their staff assistants would be the most useful to see. This was vital since the Sierra Club, with its large membership, was the source of most of the volunteer lobbyists. Throughout the long campaign, Debbie kept in close contact with the key staff assistants to the bill's sponsors in the House and Senate, responding to their questions and requests. She would use her accumulated knowledge to make out a "dance card" for each volunteer, listing persons to try to visit. Usually, it was up to the volunteer to call and schedule his or her own appointments but teams of two or three would often work together. Afterwards, a report of each meeting would be scribbled and returned.

The way our legislative system works, lobbying is essential. Unprofessional, even naive volunteer lobbyists from "back home" are often more effective than the professionals housed in Washington. The lobbying effort for the Desert Bill required constant refueling with new faces. Potential lobbyists gained fresh inspiration from the occasional wilderness conferences sponsored by the California Wilderness Coalition and, between such conferences, from seminars on the Desert Bill's progress. One successful seminar in December 1988 drew 100 participants to a ranch outside Fresno to hear veteran desert campaigners Judy Anderson, Jim Dodson, Jim Eaton, and Peter Burk open the proceedings. Others with lobbying experience then conducted workshops to help participants develop their skills in presenting the message. More likely than not events such as this would be organized by the tireless Jeff Widen and made possible by contributions from Recreational Equipment, Inc. (known throughout the West as "REI"), a network of stores that faithfully supported the cause.

Before the first lobby week was held, Debbie Sease and Terry Sopher of the Wilderness Society smoked the pipe of peace, agreeing not to compete, to "claim jump," or to hog the press. Such close cooperation has not always been the case when major conservation organizations are involved in the same long campaign. Here, it was highly successful. Always under pressure in a cramped office filled to the ceiling with documents, Debbie radiated goodwill and, by her devotion to the task, the hope of eventual victory. It might not have occurred without her.

Volunteer lobbyists urging the merits of the bill in Washington, D.C., usually had two overall objectives—to garner new co-sponsors for the bill, or to thank members of Congress or Senators for co-sponsoring and to remind them, once again, why it was the right thing to do. Over the long haul, co-sponsors needed encouragement that the bill was gaining strength; lobbyists needed it too. The co-sponsorship count helped. It was slow going at first, and by 1989 the count was only 5 in the Senate, 66 in the House. In December 1991, the count stood at only 12 in the Senate, 88 in the House. After the final bills were introduced early in 1993 the count reached 22 in the Senate and about 100 in the House. These last figures grew more swiftly in 1993–94 as the bill made its way through the last committee hearings. The final count was 47 in the Senate and at least 250 in the House. "Never give up" was the engine that drove the count and kept the Desert Bill alive.

"Phone banks" stimulated members of the Sierra Club into action during co-sponsorship efforts for the Desert Bill. It was found that a typical mailed action alert—asking for a letter to a legislator, for example—would achieve about a 10% to 15% response. However, when the mailing was followed up by a personal phone call by a volunteer to the recipient of the mailed alert, the total response rate zoomed up to close to 70% or 80% of those actually called. The regular phone bank during the desert campaign became known as TAN for (Telephone Action Network). Ronald Good of the club's headquarters staff in San Francisco started it in 1986. When he left in 1990, Vicky Hoover, who had helped him almost from the beginning, took over to coordinate the effort. As noted previously, she worked half-time for Ed Wayburn at the Sierra Club but she simultaneously contrived to be a full-time volunteer. Good had developed a list of local volunteers—perhaps 30 to 40—who agreed to come to the Sierra Club office occasionally for evenings of phoning on a conservation issue. They came partly because they were not required to ask for money but merely to request a letter or a call on an important issue. They found respondents generally willing to help. A few volunteers stayed with the effort year after year. Phone banks were also occasionally organized in Los Angeles and San Diego, but the San Francisco TAN was the principal effort.

TAN evenings were held at Sierra Club headquarters every other week—at critical times, every week. It was common to have from five to ten volunteers in the office from one to three hours each time. Apart from a telephone, a briefing sheet, a list of names and phone numbers, and Hoover's ever-cheerful encouragement, the only things needed were coffee and pizza, which were supplied. Hoover summed it up: "You really had to like pizza to be a phone bank coordinator."

" Remember,
the most powerful
religions of the world
were born of
desert metaphysics—
extremes of desert visions.
Moses, Jesus and Mohammed
were men of the desert.
It was their home.
The sea was all right
for special effects—
part it or walk on it—
but if they had serious business
with God or the devil,
they went to the desert."

—Michael Ventura

Bedeviled On All Sides, The BLM Tries To Hold Its Ground

CHAPTER EIGHT

The Incredible Keynot Mine Case

A prolonged and significant episode covering periods both before and after introduction of the Desert Bill in 1986, and involving management of mining by the BLM under the Desert Plan, left many in the conservation community in grave doubt that the BLM could be trusted to protect fragile desert resources. This was the Keynot Mine case.

In November 1980, a certain D.B. McFarland—operating, with investors, as Far West Exploration, Inc.—submitted to the BLM a plan of operations for the reopening of an old mine, the Keynot, high in the Inyo Mountains Wilderness Study Area, recommended in the Desert Plan as "suitable" for wilderness designation. He proposed to rework the mine tailings using a cyanide vat leaching process and to blast and bulldoze an access road up the incredibly steep mountain slopes of the WSA that would cross one of the few stands of ancient bristlecone pines found on BLM land. The road would be used to ferry up his employees, mining machinery, chemicals, explosives and other equipment.

Shortly before the plan was submitted, Douglas Kari and a group of his friends were hiking in the Inyo Mountains. They were startled by an explosion coming from the 8,000-foot level and made their way to the old mine site where McFarland was engaged, he told them, in "exploding old dynamite for safety reasons." Kari had co-founded Desert Survivors in 1978; its purposes were to explore the desert and to stimulate interest in the protection of wild desert lands. Here was something that needed investigation. Soon Kari was reviewing McFarland's proposed plan of operations. He was horrified by what he read.

A friend of his, Rollin Enfield, active in the Sierra Club, brought the matter to the attention of the Club. He also introduced Kari to Earthjustice Legal Defense Fund (formerly the Sierra Club Legal Defense Fund). Enfield and Kari brought to the table the evidence and documents Kari had accumulated while protesting McFarland's proposal. The Fund was convinced that the case had merit and decided to take it on. Kari was to provide it with invaluable assistance.

Meanwhile, in the fall of 1981, the BLM had prepared an Environmental Assessment (EA), a Mineral Report, and had issued its decision approving both the plan of operations *and* construction of the proposed road. The EA concluded that the proposed road would "permanently impair the wilderness attributes" of the Inyo Mountains WSA; nevertheless, it solemnly determined that McFarland held a "valid existing right on the date FLPMA was enacted." Therefore, he could operate the mine and construct his access road even if this took place in the midst of a WSA of surpassing beauty, since he would not be bound by FLPMA's nonimpairment standard, discussed in detail earlier.

Representing both the Sierra Club and Desert Survivors were Legal Defense Fund veteran Larry Silver and legal assistant Deborah Reames. As time progressed, Larry would turn over most of the work to Deborah. They appealed the BLM's decision to the Interior Board of Land Appeals and submitted a 95-page brief to show, among other things that

- A "valid existing right" under all the decided cases and the BLM's own regulations signifies a claim with a reasonable prospect of being mined at a profit both on October 21, 1976 (FLPMA's enactment) and at the time of the proposed exercise of the right (1981).

- There was no such prospect of mining this site at a profit, either in 1976 or in 1981. Three experienced mining engineers analyzed the BLM's Mineral Report on the claim. One stated "the most astonishing thing was not only the number of errors but the magnitude of the errors" made in the Mineral Report. The second referred to the report as "plagued with errors and questionable information." The third reported, "This Mineral Report is the poorest I have ever seen." First, the BLM overestimated the size of the tailings dump by 375%. Second, it erroneously calculated the gold content of the dump. Using the BLM's estimates, the dump currently had a value of $4,047,000. Correctly calculated, its value was $798,000. The size of the underground ore blocks was overstated by a magnificent 2,700% because, in converting cubic feet to tons, the factor for converting cubic *yards* to tons had mistakenly been used. The BLM's 1982 estimate of the value of the underground ore reserve was $17,954,620; the actual value was less than $664,000.

- The BLM had never assessed whether the ore was amenable to cyanide leaching (there were various possibilities which could have prevented this) and had never estimated the (very large) water requirements required to process the anticipated daily tonnage by cyanide leaching. The BLM never assessed whether such a quantity of water was available on these dry mountains. An expert hydrologist noted that even if it were possible for McFarland to tap all possible water sources, "the costs of constructing a storage facility [for water] at the mine site and pumping [the water] to the storage area would be phenomenal." It appeared that the BLM had never considered this cost, or the cost of: providing milling and mining equipment, constructing a power generating facility and a mill at 8,000 feet, complying with environmental laws, or performing the required reclamation. The cost of interest was not considered, even assuming that fixed and working capital could be raised. The BLM's generalized estimate of per ton costs was based on cyanide *heap* leaching, a process McFarland had no intention of using, which is far less expensive than the cyanide *vat* leaching which he would have to use.

For these reasons all three engineers calculated there was no possibility of profitable operations either in 1976 or 1981, and hence the mining claim could not possibly constitute a "valid existing right."

Even if the mine was estimated to be profitable, the brief asserted that the BLM had failed to note that the claim was conclusively abandoned in 1979 when the then claimant had failed to satisfy the recording requirements expressly set forth in FLPMA. There could therefore be no "valid existing right" to operate the mine. Moreover, the BLM had approved the plan of operations in violation of law and of its own regulations because it had failed to conduct the consultations mandated by the National Historic Preservation Act. Though it had freely admitted this was required, no good explanation was offered for that failure. The BLM had failed to comply with the law requiring meaningful public participation in preparing the EA. There had been repeated requests for public hearings, the case having generated heavy coverage in local media and controversy throughout the state. People had asked for at least one in the Bay Area and one on a weekend which interested parties throughout the state could attend; however, the BLM held only one public meeting in the town of Independence (in the Owens Valley) on a Wednesday evening. At the time of the meeting most of those attending had not received the draft EA, yet they were given *less than a week* to submit comments on that document.

Finally, the plaintiffs observed that the EA utterly failed to comply with the legal duty under NEPA to analyze and evaluate reasonable alternatives to the actions proposed to be taken. This was particularly egregious in regard to the access road. Given the tremendous damage the road would do, up and down steep slopes sometimes at elevations between 9,800 and 10,000 feet, and its cost, the obvious alternative was the use of a helicopter. This was mentioned by the BLM in an amendment to the EA, but in only seven lines of text with no cost comparison. Assuming that the mine itself could be operated at a profit, which was demonstrably impossible, the plaintiffs' engineers estimated the cost of the access road's construction at $800,000 to $1 million and the required reclamation at an additional $1 million and possibly double that figure. The cost of nondamaging helicopter access was not calculated but was believed to be significantly less.

Could the attorneys and their engineering experts, with Kari's help, have found anything *more* that was wrong with the BLM's work?

Faced with this devastating critique, McFarland withdrew his plan of operations and with it his road construction project, thus saving the BLM overwhelming embarrassment and mooting the appeal by the Sierra Club and Desert Survivors. Late in 1982, however, he filed a new plan of operations without the access road, expecting to use a helicopter. In the spring of 1983, the BLM approved the new plan, disregarding the data in the earlier brief and rejecting the protest of Desert Survivors. At this point Kari, now a law student, took the lead in preparing an appeal to the Interior Board of Land Appeals (IBLA) of this second BLM decision which gave McFarland the go-ahead. Under the IBLA rules, the filing of this appeal suspended McFarland's newest plan of operations until the appeal could be heard.

The Planning Commission of Inyo County also approved the new plan of operations with a required $50,000 surety bond intended, but grossly insufficient, to guarantee proper reclamation. This bond, in accordance with the BLM's request, was to run in favor of both the county and the BLM, and McFarland was specifically instructed that the bond must be issued and returned to the county prior to any mining activity. No bond was ever issued. The BLM never checked to see if one had been issued, later informing Kari that it "forgot to follow up on the bonding requirement." McFarland went ahead without delay, using a helicopter to transport to the site tanks, generators, a bulldozer, conveyors, and other equipment, plus quantities of chemicals including 28 fifty-gallon drums of sodium cyanide. At this juncture, the Interior Board of Land Appeals decided the pending appeal. It found in favor of Desert Survivors and set aside the BLM's approval of McFarland's plan of operations. Kari and his friends took another hike high into the Inyos. They discovered what had happened at the Keynot Mine, and provided the BLM with photographs of rusty cyanide drums left in the open along with leaking drums of other chemicals. All posed an immediate threat to both human and animal life and to water quality. Out went instructions from the BLM to McFarland to clean up the site. But McFarland was now broke and there *was no bond*! Nothing happened for a year; finally, the California Regional Water

Quality Control Board issued an order requiring McFarland, and if he did not act promptly, the BLM to remove the chemicals. As the reader may have surmised, it was the BLM that had to comply with the order, at a cost to the taxpayers of $27,000.

What about the abandoned tanks, bulldozer, and machinery? Alas, they are still rusting away, high in the new Inyo Mountains wilderness area. The BLM currently states that it has no funds to remove them—they may be a permanent monument to an egregiously sloppy instance of administration of federal law. In 1989, the Bureau was hoping that the abandoned materials might be removed in a military training exercise, saving the Bureau, according to its own estimate, over $100,000. It never happened. Could at least some further cleanup of the mess left by McFarland be done without cost? It could, and was, through the cooperation of a team composed of volunteers led by Steve Smith from the BLM's Ridgecrest office along with Doug Kari and his friends of Desert Survivors.

There is one painful sequel to this incredible story that deserves to be told. The indefatigable McFarland was back in 1989 with another plan of operations to open the Keynot Mine. Again, his submission to the BLM included construction of a devastating access road through the mountains. Not daring to take a chance on what the Ridgecrest office of the BLM might do, Doug Kari and Desert Survivors mailed an alert to its members asking for letters of protest to be forwarded to the Ridgecrest office of the BLM. The mailing stated that such letters could say, among other things, that the proposal "would involve the felling of hundreds of ancient bristlecone pines." On receipt of the letters (one of which included a copy of the notice which generated them) Lee Delaney, head of the Ridgecrest office, sent an angry letter to Kari, asserting that "the most blatant misstatement [in the notice] is that hundreds of ancient bristlecone pines would be felled." This he said, was "a gross piece of misinformation." He added, "We do not need lies, half truths and innuendo" and instead proposed "open and honest communication." Kari's reply was swift. Courteously, he observed that earlier events in the Keynot Mine case had occurred before Delaney had come to Ridgecrest. He then had the satisfaction of writing:

> *That statement [in the notice, about the bristlecone pines] is based on information developed by your office...the road proposed [in the new plan] is substantially similar to the road proposed in Plan No. 1 filed with your office in 1980. Your office concluded that construction of a 3/4-mile stretch of the road proposed in Plan No. 1 would result in the felling of up to seven bristlecone pines for every 100 feet of travel, a loss of as many as 277 trees. Your office characterized this as "an irretrievable impact...*

Delaney did not respond. At last McFarland, who owed the BLM the $27,000 it had cost to remove his cyanide drums, had submitted a plan that the BLM did not approve.

★ ★ ★ ★

The Keynot Mine had a significant influence on Doug Kari's career. The case was not yet over when he graduated from law school in 1985. It was important for him to join a law firm which would permit him to bring the case, on a *pro bono* basis, with him. He chose an eminent San Francisco firm, Orrick, Herrington & Sutcliffe, which was glad to have both Kari and his case. When the Desert Protection Act was introduced, Kari brought the growing Desert Survivors organization into the front line of the act's supporters. He also helped to persuade the BLM of the value of giving notice to interested persons of proposed mines, test drilling, or other potential disturbances of desert wilderness study areas and (since 1994) desert wilderness areas. Such notice would allow him or others to review the proposals, visit the project sites and, if necessary, warn of potential problems in the approval process before it was too late.

The Park Service Toes the Party Line

> *In all of the California desert there is no finer grouping of different wildlife habitats than in the East Mojave, both from the viewpoint of the total number of species and the*

*total number of animals. The Kelso Dunes, Providence
and New York Mountains, and the Cima Dome are
the finest examples of their particular habitat types in
California, as well as being the best preserved at
this time.*

Sound like a Sierra Club activist in a Congressional hearing on the
Desert Bill? It's not. Instead, it is a direct quotation from a 1979
report by the BLM's own Desert Plan staff sent to Howard Chapman,
Regional Director of the National Park Service for California,
Arizona, Nevada, Hawaii, Guam, and Saipan.[47] The staff report
added that two desert areas in particular, the East Mojave and the
Eureka-Saline Valleys northwest of Death Valley, "appeared to
qualify for national park or national monument status."

It made sense for the study, on which the report was based,
to be done by the BLM Desert Plan staff. Its people were crisscrossing
the entire California desert in the late 1970s, examining and
evaluating its resources and trying to subdivide the desert into areas
appropriate for different levels of "use." By statute, that study had to
report on lands appropriate for wilderness designation. By common
sense it also produced a report on lands appropriate for parks.

The final Desert Plan, however, failed to recommend
any land for parks despite the findings of the Desert Plan staff. After
all, it was the BLM's Desert Plan and the land was under BLM
jurisdiction. FLPMA had not expressly told the BLM to look for
land appropriate for park purposes. User groups with which the BLM
was used to dealing—grazers, miners, off-roaders—all wanted to see
the land remain under the control of the BLM, the agency with the
multiple-use mandate.

Shortly after the Desert Bill was introduced in Congress by
California's senior Senator in 1986, the Director of the National
Park Service in Washington asked Howard Chapman and his staff in
the National Park Service's Western Regional Office to analyze the
three areas which the bill proposed to transfer to the Park Service—
the East Mojave National Scenic Area and the additions to Death
Valley and Joshua Tree National Monuments. Chapman set his staff

to work and a year later, in January 1987, they produced their analysis and report.

The conclusions of Chapman's report were straightforward. Evaluated in light of Park Service policies relating to new units, the report concluded that, on balance, the proposed Mojave National Park met all three new unit criteria. The criteria were "significance," "suitability/feasibility," and "management alternatives." The status of the area as a "National Scenic Area" was reviewed together with the BLM's published management philosophy for the area. The report noted that with a "commitment to preservation" the BLM could make the scenic area an outstanding national area but observed that the BLM had been, and remained, committed to managing that area on a multiple-use basis.

As to the additions to Joshua Tree National Monument, the report concluded that the proposed Coxcomb and Eagle Mountain additions would be appropriate and desirable and also that national park status was appropriate. All but a fraction of the proposed Death Valley additions were deemed desirable, the proposed wilderness area designations made by the Desert Bill within the present Death Valley National Monument boundary were found consistent with the Park Service's long-standing recommendations, and the change to national park status was recommended.

When it reached Washington, the report was dismissed. The Reagan-Bush Administration stated, through the Department of Interior, its position that interstate highways, railroads, mining claims, and utility corridors made the scenic area unworthy to be a park. The Park Service, it said, would consult with the BLM on any additions that might be needed to Joshua Tree and Death Valley National Monuments. Thereafter, according to Chapman, no further reference was made to the report that had been prepared by his staff professionals. Chapman sensed the cloud under which he was now operating. He bore ultimate responsibility for that report. The work had been done and its conclusions were reached by *his* staff on *his* watch. His superiors had repudiated it. He believed he had no choice but to retire. He did so in May 1987.

Chapman's retirement cost the Park Service a man whose judgment and ability had gained him respect and advanced his career. His years of public service took him from Seasonal Park Ranger in Yellowstone, to District Park Ranger in Shenandoah, to Park Superintendent in Grand Teton, and finally to Western Regional Director with supervision over 44 national parks.

Less than three months after retirement, he was asked by supporters of the Desert Bill if he would like to testify in the first Congressional hearing on that bill, scheduled by the Senate Subcommittee on Energy and National Resources for the third week in July. He thought about it and said he would.

In his testimony,[48] Chapman first stated that it remained his firm belief that the Mojave National Scenic Area and the two National Monuments, Death Valley and Joshua Tree, with their proposed additions, "fully met the criteria for inclusion in the National Park System." He then paid tribute to the dedicated professionalism of those BLM land managers with whom he had often worked. He would not criticize the BLM's integrity. However, he said, "there was a very evident divergence in our mission and philosophies." He referred to the words of much-honored former National Park Service Director Newton B. Drury who had said that if we whittle away at areas of park quality, "we must recognize that all such whittlings are cumulative and that the end result will be mediocrity. Greatness will be gone." He said he had observed the pursuit of multiple-use opportunities under the BLM in the proposed Mojave National Park, referring, as an example, to the proliferation of unauthorized roads. These, he said, "are the whittlings that Director Drury spoke of that will, sooner or later, reduce greatness."

Chapman found it refreshing to be freed from the limitations that inevitably circumscribe the ability of a field manager in a bureaucracy to express his views openly. He had found his voice. He was to become one of the strongest advocates for the Desert Bill. He possessed an impressive presence and spoke with measured dignity. One could instantly sense the depth of his experience and concern. There were no fireworks, but a listener was unlikely to forget his message, which became more eloquent with each appearance before a Congressional committee.

Two years later, on July 27, 1989, Chapman was again called upon to testify, this time before the House Subcommittee on National Parks and Public Lands in *its* first hearing on the Desert Bill.[49] He decided to speak of a matter that gave him the deepest concern. "Since 1980," he said, "the National Park Service has never been permitted by the Interior Department to present its professional opinion on park matters and thereby be held accountable by Congress...The Department has either changed, or kept under wraps, such professional reports in order to present its political position to the Congress."

Finally, in September 1991, he testified again before the renamed House Subcommittee on General Oversight and California Desert Lands.[50] His testimony was now more pointed than ever. As to the excuses the Administration had given for rejecting the Mojave National Park proposal, he expressed puzzlement and astonishment. No interstate highways invaded the proposed park land—they existed only along its boundaries. Not multiple rail lines but only a single railroad crossed the proposed park, and trains rarely stopped inside the proposed boundaries. The Park Service, he noted, had found value in the entry of a railroad into Grand Canyon National Park to solve automobile gridlock problems there. It was true that corridors for utility lines were expected to cross the proposed Park. Yet such concerns, he observed, "had not stopped the Park Service from approving a utility corridor in one of the country's most significant historical parks—Colonial National Historical Park in Virginia"—and the Service had also allowed high voltage lines within Yosemite and Yellowstone to serve government and concessionaire operations. He also noted that "our country has set aside in its National Park System less than 3% of our land area, yet other countries of the world which have followed our lead, such as New Zealand and Costa Rica, have set aside up to 10% of their land to protect their natural and cultural heritage."

In conclusion, he added that because the East Mojave was "a contiguous area with an existing road system little, if anything, would be required to be built to provide access for the visitor or to administer and protect the park." The access already in existence would be valuable in assuring fulfillment of the Congressionally-mandated mission of the Park Service to provide for the education, use and enjoyment of the public. He closed with the most pregnant statement of all:

> *This Congressionally mandated mission [of the Park Service] should answer the critics who choose to argue that becoming a park would be locking out the public. In actuality, restrictions would only affect those activities that would destroy the very things the park was established to provide and protect for all citizens.*

The Contest for Support

After the Desert Bill was first introduced in the Senate in 1986, Ed Hastey, California Director of the BLM, considered what he might do. For years he had been visiting BLM offices around the state. Local governments in California received millions of dollars from the BLM each year under the Payments in Lieu of Property Taxes Act; it was not surprising that he had many friends among public officials in rural counties from border to border. He was now ready to ask those friends to help him turn back this new effort to reduce the turf under his jurisdiction.

Ed Hastey, veteran California Director of the Bureau of Land Management.

Courtesy of California State Office, BLM

Hastey was articulate, affable, ready with a laugh, easily approachable, and totally convinced that the BLM under his leadership, with only an occasional human lapse, was properly balancing protection of desert resources with consumptive uses of the desert. He radiated conviction without being heavy-handed about it. In short, he was every inch the effective politician whom the Bureau needed for the contest that was developing. Moreover, he was ready to spend significant amounts of his time.

Inyo County was the first to adopt a strong resolution opposing the Desert Protection Act. Its supervisors became Hastey's allies to help persuade other counties to do the same. Tulare County fell into line and soon there were others. Hastey was making swift progress.

Nobby Riedy recalls a taste of Hastey's influence in 1986 after he had returned to California on the staff of the Wilderness Society. Someone was needed to present the position in favor of the Desert Bill at a meeting of the California Association of County Supervisors. Nobby was tapped and, when he appeared at the meeting, was accorded the honor (handicap?) of speaking first. He did so to his own satisfaction, at least. Then the moderator turned to Hastey with the words: "*Now*, we'll hear from Uncle Ed." In an instant, Nobby realized he had been beaten.

The proponents of the bill recognized that endorsements were important, as in any political contest. Judy Anderson, Sierra Club Desert Committee chair, asked people to take action in their own cities and counties. Few volunteers, however, knew how to go about it. Peter Burk stepped in. He knew how to find local citizens who were sympathetic to desert protection and who might be persuaded to ask their city councilmen or county supervisors to sponsor a resolution endorsing the Desert Bill. He drafted such a resolution and put together a packet of information about the bill to send out.

Burk had heard rumors about what Ed Hastey was doing and learned of the resolution adopted by Inyo County. By using a *nom de plume*, he obtained accurate information about what counties had taken action. To his surprise, he learned that 23 countries, most of them in the foothills and mountains of the long chain of the Sierra Nevada and in the far north, plus the major desert county of San Bernardino, had already adopted resolutions in opposition. It was time to get moving.

What about support from cities? City governments might be more attuned to the recreational needs and desires of urban populations than rural counties. Four different polls had shown strong support for desert protection among the California population at large, even including those living in the desert. It would be a splendid thing if Riverside, seat of its own desert county and headquarters of the Desert District of the BLM, would pass a supportive resolution. Burk had old friends in Riverside to whom he sent his draft resolution and information about the Desert Bill. His friends responded quickly. Riverside became the first important city to endorse the bill. Burk had already sent his draft resolution and accompanying information to friends in other cities in southern California and would press them for action. And, to the extent possible, he would focus special attention on the desert area. It would not be easy, and Hastey had drawn the first blood.

Meanwhile Gary Patton, a young county supervisor in Santa Cruz County south of the San Francisco Bay, had learned that a major desert conservation bill was pending in Congress. He was a long-time member of the Sierra Club and had been in the habit of asking his fellow supervisors to endorse conservation measures. This was obviously a matter of large significance. He recalls asking Senator Cranston for a copy of the bill and using the bill's language to draft an endorsing resolution that he sent, with a letter, to his colleagues. His colleagues responded collegially by passing it without delay in January 1988.

Soon Patton received a phone call. It came from Vicky Hoover, chair of the Wilderness Committee for the San Francisco Bay Chapter of the Sierra Club. She was surprised and delighted to have heard about Santa Cruz County's action and told him so.

Hoover had been a Sierra Club outings leader and frequent peak climber in the Sierra but had never explored the California desert, apart from a few car camping trips with her family to Death Valley. Her attention was attracted when the new Desert Bill was introduced. She was particularly intrigued by the concept of a Mojave National Park. At a Sierra Club meeting in San Francisco, she asked Elden Hughes if he could give her some pointers about places to see on a trip to the Mojave and how to get to them. Hughes, sensing potential help for the Desert Bill campaign, wrote up a four-page list by hand for her.

She reached the Mojave for the first time in the Christmas season of 1986 with a few Bay area friends. They climbed lofty Clark Mountain in the snow, as one might have expected of her, visited the Kelso dunes, Fort Piute and other points of interest, and went on to Joshua Tree National Monument to hike through its Wonderland of Rocks and climb Ryan Mountain at sunrise. She became thoroughly hooked.

The following Christmas she led a San Francisco Bay Chapter group of 14 to the Mojave, focusing on three mountainous WSAs that they had impulsively decided to "adopt": the Old Woman, Turtle, and Whipple Mountains WSAs. Now, less than a month later, she had in her hand a copy of Santa Cruz County's desert resolution and reproduced it for her Sierra Club friend Lawrence Fahn, active in Marin County.

Hoover had meanwhile taken on the leadership of the Bay Chapter's Wilderness Committee and had decided to make the Desert Bill, which clearly involved the major current campaign for wilderness in California, that committee's chief endeavor. Here was something concrete to do and she plunged into it. Hughes had been right. She was also part-time executive assistant to Ed Wayburn, Honorary President of the Sierra Club, who encouraged her and agreed to sign letters asking individual supervisors for help in obtaining county endorsements. She corresponded with active Sierra Club members in northern California cities and counties and sent them Gary Patton's resolution as a model, asked them to do what they could with supervisors or city council members whom they knew, and kept after them. San Francisco she retained as her own pet project and it was first to respond, this time with a joint city-county resolution introduced by Supervisor Carol Ruth Silver. Marin County (with the help of Lawrence Fahn), Santa Clara County (helped by Bernadette Ertl) and Alameda County (prompted by Alan Carlton and Gayle Eads) followed suit in the next few months. Contra Costa County was close behind.

Peter Burk and Vicky Hoover were now in contact and with a few exceptions focused their efforts, respectively, on the two halves of the state, always making sure that copies of resolutions that had been passed reached key Senators and Members of Congress. This was labor-intensive. It sometimes involved sending the county clerk envelopes that were pre-addressed to all members of the California Congressional delegation. Would cities in the desert be interested? It wouldn't be as easy as cities and counties in other parts of the state, whose populations were not involved in economic activity in the desert. Burk made an ally of Buford Crites, city councilman and later mayor of Palm Desert. Together they were able to obtain endorsements from important cities in the most populous area of the California desert, the Coachella Valley—Palm Springs, Palm Desert, La Quinta, Rancho Mirage, and Desert Hot Springs.

Other friends of Burk's were able to bring in Redlands (with the help of James Poss), Ontario, Upland and Yucaipa—sizable cities of the great desert county of San Bernardino, although not themselves located in the desert.

Camille Morgan in San Diego was a young woman of enormous energy and dedication, a leader of the San Diego Chapter of the Sierra Club, who had organized many trips to the desert. Burk called her and she responded enthusiastically. She ultimately obtained the support of both the city and county of San Diego as well as the cities of Coronado, Poway, and Escondido. Another county that might prove favorable was Santa Barbara. Burk got hold of Frank Fetscher and Charles Eckberg, who carried the ball in Santa Barbara County with assistance from Jeff Widen. In a book on state government, Burk found the names of the supervisors of Placer County in the gold rush region. Ever brash, he called one of them, explained what was wanted, and the supervisor at the other end of the line said he'd present the resolution. It passed!

Meanwhile, Burk and Hoover and numerous local volunteers to whom they sent information added the counties of

Contra Costa (assisted by Ro Aguilar), San Mateo, Sacramento (assisted by James Middleton), and Monterey, and the cities of San Mateo, Davis, Visalia, Vallejo, Fairfield (assisted in several by James De Kloe), Salinas, Sacramento, Berkeley, Oakland (assisted by Alan Carlton), Santa Barbara, Fresno (assisted by Paul Mitchell), Del Mar, Ventura, Irvine, Visalia (assisted by Brian Newton), and Hemet. Jeff Widen was always helpful.

Burk kept hammering away on Barstow, his hometown in the center of the Mojave Desert. Finally, he persuaded the city council to change its position from opposed to neutral. It didn't last very long—the council recanted—but it was nevertheless a monument to persistence. He also persuaded Alpine County to change its position from opposed to neutral early in 1990. Hoover got the help of Bill Floyd to shift Nevada County to neutral in September 1990.

Others took up the cause. Ray Williams, chair of the San Jacinto chapter of the Ikes (Izaak Walton League) had succeeded, with much effort, in gaining support for the Desert Bill from large, midwestern chapters of the Ikes. He obtained qualified support from the national office, though not (to his disgust) from the largest California chapter. Williams took Burk's call and obtained supporting resolutions from the cities of Irvine and Whittier.

Finally, it was time to go for the big one, Los Angeles County. Burk called on Dick Hingson, conservation coordinator of the Sierra Club's Angeles Chapter, to assist. Lucien (Lu) Haas, who had once worked for Senator Cranston, helped put together a strategy to gain a favorable majority on the Board, with Supervisor Edmund D. Edelman as the mover. Elden Hughes came forward at the key supervisorial meeting to lead the testimony and response to questioning. It turned out to be a vigorous hearing with vociferous opposition from ORV and motorcycle organizations. Weakening amendments were overcome. The final vote was 3–2 for the resolution.

As we have seen, Nobby Riedy hadn't come off too well when he had the temerity to go head-to-head with the redoubtable Ed Hastey. Would Hoover do any better? Someone had informed

Jeff Widen that Hastey had put an item asking for a resolution to oppose the Desert Bill on the agenda for the State Parks and Recreation Commission meeting at Pacific Grove in August 1988. The notice was short. Would Hoover, who was the closest, speak for the desert? She hastily arranged the $2^{1/2}$-hour drive and signed in at the meeting as a speaker. After most of the business of the meeting was over, Hastey made his presentation. The commissioners asked if anyone else wished to speak. Hoover stood up and told the commission of the support that had been building for the Desert Bill, the organizations behind it, the editorials in major newspapers, and asked the commissioners not to take a position until they could hear more detailed presentations from both sides. They asked her a few questions and agreed to table the issue. Hastey had not realized a proponent had come to the meeting. He left, she said, tight-lipped and shaking his head in dismay over what had happened.

Although the Desert Bill's proponents succeeded in obtaining supporting resolutions from fewer counties than Hastey (15 to be exact) theirs were larger, aggregating well over half the state's population together with 35 cities, including the 8 largest in the state. The aggregate population of favorable cities and counties far outweighed the population figures of the many small counties and cities which had registered opposition to the bill. Asked much later about the outcome, Ed Hastey smiled and observed, "They beat me." Almost without exception, this was due to the efforts of volunteers and was to have a significant impact on the ultimate success of the Desert Bill.

★ ★ ★ ★

Robert Cates was a mechanical engineer working at Litton Guidance and Control Systems, a division of Litton Industries, Inc. He was also an avid hiker and mountaineer who had come to love Joshua Tree National Monument.

Surprised by the lack of information about the monument, especially when compared to the plethora of books, magazines, and articles dealing with Death Valley, he decided to put together an illustrated visitors' guide to Joshua Tree. In his words, "It was a niche just waiting to be filled."

Assisted throughout by his wife Maureen and drawing upon Sierra Club hiking acquaintances for companions in field research, he assembled a fat notebook of historical and cultural information about the monument as well as its natural history. It never occurred to him, he said, to seek a publisher for the resulting guidebook. He and Maureen simply created their own company, Live Oak Press, printed up 5,000 copies, and sent samples to potential retailers. In the book he told wonderful stories about the monument, including that of Minerva Hamilton Hoyt, no "sun-hardened desert rat" but a prominent society matron in Pasadena, who had asked then-Governor James Rolph of California to introduce her to newly elected President Franklin D. Roosevelt. She bearded the President in the oval office and told him he should act to establish a national park or monument in the area. Thereafter she held his feet to the fire and, three years after their first meeting, she prevailed; Joshua Tree National Monument was established by the President's proclamation.

Demand for Cates' book was high, especially at the monument's visitor centers where it continues to sell, joined by an ever-growing host of Johnny-come-lately competitor publications. The revised edition, taking into account the adjusted boundaries and change of status from national monument to national park, was issued in 1995.

After the Desert Bill was introduced in the Senate, Cates found he had several acquaintances in the workplace who were hard-core off-roaders opposed to the proposed legislation. For a while, he gave them copies of articles in the magazines of conservation organizations to introduce them to the problems caused by abuse of the desert by careless off-roaders. "Any form of criticism of their adopted life style just made them madder," he said. He noted that they were long on complaints about the double-damned government and its restrictions on their "right" to use the desert as they chose, but short on doing anything about it. Annoyed, he decided that *he* would do something, quietly and independently, to help the Desert Bill pass.

Cates had seen a memorandum from the Wilderness Society in 1987 listing some 300 scientists as supporters of the bill and thought he could do better than that. What he needed first was a good solicitation kit. He started with an inspirational letter written by Dr. Robert Stebbins, the great naturalist at the University of California, Berkeley. Editing that letter down to one page, he sent it to Stebbins for approval. He next procured a strong one-page letter from Professor Arthur Montana, chair of the Department of Earth and Space Sciences at UCLA, a strong supporter of the bill. Printing them back-to-back on a single sheet of paper, and including several preprinted endorsement petitions, he had what he needed in the way of a kit.

Who to contact? Most of the original 300 endorsers represented UCLA and UC Berkeley but the original Wilderness Society solicitors had obtained a fair sprinkling of representatives of other institutions, evidently by circulating early petitions at several national scientific gatherings. Off went his kits to these original endorsers, along with a request to circulate the solicitation packet in their respective departments and institutions.

The response was overwhelming. Every week's mail brought in filled-out petitions. In the meantime, Cates spent several weekends at the UCLA Research Library searching the scientific literature for works dealing with aspects of the California desert. The authors of these pieces then would find one of his kits in their mail. He estimated that he obtained a 90% return rate on his investment: that is, nine out of ten contacts eventually resulted in returned endorsements. He never received a negative response.

Cates prepared a specific letter of endorsement that he circulated to the executive directors of seven major botanic research gardens and arboreta around the nation. It was signed by every executive director and formally entered into testimony at the 1989 House subcommittee field hearing in Barstow by Dr. Thomas Elias, then serving as executive director of the Rancho Santa Ana Botanic Garden in Claremont, California. By 1991, Cates could list more than 1,600 scientists and academicians nationwide who had endorsed the bill, including 136 scientists and educators from the great California universities, UCLA and UC Berkeley. The list, submitted in petition form to

Congress, also represented a corps of scientists who could be and were drawn upon to testify before Congressional Committee hearings in Washington and California. It was a prime example of a highly successful, invaluable, self-imposed task done by a single volunteer.

The BLM's Actions Contradict Its Words

At last, a big chunk of California's vast desert wins national status (but how much protection?)

—*Sunset* Magazine, September 1981

The "big chunk" referred to in the magazine was the area in the eastern Mojave Desert between interstate highways I-15 and I-40, first proposed in the 1970s for National Park status in bills introduced in the House by Congressman George Brown (Democrat, California). Later in the 1970s the area was found to deserve National Park status by the BLM's own Desert Plan staff, a recommendation rejected by the BLM as we have seen. Finally, in 1980—without prior opportunity for public comment—it was designated the country's first "National Scenic Area" by the Desert Plan and by proclamation of the Secretary of Interior. It was officially called "East Mojave National Scenic Area" (EMNSA). *Sunset Magazine's* question was highly pertinent. No precedents, no standards of any kind, existed for a "National Scenic Area." This was a genuine "first" and the BLM could write on a clean slate. Could this possibly mean something akin to a park? Could it be a place in which enjoyment by the public of undisturbed scenic beauty had the highest priority? The conservation community placed no bets and waited to see.

There was not long to wait. On August 1, 1981, the BLM issued its "Management Philosophy Statement" for the EMNSA.[51] It said: "The National Scenic Area designation does not add a new layer of guidelines or regulations. It simply establishes a boundary around an area of high resource value and sensitivity." Following this unpromising beginning, the statement went on to list the BLM's management goals for the area, including, "make the region a demonstration showcase for multiple-use management" and "assure retention of the balance between use and natural values." As *Sunset* put it: "...the BLM hopes to prove it can protect an area's scenic, cultural and recreational riches, yet still permit traditional uses like mining and cattle grazing. How this will work remains to be seen."

In the years that followed, a few modest steps were taken which did not amount to much more than business as usual under the Desert Plan. A manager of the area and a Natural Resources Specialist were appointed. The ranger force was augmented. Big-game guzzlers were installed. Some enclosures were placed around water holes to protect them from wild burro damage. Signs were put up, a few petroglyph sites were fenced and others inventoried. Management plans for all ten grazing allotments in the area were completed. Access guides and a brochure for the area were published, and an interpretive program was implemented.

This was a far cry from what some had hoped for. For example, even if hunting regulated by State Fish and Game was to be allowed to continue, why was it thought necessary to allow casual shooting in the EMNSA at targets, rocks, cans, or whatever? The BLM's guides, brochures, campground improvements, and interpretive programs emulated those of a park or national monument. They constituted an invitation to the public, to families with children, to those interested in the study of nature and the enjoyment of outstanding scenery to come to this particular area. Were not such invitees entitled to better protection, particularly when huge areas of BLM desert lands, largely unvisited by the public, were available for casual shooting? Illustrative of such concerns was the statement of Jim Cornett, Curator of Natural Science at the Palm Springs Desert Museum, quoted in *Defenders*, the magazine of Defenders of Wildlife for January/February 1990:

> *I've watched people with cowboy holsters drawing pistols and shooting Joshua Trees as if they were having a gun battle with some desperado...People will buy shotgun*

shells that have big lead slugs that leave gaping holes. I've seen wild horses shot in the neck. I've seen people shoot fringe-toed lizards and desert iguanas with shotguns. I've asked why they were doing that and they say, "For fun."

He added that it was not unheard-of for some of these imitation cowboys to shoot at people.

Major disappointments came swiftly. These included the attempted deletion, in the 1982 Desert Plan Amendment process, of 140,000 acres of the EMNSA, subsequently reduced after public outcry to 47,000 acres, and the reauthorization of the Barstow-Vegas motorcycle race on a route which passed through part of the EMNSA.

Howard Chapman, former Western Regional Director of the National Park Service, was amazed that the BLM would continue to allow mining of cinders in the Cinder Cones National Natural Landmark, an area of the EMNSA specially set aside for its scenic and geological qualities.

After the California Desert Protection Act was introduced in 1986, calling for the EMNSA to become a National Park, the BLM speeded completion of a comprehensive management plan for EMNSA. Were they trying to pull the teeth of park advocates? Some thought so. A 208-page Draft Plan and Environmental Assessment was released early in June 1987, almost six years after the BLM's "Management Philosophy Statement" for EMNSA had first appeared.

A number of features of the Draft Plan were welcomed as steps in the right direction. These included

- Limiting the use of all-terrain vehicles (ATVs) to specifically permitted or officially authorized uses only, where careful supervision and control was feasible.

- Closing a number of vehicle routes; opening one closed route; closing some desert washes to vehicle travel.

- Improving two campgrounds; permitting cars to be driven outside designated camping areas only in or to points "immediately adjacent" to roads, rather than 300 feet on either side as permitted under the 1982 Desert Plan Amendments.

- Reclassifying 120,000 acres from "moderate" to "limited" use designation.

- Making approximately 60,000 acres off-limits to mining, except on valid preexisting mining claims, but not to mineral leasing.

- Generally considering "wind farms" and other large commercial developments incompatible with the objectives of the plan.

- Establishing "no-shooting" zones for public safety around developed campgrounds and recreation sites and the Piute Creek ACEC. Closing the eastern Granite Mountains, Kelso Dunes and Caruthers Canyon to firearms except for hunting.

- Relocating one utility corridor one-half mile to the east, eliminating the portion inside the EMNSA.

- If funds could be obtained, adding additional employees and continuing to acquire private inholdings to reduce disturbance of wildlife habitat.

- Further developing desert information outposts, interpretive programs, trail guides, bulletins, a better signing program, and increased surveillance of unauthorized activity in sensitive areas.

Many had hoped that shooting, except for hunting, would be prohibited in the Final Management Plan for the EMNSA. It was understood that John Bailey, the Chief Outdoor Recreation Planner for the EMNSA, had specifically recommended this. He had also recommended the prohibition of ATVs in the area and this was accepted, with exceptions, in the Draft Plan.

A year later, in May 1988, the Final Management Plan was issued. Overall, it was a significant retreat from the Draft Plan. The prohibition against ATVs was gone. Acreage withdrawn from the further location of mining claims was reduced from 60,000 to 48,000 acres. The Draft Plan had proposed closing to shooting (other than hunting) three sizable areas which attracted many visitors. The Final Plan eliminated closure to shooting for the two largest of these areas: Caruthers Canyon and the Kelso Dunes. Gone was the strong statement of the Draft Plan that wind farms and other large-scale energy production facilities should not be permitted in the EMNSA. Finally, no restrictions on grazing were either proposed or adopted.

The contrasts between the draft and final management plans illustrate the contradictions that had plagued BLM management and planning from the beginning. Referring again to the Kelso Dunes, the Draft EMNSA Plan, on page 12, says the dunes have been closed "to vehicle use since 1973 to *protect vegetation.*" According to BLM's own analysis in the Final Plan, page 120, the Kelso Dunes is one of only five areas in the EMNSA which support wild vegetation considered either "highly sensitive" or "very sensitive" to habitat disturbance. Despite such facts, and the arguments based on them vigorously asserted by the conservation community ("concern was expressed" says the BLM), the agency could not bring itself to close the Kelso Dunes to cattle grazing. Again, the Kelso Dunes is one of the two or three most popular sites in the entire area for visitors. Nevertheless, the BLM rejected its own staff's Draft Plan to close the dunes to casual shooting.

The problems with ATVs illustrate another contradiction, this one stemming from the phrase in FLPMA that use of off-road vehicles should be permitted "where appropriate" in the California desert. How could such recreation be appropriate in "a very special place" possessing "beauty in a raw, untouched sense," to use the BLM's own words for the EMNSA on page 3 of its Final Plan? The staff, on page 52 of the Draft Plan, stated in essence that ATV use was inconsistent with the purposes of planning for the EMNSA, observing that ample opportunities for ATV use are available in nearby free play areas. Rasor, Dumont Dunes, and Johnson Valley play areas were all mentioned. Their use in the EMNSA, according to the Draft Plan, would be appropriate only during "permitted events…tightly controlled for resource protection" or involving "volunteers with authorization from BLM to use ATVs at specific times on specific routes." The Desert District staff's view was rejected.

The conservation community came to regard the astonishingly weak Final Management Plan for the EMNSA as additional evidence for its urgent message to the country at large: A national park is needed if the outstanding natural resources of the EMNSA are ever to obtain adequate protection.

★   ★   ★   ★

The late 1980s witnessed a further BLM effort to counter the thrust of the desert legislation then in Congress.

In 1987 the Western Regional Office of the National Park Service had recommended the new national parks proposed by the Desert Bill, including much of the proposed additions to Death Valley and Joshua Tree. This recommendation was rejected by the Administration through the Interior Department. But on June 5, 1987, the Acting Director of the National Park Service prepared a memorandum stating, "We intend to explore in cooperation with the BLM administrative adjustment to the boundaries of Death Valley National Monument and Joshua Tree National Monument to include resources that we have determined to be important...our proposal would add approximately 1,162,080 acres [to Death Valley National Monument]. With regard to Joshua Tree...our proposal would add approximately 156,500 acres."[52] These additions were only a little smaller than what had been proposed in the Desert Bill itself! This was definitely *not* what the BLM had in mind—giving up anything like that much turf to another agency, even to a sister agency in the same department of government.

Discussions between BLM and Park Service personnel in California began late in 1987 or early in 1988. By the time the BLM had settled on the acreage it would propose to give up to the Park Service, the amount had been whittled down to less than one-fifth of the acreage which the Park Service had initially indicated it desired in order to achieve more manageable boundaries and to round out ecological and topographic areas inside the two monuments.

In May 1988, information concerning the proposed transfer became public. After "scoping meetings" had been held, the California office of the BLM, as "lead agency," published a Draft Environmental Impact Statement in July 1988 describing its proposed amendment to the Desert Plan to transfer 4,480 acres to Joshua Tree and 242,850 acres to Death Valley.

When questioned by the *San Bernardino Sun* about this inconsequential outcome of the discussions between the two agencies, Elden Hughes commented: "To say this document has fully addressed the situation is like erecting a pup tent in downtown Los Angeles and saying we have fully addressed the homeless situation."[53]

Nor was the Draft EIS to be the last cut in the original wish list of the National Park Service. Months of inaction followed the comment period and the public hearings on the Draft EIS, during which the BLM obviously scratched its collective head on how much land it was prepared to give up to a sister agency whose resource management policies focused on protection. A year following the Draft EIS, a final version was printed. It reduced the Death Valley additions from 242,850 acres to 103,750 acres and changed the Joshua Tree addition from 4,480 acres to 4,800 acres.[54]

Did the BLM thereby pass up its best chance to avoid losing the East Mojave to the Park Service? The opinion has been expressed that had the BLM acceded to the original Park Service request for a significant expansion of the two desert national monuments, such action might have reduced the impetus behind the campaign for the Desert Bill.

Nothing further came of the proposed transfer of lands during the next two years. It had been reduced to insignificance. The BLM was occupied in trying to put together its final recommendations for wilderness designations in the California desert and elsewhere in the state. Finally, in June 1991, that process was completed, and the Secretary of Interior forwarded the BLM's wilderness recommendations to Congress. These recommendations achieved legislative form a month later with the introduction, as the Administration's bill, of H.R. 3066, entitled "California Public

Lands Wilderness Act." Included at the end of the Administration's bill was the final version of the proposed transfer of BLM lands to the National Park Service, described above. It was destined to have a short history. After several months it was dropped as the House finally moved to schedule floor debate on H.R. 2929, the bill for the California Desert Protection Act.

"Easily Scarred and Slowly Healed"— the Castle Mountain Mine Case

> *The Federal Bureau of Land Management is currently waging a furious battle against Sen. Alan Cranston's bill, S. 7, to provide greater protection for large areas of the California desert, arguing that its own management of those properties is perfectly adequate to safeguard the land and the wildlife that depends on it. But BLM's involvement in a controversial gold mining scheme itself makes the case for Cranston's bill.*
>
> — Editorial in the *Sacramento Bee*, May 27, 1988

What caused the *Bee* to speak so harshly of the Federal agency that manages most of the public land in California? Possibly the *Bee's* editorial writer was aware that Congress itself had included in the Federal Land Policy and Management Act of 1976 the following evocative phrase: "The California desert environment is a total ecosystem that is extremely fragile, easily scarred and slowly healed." The "controversial gold mining scheme" referred to by the *Bee* would produce two or more truly monstrous scars in the desert that would, as a practical matter, *never* be healed.

Early in the 1970s, at the urging of the U.S. Bureau of Mines, mining companies became interested in a process that enabled the profitable extraction of gold from extremely low-grade ore or alluvial sands. In these situations the gold is so finely divided that it is invisible to the naked eye, and the gold-bearing ore cannot be assayed by conventional means. It was referred to quite graphically as the "cyanide heap–leach open pit process." No longer would veins of gold ore have to be followed into the mountain by laboriously constructed underground tunnels. No longer would a crumbling headframe and small tailings piled on the mountainside remain behind as picturesque reminders of man's age-old search for a fortune in gold. Low-grade, gold-bearing rock, gravel, or sand could be removed with the heaviest available equipment, the overburden of waste rock left in a pile to one side, the ore piled up in heaps atop thick plastic pads, leaving behind an open pit or pits hundreds of feet deep. A cyanide solution would be sprayed on each heap and, trickling through it, would dissolve much of the gold and be collected in a pond at the bottom of the heaps. Refining processes would then recover the gold. After this was accomplished, much of the cyanide solution could be reused. The end result after the ore body was exhausted: vast, unsightly open pits, huge piles of waste rock and leached ore, and hundreds of acres of roads and other disturbed areas that had been used for structures, machinery and other purposes. Structures could be taken down but regrowth of vegetation around the pits would take many years, particularly in the desert, and the great pits themselves would remain, forever unreclaimed.

Nevada was to see the first massive development of heap-leach, open pit gold mines. By 1987 more than 60 of them pockmarked the land in that state. The California desert escaped until 1981, when the Picacho Mine went into operation in Imperial County. By 1987 there were five additional open pit gold mines in the California desert, including the gigantic Mesquite Mine east of Brawley, then expected to become third largest in the country.

Many of these mines were owned by foreign companies, often Canada-based. Such companies could hardly believe their good fortune. They could extract gold worth hundreds of millions of dollars without paying a cent to the U.S. Government for the right to mine the public lands in the U.S. and without paying any royalty whatever to the U.S. Government (and hence indirectly to the taxpaying citizens of the country) for the gold they obtained. It was too good to be true—but it was true. It happened thanks to the obsolete U.S. Mining Law of 1872, fiercely guarded from fundamental reform to this day by the mining industry.

So it was that in 1987 another foreign mining company arrived in the California desert. The Viceroy Gold Corporation of Vancouver, Canada, had a plan of operations for a gigantic new heap-leach open pit mine[55] on a 2,750-acre site. It required two open pits; the largest covering 110 acres and reaching down 600 feet—deeper than the Washington Monument is high. It would bulldoze and pile up 90 million tons of earth, enough to fill the Los Angeles Coliseum more than 30 times. As much as 3,000 tons of cyanide would be used at the mine each year. The swiftly developing heap-leach process was now capable of profitability with ore containing as little as three hundredths of an ounce of gold per ton of ore!

This mine was to be located in the northeastern part of the East Mojave National Scenic Area (the "EMNSA")—the area for which the BLM had just released its Draft Management Plan. In that plan, the BLM had referred to the EMNSA as "a unique area of special significance."[56]

The Castle Mountain Mine, a cyanide heap-leach open pit operation.

Courtesy of Larry Tapper

By the time the conservation community learned of it in December 1987, Viceroy Gold's plan of operations for the "Castle Mountain Project" had been approved by the BLM. The plan was approved even though it was accompanied by only a minimal environmental assessment, with very little in it about reclamation. Viceroy Gold was almost ready to begin the necessary blasting.

There was no time to waste. A coalition of conservation organizations, ultimately including the Wilderness Society, Sierra Club, California Wilderness Coalition, Natural Resources Defense Council, Desert Survivors and Citizens for a Mojave National Park, turned to Earthjustice Legal Defense Fund's Deborah Reames for help.

Reames came to the Legal Defense Fund in 1977 as a full-time legal assistant, or law clerk. It is rare today in California for someone to become a practicing lawyer without graduating from an accredited law school. In the old days, however, it was not uncommon for young aspirants to read the law in the office of a practicing lawyer and thereby qualify for admission to the bar. This route to the profession is still open in California, although in recent times it has required the aspirant to submit monthly examination papers on legal topics over at least four years. Deborah took this route. In 1981 she passed her "first-year bar exam," was certified to practice law under supervision, and began directly counseling clients and arguing motions. Three years later she became a full-fledged member of the California Bar. It is likely that her years of hard experience were more than equivalent to the course of study at a good law school. By 1987 she had become widely respected as a fearless advocate and rawhide-tough negotiator. In 1991 she received the Sierra Club's William O. Douglas Award, the citation referring, among other things, to her "skilled and tenacious efforts" to protect the California desert and reform the 1872 Mining Law.

Earlier in her career, although only a law clerk at the time, she had handled much of the work on the Keynot Mine case. She was involved in the successful fight to overturn the BLM's decision opening the Panamint Dunes to ORV use in 1982. She was also engaged in the long struggle to protect the desert's wildlife and scenic resources from the impacts of the Barstow–Vegas motorcycle race.

Assessing the case at hand, Reames quickly realized that there was nothing her clients could legally do to put a complete stop to the proposed mining project. The 1872 Mining Law essentially authorized Viceroy to go ahead if it held a claim to a valuable deposit of hard rock minerals on public land, and Viceroy complied with such reclamation of the mine site as the BLM and the County requested. But the BLM's own regulations, not to mention its stated interest in seeing an area like the EMNSA appropriately protected within the law, cried out for more study of the environmental impact of this mine and for a truly thorough reclamation plan. On its face, the company's plan of operations was grossly inadequate.

Reames promptly filed a formal appeal to the Interior Board of Land Appeals demanding preparation of a full-scale environmental impact statement (EIS). The filing of this appeal brought the matter to the attention of State BLM Director Ed Hastey. He reacted by moving to set aside the agency's approval of Viceroy's plan of operations, requesting that a new plan be prepared, and setting in motion the procedure for preparation of the full EIS Deborah had requested. It was a good start.

From the beginning, the Wilderness Society was particularly active in the case. Patty Schifferle, head of its western regional office, prepared a valuable background report on the extent and the absence to date of adequate regulation of cyanide heap-leach gold mining. Norbert (Nobby) Riedy, then posted from Washington to the society's San Francisco office, prepared the conservation group's comments on the issues. Together they brought into the picture Professor Robert Stebbins of the University of California, Berkeley, whom we first met in "Showing off the Baby" (Chapter Seven), hydrologist Dr. Robert Curry, and U.S. Geological Survey desert expert Dr. Howard Wilshire. Quickly, these experts indicated their concerns in a private scoping session with BLM officials on the issues to be addressed by the EIS. A major concern was the potential effect on Piute Spring of the planned withdrawal of large amounts of groundwater for the needs of the mine. This precious spring, located 16 miles from the mine site, was the source of the only year-round flowing stream in the EMNSA. Other immediate concerns included the danger to wildlife from open cyanide ponds, even though netting might be stretched over them, and lack of a thorough revegetation plan. The company's early response to all of these concerns was uniformly negative and its new plan of operations highly unsatisfactory.

It took nine months, until March 1989, for a Draft EIS to be produced by Environmental Solutions Inc., a private firm paid (as was customary) by Viceroy Gold to do the necessary work. It was an improvement over the original EA but it still failed to provide an adequate reclamation plan, it failed to adequately mitigate the damage to desert tortoise habitat and desert vegetation, and it failed to adequately address the serious concerns of the conservation organizations about groundwater withdrawal. By this time, the press and others had become interested in the issues and had reviewed the Draft EIS. The California Attorney General's office filed a set of critical comments. Particularly noted by the press was the conclusion reached by the Draft EIS that, based on the mitigation measures incorporated in the draft, the project would have "no significant environmental impact." Said the *San Bernardino Sun* on April 22, 1989:

> *It is one thing to argue the relative merits and values of preserving the virgin nature of the desert against the need to engage in economic activities such as mining. Such a debate may or may not lead to the conclusion that some environmental disruption is necessary to sustain economic activity. But to argue, as the BLM has been doing in this case, that such a massive operation as this can be undertaken with minimal disruption of the desert, is ridiculous. If this project meets requirements for a designated National Scenic Area, then how can the BLM maintain credibility as an advocate of environmental preservation?*

Meanwhile, conservation organizations had not been idle. Jim Dodson (for the Sierra Club) and Johanna Wald (for the Natural Resources Defense Council) joined Nobby Riedy in analyzing the Draft EIS and preparing an extensive critique. The experts had completed a careful study of the case and had prepared ominous written reports. Ed Hastey was now instrumental in bringing the parties together to negotiate. At the first session, the conservation side disputed the conclusion of the Draft EIS that the project's newly assessed (and increased) water requirements could be taken from groundwater without affecting water flows at Piute Spring. The experts recommended a careful monitoring plan for groundwater levels at the mine site and for water quantity and quality at the spring. They wanted certain trigger levels that called for various actions by the company, including the cessation of mining activity if a particular low level of water flow from the spring was reached. After many hours of resistance at the first session, the company agreed.

At a second vigorous session, this time regarding concerns for wildlife, more progress was achieved. Dr. Kristin Berry, the BLM's tortoise expert, joined in, bringing persuasive ideas to the table. The company agreed to several remedies. It would build a new access road which would lessen the impact on the desert tortoise, reclaim a number of existing roads in the area of the mine, consider a closed storage rather than an open pond cyanide system, install specially designed protective fencing recommended by Professor Stebbins around the entire mine site, and use a drip irrigation system for its heap-leach pads rather than sprinklers.(Drip irrigation would avoid wind dispersal of the cyanide spray and the pooling of the solution on top of the mounds, both attractive to birds.) At the third session, the company agreed to a proposed closed cyanide storage system using tanks rather than open ponds, in which the evaporation loss would be high. This enabled the groundwater requirement to be reduced by more than 50%.

The negotiations continued for another full year and Viceroy Gold agreed to further innovative reclamation improvements. This included compensating for the damage it would inevitably do to the environment by filling two clay pits left over from former mining operations with overburden from its own pits. It would also establish a desert nursery to preserve cacti and other desert plants which would be replanted on the site once the expected ten-year life of the mine has ended. Past reclamation plans at other mines in the desert generally provided little more than spray seeding of the area when the mine was abandoned, typically resulting in little revegetation. In this instance reclamation was to be done in stages. As a particular area was used up, specified percentages of density and diversity of vegetation were required to last through a stipulated period of years, including one year with no artificial watering, before relevant portions of the reclamation bond would be released. It was necessary to appeal directly to Ed Hastey to have these and other concessions by the company included as detailed, enforceable stipulations attached to the Record of Decision of October 31, 1990. Hastey cooperated and it was done.

Final settlement of the dispute was reached by a formal agreement (to which the BLM was not a party) on November 7, 1990. Its provisions were unprecedented. In addition to the measures agreed to in the earlier negotiating sessions and embodied in the Record of Decision, final bargaining established a "Revegetation Review Committee" to oversee Viceroy Gold's progress throughout the mine's life and included provision by the company of a $2 million fund for "environmental enhancement," to be conservatively managed by the independent Trust for Public Land. The conservation organizations could elect to have this fund, grown larger through accumulation of interest, used following closure of the mine to pay for such backfilling of the smaller of the two huge pits produced by the project as could be done with the money then available.

This was the climactic achievement. Both the BLM and San Bernardino County authorities had absolutely refused to require any backfilling of the pits. On no other occasion in the history of heap-leach, open pit mining had this been required, and the BLM was not about to be the first agency to try it. Public policy arguments failed. But provision in the agreement for the special fund to be established at the outset and used for backfilling at the option of the conservation organizations struck hard at the assertion of the mining industry that backfilling of such pits would render mining operations uneconomical. Deborah Reames expressed the solemn satisfaction of the conservation community: "The central concern with this kind of mining operation is that, after reaping huge profits from the public lands, the mining companies, paying no royalty, leave the public with nothing more than pits. This agreement demonstrates that this need not be the case."[57]

★ ★ ★ ★

One might well ask: "What was the true outcome of the Castle Mountain Mine case? What did the efforts of the conservationists, their experts and their counsel, sustained over several years, accomplish? Did Castle Mountain establish new standards which, in future years, similar mining projects would be required to adopt?"

It did, to some degree, although mainly in minor respects. There would be no more massive open pit gold mines on public land in California without the prior preparation of a full-dress EIS. Otherwise, most of the ideas generated by the Castle Mountain case were thereafter applied with little uniformity or consistency. No subsequent operations confined the cyanide to metal tanks. In two instances, but not in others, "pregnant" cyanide solution ponds were to be covered with hard plastic to protect birds and other wildlife. For similar reasons, and to conserve groundwater resources, drip irrigation of leach pads rather than spraying the tops of the pads was proposed for most, but not all, subsequent projects. Some plant salvaging has been required for subsequent projects, but only one venture other than Castle Mountain proposed to establish a revegetation review committee. Several, but not all, projects established "success" standards for revegetation based on stipulated percentages of plant diversity and density following reclamation. In only one subsequent project did the final EIS recognize a need to contour the slopes of waste rock piles and leach pads to approximate natural landforms and improve the possibility of successful revegetation.

A loose standard grew out of Viceroy Gold's agreement to refill several small, old pits on a nearby area previously disturbed by clay mining and revegetate the area. Subsequent mining operators have been asked to come up with comparable "offsite reclamation" projects. California State BLM Director Ed Hastey's effort to describe this policy in writing in 1994 proved difficult for the mining industry to swallow and he withdrew it; however, he has stated that the policy remains in effect in unwritten form. The reasoning behind the policy is made clear in the agency's abortive 1994 Instruction Memorandum, which included an ominous prediction:

> ...the number of non-backfilled pits will increase to add to the cumulative impacts that encumber the public lands. To compensate for these impacts, it makes good sense, from ecosystem management and public interest standpoints, to ask the project operator to provide some equivalent off-site reclamation when open pits or other areas are left unreclaimed...the amount of off-site compensation will be determined in a case-by-case basis but it will be commensurate with the area left unreclaimed in the pit, overburden and leach pad areas.[58]

"Makes good sense?" Must the number of huge, *unreclaimed* open pits inevitably increase, as Hastey observed, leaving behind a cumulative impact of unimaginable proportions on the land? How can a modest off-site "mitigation project," desirable as it might be, to clean up old trash and hasten the revegetation of a previously disturbed area possibly offset the impact of an open pit hundreds of feet deep and hundreds—even thousands—of feet across, never to be reclaimed?

The California state office of the BLM has continued steadfastly to refuse to require open pits to be backfilled by the operator, despite the modest opening provided by the agreement of Viceroy Gold to establish a special fund that could later be used for partial backfilling of a pit at the Castle Mountain Mine. When more than one pit is planned, the agency now encourages the miner to plan to backfill the first pit with waste rock from the second while the second is being dug *if* the miner considers this feasible. Some miners have found that this "sequential backfilling" actually saves money. But the last pit in a sequence of pits is never required to be backfilled. This is the end result of the BLM's interpretation of the 1872 Mining Law.

However, the Federal Land Policy and Management Act of 1976 (FLPMA) incorporated a significant amendment of that law which deserves far more attention than it has received: "In managing the public lands the Secretary [of Interior] shall by regulation or otherwise take *any action required to prevent* unnecessary or *undue degradation of the lands* and their resources *or to afford environmental protection*." (The emphasis is the author's.) In another section, the statute refers specifically to the California desert with these words: "...all mining claims located on public lands within the California Desert Conservation Area shall be subject to such reasonable regulations as the Secretary [of Interior] may prescribe. ... Such regulations *shall provide for such measures as may be reasonable to protect* the scenic, scientific and environmental values of the public lands of the California Desert Conservation Area *against undue impairment*. ..."59

A serious question may be raised as to whether, since 1976 (the date of FLPMA's adoption), successive Secretaries of Interior have properly carried out this unqualified mandate, which is to prevent *"undue"* as well as "unnecessary" degradation of the public lands and which specifically *amends* the 1872 Mining Law. Dictionaries define the word "undue" in straightforward terms to mean "inappropriate," "excessive," "unsuitable," "improper," "unrightful." Most often cited as a synonym for "undue" is the familiar word "inappropriate." On its face, this concept differs significantly from the concept "unnecessary."

Take, for example, a new open pit gold mine presently under review in the California desert. It is to be sited in a pristine desert area long classified by the BLM for "limited" use, hence, in the words of the *California Desert Plan Draft EIS*, "oriented toward giving priority to the protection of sensitive natural, scenic, ecological and cultural resources while placing limitations on other uses which may conflict with these values."[60] The land in question contains sites sacred to an existing Native American tribe. The "proposed action" for this mining venture, tentatively approved at the time of this writing by the BLM, would leave the largest open pit unbackfilled and hence unreclaimed. That pit is scheduled to be over 800 feet deep, over 4,000 feet long and over 2000 feet across.

Would this constitute undue (*i.e.* "inappropriate") degradation? It might not if gold were a strategic metal and in very short supply. It is neither. It might not if the "proposed action" was in keeping with the wishes and desires of the public. As previously described, *all* of the independent polls taken during the development of the California Desert Plan (and a subsequent Field Institute poll in 1988) showed that large public majorities wanted greater protection of the desert environment and *not* more mining. It might not if the area in question were already torn up by historic mining activity, including other unreclaimed open pits. That does not apply. The question would seem to be: In the absence of *any* of these obvious factors, how could anyone reach a rational conclusion that, on this land, such degradation is other than inappropriate?

In 1997 Secretary of Interior Bruce Babbitt ordered a thorough review and revision of the BLM's "3809 Regulations," (43 CRF § 3809) dealing with hard rock mining, observing "It is plainly no longer in the public interest to wait for Congress to enact legislation that corrects [their] shortcomings."[61] Will the changes ultimately made during this revision of the regulations put a stop to the enormously destructive processes now used to extract minute amounts of gold from the public lands? Will they conform more fully to FLPMA's mandate to protect the desert against "undue degradation" and, in addition to safeguard the scenic, scientific and environmental values of the *California* desert against "undue impairment?" Will they include standards that require *full* reclamation of gold mining sites, including (except in the most unusual circumstances) the backfilling of all open pits?

It is likely to be a long, hard row to hoe.

Fadeout for Barstow–Vegas

You're acting like a bunch of little Nazis. If you want to stop my first amendment rights that's a decision you're gonna have to live with. Now, I'm going to fire this machine up and I'm going down the road.[62]

—Rick Sieman

And this he did, on a motorcycle decorated with a plastic desert tortoise, closely followed by three others and cheered on by a crowd of about 100 fellow cyclists and supporters gathered to defy "the Feds." They were chased by two governmen helicopters (plus two from the media) and a passel of law enforcement officers.

Courtesy of *San Bernardino Sun*, Ken Jolly

It was the last hurrah of the radical wing of the Barstow-Vegas race promoters. They were finally confronted on that Saturday morning of the 1990 Thanksgiving week-end by a BLM order closing to public entry all BLM land (including the traditional starting area) used for the race in the past. The order was prompted by the off-roaders' vehement threats to run the race despite the lack of a permit. This time the BLM's order was to be enforced. The BLM had roped off the old starting line. Guarding it was a powerful force of BLM rangers, San Bernardino County deputy sheriffs, and State Highway Patrol officers.

The four who had determined to go down in flames (well, not quite) turned the defenders' flank by slipping around the end of the rope in a cloud of dust and headed east. It took quite a while for their pursuers to catch all of them, but catch them they did, then applied the cuffs and took them off to the local sheriff's station for booking. In a subsequent jury trial each was fined $850[63]—a tiny fraction of the expense incurred by County, State and Federal governments to enforce the law against those who took it into their own hands, Wild-West style. (Six others were also arrested.)

What had brought about this bit of semi-violent desert drama?

The story goes back to the mid-1960s, when the San Gabriel Valley Motorcycle Club first organized a race through the Mojave Desert on Thanksgiving weekend. It started near Barstow and ended at the Nevada border (later extended to a short distance west of Las Vegas). The Club laid out its own course, no permit being required at the time. This was the event that awakened a startled Russ Penny to the risks posed by uncontrolled off-roading on BLM desert lands.

As described earlier, the race soon grew in size and was promoted throughout the country. After the BLM conducted a thorough study during 1974 of the environmental impact of the race, followed by a careful post-race review, the agency halted the race by refusing a permit. For each of the next eight years the BLM stuck to its decision not to permit the race but was unable to enforce it. The story of the organization of illegal Barstow-Vegas "protest" rides during those years has been told in detail elsewhere.[64] As has been previously described, the BLM decided to permit the race to resume in 1983, and conservation organizations were unsuccessful in overturning that decision by court action.

Permits for the race were issued in each of the years 1983 through 1988, during which time it became co-sponsored by District 37 of the American Motorcyclist Association (the "AMA"). While continuing to oppose the race, conservation organizations monitored each race to assess the damage done.

Meanwhile, the case for listing the desert tortoise as an endangered species had become unchallengeable. On May 31, 1989, the Environmental Defense Fund, Natural Resources Defense Council, and Defenders of Wildlife petitioned the Fish and Wildlife

Service a second time to list the tortoise as endangered. They supplied new information about its precipitous recent decline, and served notice of their intention to sue for the listing at the end of the statutory period of 60 days.

The original turtle form evolved almost 200 million years ago and has remained remarkably unchanged since. Tortoises, the land form, appeared somewhat later. Close forerunners of today's desert tortoise were active in dry habitats 33 million years ago, leading to the frequent reference to the animal as a "living fossil." It is widely regarded in scientific circles as an "indicator" species—its numbers reflect the health of desert wildlife in general. By 1988 the BLM's own data, collected by staff research scientist Dr. Kristin Berry, showed an estimated 90% decline in the tortoise population of the western Mojave Desert during the previous several decades. Study plot data from eight sites indicated that populations had declined at rates of up to 11% per year for each of the previous six to eight years. Nevertheless, according to an article in the *Los Angeles Times* on May 24, 1989:

> . . . *Ed Hastey (the* BLM *State Director), acting against the advice of his own staff expert, asked the California Department of Fish and Game to wait up to four years before listing the desert tortoise as a State-threatened species. He said* BLM *needed the time to develop its own tortoise protection program.*

The California Department of Fish and Game was not persuaded. It listed the tortoise as a threatened species in June 1988. This was encouraging but of limited practical value, since more than 70% of tortoise habitat was on Federal land where the State's action would have little effect. Federal action would be necessary to secure adequate protection. Would the U.S. Fish and Wildlife Service in the Department of Interior follow the decision of the State Fish and Game Department? It would, spurred into action by the 60-day notice from the group of conservation organizations. On August 4, 1989, it published an emergency determination of endangered status for the

Mojave population of the tortoise, defined as all tortoises north and west of the Colorado River. In its brief statement of reasons, after referring to the critical deterioration of tortoise habitat, the U.S. Fish and Wildlife Service stated:

> *Competitive off-highway vehicle racing events adversely impact tortoise habitat. They usually involve several hundred race participants and thousands of spectators. The camping and race start-to-finish areas receive intensive vehicle use and become devoid of vegetation. Tortoises are eliminated from these areas entirely due to loss of food, cover, and burrow sites. Affected areas become enlarged with continual use. Vehicle route proliferation has occurred in many areas and can result in a significant loss of habitat.*[65]

The BLM proposed again to authorize the race for the Thanksgiving weekend in 1989. It did so despite the actions of the two wildlife agencies and in the face of the alarming fact that the Barstow-Vegas race would cross at least three large areas designated by the BLM itself as critical desert tortoise habitat.

An unsympathetic judge had thwarted the conservation community in 1983 in its effort to stop reauthorization of the race. Now, the tortoise listing gave conservationists fresh ammunition. They were determined to try again. Deborah Reames of Earthjustice Legal Defense Fund, representing a group of conservation organizations, notified the BLM's State Director they would challenge the decision to allow the race to proceed. Director Hastey responded by inviting the group to discuss the issue with him and the AMA, the principal race proponent.

Three people represented the conservation side in these discussions. Deborah Reames and Jim Dodson are familiar names in the fight for desert parks and wilderness. The third negotiator was George Barnes, a systems engineer from Palo Alto, California. George came from a family of desert explorers. While in college, he was a summer employee at the China Lake Naval Weapons Center in the Mojave Desert. His college graduation present in 1958 was a 4-wheel drive Jeep, which he used during the next dozen years as a desert explorer and technical climber. He came to know the desert as well as, and perhaps better than, any other single person. His advice was sought from the beginning, as boundaries for wilderness areas in the Desert Bill were being drawn.

Early in the 1970s the Barstow-Vegas race became Barnes' prime concern. From 1975 through 1982, he and others he recruited monitored the "protest rides" on the race course when permits to run the race were denied by the BLM. In 1978 and 1979 the BLM tried to halt these rides by court proceedings, which were largely a failure. Daunted by lack of adequate funds for enforcement and by violent threats to BLM personnel by a few of the protesters, the BLM finally abandoned any serious effort to enforce its permit requirements. Nevertheless, Barnes and his friends were on the scene every November. By 1979 he estimated that at least 2,000 protest riders and an equal number of spectators were on the course for the traditional Saturday after Thanksgiving. Embarrassed by its failure to enforce its own rules, the BLM decided to legalize the race in 1983. The annual vigil by Barnes and his friends continued, with written reports of their findings. Now, in 1989, he was ready with suggestions that might lead to significant change.

Hastey opened the discussions by reviewing what the BLM had decided to do in response to the threat of suit. It had modified the course of the race substantially. The mass start would occur this year by special permission on the property of the Fort Irwin Military Reservation. The route would then proceed eastward along southern California Edison's pole line road and would not invade the EMNSA or any of the WSAs that bordered the route. Barnes, Reames, and Dodson pursued a single objective. They wanted the BLM to stipulate far stronger conditions for the race than they had in the past. The goal was to control the racers and spectators, minimize damage to tortoises, and also to determine once and for all whether strong controls would work.

The AMA agreed to key stipulations. It may have realized that Deborah's clients would win the suit if it was brought. Among other things, the stipulations restricted the course to a width of 25 feet where it crossed critical tortoise habitat and required that the edges be carefully flagged. It was clearly understood by the conservation side that the BLM would check the flagging on the ground before the race proceeded. The race went forward and the stipulations were closely monitored both by BLM staff and the volunteers led by George Barnes.

Following the race, both the BLM monitors and monitors from the conservation groups agreed that many of the stipulations for the race had been seriously violated. The BLM counted 23 violated stipulations out of a total of 97. In the language of the BLM report:

> *The data collected indicates that the actual course utilized by the racers was routinely wider than the stipulated width particularly through desert tortoise habitat. Straying of many racers off the course resulted in additional trails and individual tracks far outside the stipulated course.*
>
> *Flagging was sporadic and spaced at distances too great to adequately delineate corridor boundaries. Most of the barrier ribbon placed along the race corridor appeared to be intentionally driven over. Many areas had trails 3 to 6 feet wide established immediately outside placards with arrows pointing inward. The presence and attempts of [AMA] race marshals and BLM monitors to enforce the width of the race corridor proved to have little effect.[66]*

But Barnes had something even more specific to report to the BLM. Following the course immediately after the last competitor had passed, he discovered that the BLM had failed its obligation to inspect the flagging of the course before the race took place. Much of the required flagging had never been put up. Further, Barnes had been informed by a BLM race monitor that uninspected AMA flagging had entered the Hollow Hills WSA in violation of the stipulations. He found it to be true.

On December 6 he brought this information directly to the attention of senior BLM officials. A few days later via a press release dated December 11, 1989, the BLM summarily announced to the public that it intended to disapprove any future applications not only for the Barstow-Vegas race but also for three other long-distance desert racing events. As previously described, these three races had been authorized by a last-minute addition to the BLM's 1980 Desert Plan. The basis for the December 1989 decision, according to State Director Hastey's statement in the release, included "the cumulative environmental impact of these events over the years, the sponsors' continuing problems in managing the events and the emergency listing of the tortoise as an endangered species." The announcement added that "BLM's monitoring of these events has identified recurring problems including numerous incursions into wilderness study areas, course straying and widening, and wildlife habitat and vegetative damage."

Barnes believes it possible that the agency's embarrassment over the fact that the critical flagging of the course had not been checked, and that this fact and its results would soon be announced at a press conference by the conservation groups, may have persuaded Hastey to act with unaccustomed dispatch. The conservation community called off its press conference.

The BLM had a second compelling reason to act as it did. As the agency said in its subsequent "Policy Statement,"[67] it could no longer afford the tremendous commitment of money and staff time which the race required in light of the relatively small number of racers participating (1,200 had been set as the maximum) and the fact that the "recreational benefits" of the race lasted only a day or two. Finally, in a deliciously mixed metaphor, the Policy Statement complained that the event "had become a millstone around the BLM's professional image."

The last several months of 1989 had been far from easy ones for the California BLM. Nevertheless, in the end Ed Hastey summoned up a touch of gallantry. In a letter to Deborah Reames dated December 1, 1989, he paid tribute to her for the part she had played in negotiating stipulations for the race permit. He said:

> I am often put in tough negotiating situations.... However, as difficult as they often are, such situations are workable if the parties respect each other's positions and bargain in good faith. On both counts, you rate very high in my book. I

greatly appreciate your professionalism, honesty and good humor.

In turn, Deborah gives Hastey credit for taking a strong position with the AMA to support the tough stipulations demanded by her and her colleagues.

It remains to mention briefly what occurred in the aftermath of the BLM's decision to end the Barstow–Vegas race. It was not surprising to find the BLM's announcement of no further permits for the big race (and the three smaller ones) quickly challenged by the AMA. The challenge was initiated in April 1990, after the BLM had rejected the AMA's application to run its race again in November 1990, and had issued its February Policy Paper mentioned above, to justify that decision. The paper indicated that an amendment to the Desert Plan would be developed to eliminate the four races and that further permit applications would be denied until the Plan Amendment process, which required public comment and was subject to appeal, was finished.

The AMA's lawyers thought they had a fruitful line of attack. They took the position that the Policy Paper was a "de facto" amendment of the Desert Plan, without the environmental assessment or any of the public processes required by law. They therefore asserted that denial of the permit for a 1990 race had been based on invalid agency action. They sought an injunction against any implementation of the Policy Paper until all formal requirements of law had been complied with.

The BLM responded that the Policy Paper was no more than an announcement of intention to propose amendments to the plan, that a formal plan amendment process had already begun, that an environmental assessment was also in the works, and that the AMA had failed, as required by law, to exhaust its administrative remedies before suing. Representing the conservation organizations involved in the prior negotiations, Deborah Reames moved in May to intervene in the case and filed a 35-page brief in support of the BLM's position. The District Court Judge, Solomon–like, gave each side a piece of the pie. He granted an injunction ordering the BLM to reconsider the AMA's permit application. This was to be done, however, only after an environmental assessment had been prepared. After that occurred, he said, the BLM was at liberty to grant or deny the permit in its discretion.

The BLM moved with alacrity to complete its environmental assessment, finished it in August, but then decided that a full-dress EIS, customarily paid for by the applicant, would be necessary. There was no time to complete an EIS before Thanksgiving 1990, and hence the AMA's permit application was not reconsidered. Frustrated, the AMA decided to postpone its sponsorship of a Barstow-Vegas event in 1990, dismissed without prejudice its lawsuit against the BLM, and put together for its members an alternative race on lands designated "open" east of Victorville. The alternative race was duly permitted and drew some 400 riders. The AMA has subsequently continued to sponsor some 30–35 desert motorcycle races per year within the open areas, as well as "dual sport rides" (not races) on established roads and desert routes from the vicinity of Los Angeles, over the mountains and across the desert, often as far as Las Vegas. The proposed EIS and plan amendment appear to have been put on the shelf.

The AMA took no part in the imbroglio in the desert, which occurred on the Saturday after Thanksgiving in 1990. In fact, it is understood that District 37 of the AMA, the principal sponsor of Barstow-Vegas in its later years, never condoned or participated in the illegal protest rides which occurred when permits were withheld.

The events of that Saturday after Thanksgiving in 1990 require an introduction to the notorious "Phantom Duck of the Desert." The quacking of a mysterious phantom duck had been heard as early as 1975. It turned out to be Louis McKey, an avid motorcycle racer and a principal organizer of annual protest rides over the Barstow-Vegas race course after the BLM ceased to permit the race in 1975. His close collaborator in the protest movement was Rick Sieman, editor of popular *Dirt Bike* magazine. Protest rides, of course, ended after the race was reauthorized in 1983. But not long after the BLM issued its announcement in December 1989 that it would no longer permit the Barstow-Vegas race, McKey and Sieman met to plan the protest they knew they would be sponsoring the following Thanksgiving weekend.

Keep Your Riding Area Beautiful

PLANT A SIERRA CLUBBER

Courtesy of Rick Sieman, Sahara Club, USA, Inc.

Early in 1990, Sieman had started the *Sahara Club* and its newsletter, a bawdy periodical that quickly gained readers. Some subscribers were environmentalists who wanted to keep an eye on the radical opposition and were also on the lookout for a laugh at the newsletter's intentionally outrageous commentary. In the fall of 1990 the *Sahara Club* broadcast an oblique call for a protest ride, indicating that Sieman and the Phantom Duck would be there. On October 20 a flyer was received by the BLM and many others from "the Freedom Riders" touting the coming protest. "Will you be ready for the largest-ever Barstow-Vegas Protest ride?" it asked, indicating that its invitation would reach over 50,000 people. It was to be "the Mother of all protests."

The BLM, smarting from past criticism of its inability to halt the protest rides of the late 1970s and early 1980s, determined to be ready for this one. It announced the closure to public entry of the traditional starting and pitting areas and the major routes that had historically been used for the race. At a Desert District Advisory Council meeting shortly before Thanksgiving, Gerry Hillier, BLM Desert District Manager, observed: "It looks like we're going to have a real picnic." And so it was, although the protesters who actually showed up were but a fraction of the number who had been promised.

Things remained relatively quiet throughout the spring and fall of 1991. As a precaution, the BLM again closed starting and pitting areas and the major race routes to public entry. A few days before the Thanksgiving holiday, the BLM was suddenly hailed into court by Sieman and the Duck. It was ordered to show cause why a few quiet, gentlemanly riders should not be exempted by court order from the closure of the route so they could symbolically memorialize the demise of the famous race. District Judge Gary Taylor apparently thought that was little enough to ask. He granted their request, ordering the BLM to permit them and eight others to ride (not race) along the old route.[68] Sieman exulted in the March 1992 issue of *Dirt Rider* magazine: "We used the same tactics the BLM has been using for years—we waited until the last minute to apply for legal leverage, allowing the BLM little time to fabricate any sort of defense." The BLM glumly accepted the ruling.

George Barnes tells the rest of the story. The ten permitted riders, with a BLM escort, made their way to the Nevada border without fanfare. It was essentially a "dual sport ride," using street-legal cycles also capable of rough riding off-road, and not a competitive race like those in the past when *cycle speed* was a prime factor in the damage done to desert plants, animals, and other resources. About 30 friends of the "lawful 10," having seen the others off, rode eastward out of sight, illegally crossing Soda Lake on the way. They were soon discovered by a BLM helicopter and apprehended.

In 1992 a similar dual sport ride was exempted by the BLM from the closure of the route with some 40 riders permitted to proceed to the Nevada border with BLM escort, monitored by a CHP helicopter and a BLM fixed-wing aircraft. In the event, between 20 and 30 cyclists made the ride. The following year saw the BLM tighten up on the "memorial protest," allowing about 80 riders to traverse only a short turnaround course of some six miles. By 1994 the steam had gone out of the protest and only 13 riders showed up, the Duck's machine being disabled near Baker.

The protesters never faded out completely. In 1995 they threatened to cross the new Mojave Preserve. This time, the BLM appeared at the starting line and the protesters said they were just campers with no intention of riding to Nevada. When the BLM left the scene and only George Barnes (as always) was watching the proceedings, 16 riders roared off eastward. George took off behind them, observing a bunch go under a bridge to the area south of Interstate 15. He soon caught up to find that one, Pat Martin, had crashed. His companions feared that he might be fatally injured. A call went out to the BLM for a helicopter to transport the injured rider to the hospital. Fortunately, he recovered.

When Barnes later chided the BLM for being hoodwinked by the protesters that morning, staff members of the agency vehemently denied that *any* protest ride had in fact occurred. "Very interesting," said George. "Then *who* was the employer of that ranger who rescued the badly injured protester in *your* helicopter?"

★ ★ ★ ★

In the demise of the Barstow–Vegas race, the desert tortoise proved to be a powerful factor. Following the announcement in August 1989 by the Interior Department's Fish and Wildlife Service that the Mojave population of desert tortoises was endangered and a proposed permanent rule in the fall of 1989, the service published a formal determination of threatened status for tortoise populations north and west of the Colorado River.[69] Support for the listing had greatly outweighed the opposition. The BLM joined the supporters while the Federal Bureau of Reclamation questioned the action. State agencies and commissions in California split, as expected, between the Departments of Fish and Game, and Parks and Recreation (in favor) and the Off-Highway Motor Vehicle Recreation Commission (against). The next step under the law was preparation of a recovery plan. That massive task called for an evaluation of tortoise populations and habitat in four states. Pushed by the conservation community to complete its work, the Fish and Wildlife Service issued its Draft Recovery Plan in April 1993.

Next came the announcement in February 1994 of the designation of 6.4 million acres of desert as critical habitat for the tortoise, including 4.8 million acres in California, most of it under

BLM jurisdiction.[70] The final Recovery Plan with final habitat designation was published in June 1994. Such a plan amounts to little more than a series of recommendations to landholding agencies. The Fish and Wildlife Service has limited power to enforce it. Ed Hastey had by this time become chair of the Desert Tortoise Management Oversight Group, a four-state team of State Directors, Fish and Wildlife Regional Directors and State Fish and Game Directors. In this capacity, as well as in his capacity as head of the California BLM, he signed the final Recovery Plan, pledging the cooperation of his agency and the members of the oversight group.

Still to come are action plans from the Federal land agencies for protection of the tortoise and other species inhabiting the west Mojave Desert, the eastern part of the Mojave, and the northern and eastern Colorado Desert. Such plans are not easy to produce and will be hard to monitor because of the complex checkerboard of private and governmental desert land ownership, particularly in the west Mojave. Will the plans be good ones? Will they be implemented in time?

It has been far from easy for Dr. Berry to maintain her conscientious effort over many years to monitor tortoise population trends. She was always frank and outspoken about the occurrence of damage to tortoise habitat. In 1983 she was informed that there was no money to pay for her position as research scientist and monitoring coordinator in the BLM's California Desert District. Convinced of the importance of what she had been doing, she successfully sought grants to the BLM from Southern California Edison and the California Department of Fish and Game. This funding allowed her to continue working at a BLM position until Congress became somewhat more generous in supporting BLM desert programs in the late 1980s. In November 1993, her job was suddenly transferred to the "National Biological Service," a new agency set up by Secretary of Interior Babbitt in his Department. This new agency, one more bureaucracy, did not find support on Capitol Hill; Congress later demanded that scientific research conducted by agencies such as the BLM and the National Park Service be placed, uncomfortably, under the U.S. Geological Survey. The Interior Department complied and, in October 1996, Dr. Berry was subjected to yet another transfer.

As of this writing, the USGS apparently has minimal interest in monitoring the populations of the desert tortoise and the BLM has no funds to spare for such purposes. Thus, although the recovery plan for the tortoise, which was so laboriously and expensively prepared, calls for monitoring as an essential part of the plan, and although the monitoring itself is not a matter of much expense, it appears to have fallen victim to Washington "reorganizationitis." In short, it has ceased. It would be overly kind to refer to this painful fact as an administrative lapse.

"Determine the thing
that can and should
be done,
and then we shall
find the way."

—Abraham Lincoln

In the Corridors of Power

CHAPTER NINE

Needed: A Sponsor in the House

Throughout 1985 the California proponents of the Desert Bill had pushed hard to ready the bill for introduction, to complete all maps and wilderness area descriptions, to resolve boundary problems as best they could, and to prepare data for the media. They had not had time to look beyond the bill's introduction in the Senate by Alan Cranston early in 1986. In Washington, D.C., however, an old campaigner had her eye on the next essential step—selection of a sponsor for the Desert Bill in the House. This was Debbie Sease, then director of the Sierra Club's Public Lands Program.

A logical choice for House sponsorship was Congressman Rick Lehman. His Central Valley District included part of the California desert east of the Sierra in Mono County. He was on the House Interior Committee and he had spoken out at the 1985 Wilderness Conference, stating desert protection would be one of his legislative priorities. But he had later expressed skepticism about the idea of a Mojave National Park. He might not want to introduce in the House a bill precisely like that of Senator Cranston.

A backup choice was needed. Another California Congressman, junior to Lehman in seniority, was also on the key Interior Committee. His district included the Santa Monica Bay cities and the Santa Monica Mountains. He had pressed for conservation measures in both of these areas and had a fine environmental record from the time he first became a state legislator in 1977. His name was Mel Levine.

Sease discussed the matter with Bob Hattoy. Together they made an appointment with Levine. He told them he'd be favorably inclined to sponsor the bill but would first like to talk to Senator Cranston. He did so, and the Senator mused, "Perhaps I should ask Rick Lehman first." It made sense. The Senator called Lehman, after which he told Levine that Lehman was reluctant for several reasons. His main objection was that he was genuinely lukewarm about a national park in the East Mojave. Would Levine do it? Levine agreed and also agreed that they would introduce identical bills in both Senate and House.

Thus on January 6, 1987, almost immediately after Congress reconvened, Senator Cranston introduced S. 7 and Congressman Levine introduced H.R. 371. Apart from minor changes, largely to correct boundary errors, the bills were the same as S. 2061 introduced by Senator Cranston the year before. Meanwhile, Hattoy found occasion to introduce Betsy Ford to Levine as a potential environmental aide. Ford had been an intern in the Sierra Club's Washington, D.C., office and was an ideal candidate. Levine hired her, and she came to work on January 13. Over the years that followed, Ford skillfully separated the many frivolous demands addressed to her boss for changes in the bill from those that appeared reasonable. She acquired the habit of trying the latter out on Kathy Lacey in Cranston's office and also on either Jim Dodson, Judy Anderson, or Elden Hughes, knowing they would consult with each other. She then secured the necessary map changes from Anderson, thus moving forward step by step the long and gradual process of perfecting the legislation.

California Congressman Mel Levine, original House champion of the Desert Bill.

Courtesy of Mel Levine

Congressman Lehman had been torn between his desire to be the author of a significant bill for California and the thought, or so it was believed, that his best move might be to try to broker an acceptable bill between Senator Cranston and the opposition forces. He took the unusual step of introducing, also in January 1987, two "shell" bills, one for the three proposed national parks (H.R. 361) and one for BLM wilderness areas (H.R. 279). Both bills left blanks for the acreage involved. The parks bill permitted all grazing permits in the Mojave National Park to be renewed on expiration for up to ten years. The rest was partly grab-bag, designating part of the Kings River "wild and scenic," and adding an indeterminate amount of acreage to Yosemite National Park.

Lehman did not press for action on his bills, nor were they reintroduced in subsequent Congresses. In July 1989 he refrained from testifying on Congressman Levine's newly reintroduced H.R. 780. Late in 1990, Levine quietly suggested to Lehman that they meet to see if together they could develop a bill that both could support. Lehman was agreeable and the process began. The story of this creative collaboration is yet to come. Much later Levine heaped praise on his colleague, proclaiming: "His skillful guidance, his sense of fairness and his commitment to conservation made the process [of negotiation] not only fruitful but enlightening." It was a gracious compliment. But credit for the first Desert Bill victory, achieved in the House in 1991, belongs in large part to Congressman Mel Levine.

What's Your Position, Senator Wilson?

If a bill involves land or significant interests in one state, its chances of passage in the Unites States Senate are greatly enhanced if both of the state's senators favor it. If one senator is opposed, passage may occasionally be possible but it would be a rare event. California's Senators Wilson and Cranston had known each other for many years. They had not been poles apart in their political views and had maintained a relationship, which was by no means unfriendly, ever since Wilson was first elected in 1982. In 1984 they had reached a compromise on what became known as the "California Wilderness Act of 1984," bringing many Forest Service areas into the wilderness system. Would they be able to come to agreement again?

The conservation community fervently hoped so. Wilson's aide Jim Burroughs made several trips to the desert in 1985. Senator Wilson himself visited in 1986. Volunteers who best knew the desert hosted them both. In June 1987, Wilson was invited to be the main speaker at the California Sierra Club's annual convention. Delegates from all of the club's chapters in California were eager to hear him promise support for the pending Desert Bill. He came, he referred to his support of clean air and water legislation and stressed the part he had played in reaching a compromise on Forest Service wilderness. He was warmly applauded, but his refusal to express a view on the Desert Bill was a keen disappointment. By this time his likely Democratic opponent for re-election to the Senate,

California's Lieutenant Governor Leo McCarthy, had made clear his strong support for the bill.

July 1987 saw the first Congressional hearing in Washington, D.C., on the Desert Bill before the Senate Subcommittee on Public Lands, National Parks and Forests chaired by Senator Dale Bumpers of Arkansas.[71] It was expected that Senator Wilson would speak and the conservation community waited anxiously. He was first on the program. His statement was short. He indicated he had not yet reached any judgment on the matter. But he did commend Senator Cranston "for having undertaken this ambitious effort." It was apparent that he was waiting to see which way the political winds would blow.

The balance of the hearing was relatively evenly divided between the testimony of proponents and opponents and served to confirm the positions of key players in the drama to come. California Representative Jerry Lewis, who was to lead the opposition in the House, asked to speak to the Senate subcommittee and stressed his opposition in a lengthy speech to the Senators. Senator Malcolm Wallop of Wyoming, destined to become the leading Senate opponent, made a brief appearance objecting to the holding of any hearing whatsoever on the bill since both California Senators were not in accord. Senator Cranston and Representative Levine, the bill's authors, defended their handiwork. The Reagan Administration's position was made clear by a letter from Interior Secretary Hodel, who asserted that the bill "would effectively stop most desert access" and would "brush aside all that had previously been accomplished" by the BLM's 1980 Desert Plan. These bizarre and misleading statements foreshadowed much of the rhetoric habitually used in opposition to the Desert Bill as it wended its way through the long hearing process in both Houses of Congress. It was also ironic to hear the ORV organizations, which had sued to derail the Desert Plan in 1981, now vociferously assert that the plan was just what they wanted!

A significant aspect of this first hearing was the signal given by Subcommittee Chairman Senator Bumpers. He generally favored the bill and wanted it to move it swiftly to "markup"—the full committee hearing in which votes are taken on specific amendments to revise the language of a bill before the committee votes to approve or disapprove it. He personally questioned some of the witnesses extensively.

The press in California was filled with articles about the controversy over the Desert Bill during the summer and fall of 1987. Senator Cranston made it clear in press interviews that he was open to reasonable compromise. Wilson said nothing. Early in the next year Jim Burroughs, Wilson's environmental aide, was quoted as saying, perhaps without authority to do so, that the Senator "is really not in a position to delay his involvement in this issue until after the [1988 general] election—that wouldn't sit well with the voters."[72]

At the end of January 1988, Burroughs and Cranston's environmental aide, Kathy Lacey, began quiet negotiations to try to develop a compromise that they could recommend to their respective bosses. Both were discreet—nothing was leaked about the scope or progress of what they were doing. However, Elden Hughes, whose hours of work were flexible (unlike those of his close colleagues, Judy Anderson and Jim Dodson) began to get regular, lengthy early morning calls from Lacey. She was asking for detailed factual information on subjects related to the bill, including particularly the proposed boundaries of park and wilderness areas and "precisely what was inside them." Hughes would relay her questions to those with special expertise on each area, gather all the data he could, and phone back as promptly as possible. Sometimes, he said, their calls lasted a couple of hours before he went off to work. A process of almost daily consultation developed between Judy, Jim, and Elden on strategies to move the bill forward. They became a small, working web within the broad framework of the California Desert Protection League (CDPL) operating without a chair, without a charter, and essentially without challenge. They respected each other's skills, trusted each other's discretion, and hence were entirely open with each other. There were no private agendas. Little importance escaped the attention of at least one, and what was significant was quickly shared. Their intensive consultation was to last until the drama's end, and it greatly enhanced their effectiveness year after year.

Wilson was reported as saying that it would be a good idea to delay the bill's passage until the 101st Congress, beginning in 1989, since "it's more important to do it carefully than to rush to hasty judgment."[73] Was this pure politics? Wilson would be on the ballot in California in November of the prior year. If only he could avoid taking a position until after the election, he might hope to garner a good share of the environmental vote as well as *all* of the votes of the bill's opponents. So it seemed, at least, to the *Sacramento Bee*, which editorialized:

> *A compromise might have been struck if Wilson would have said what he wanted. But Wilson never did. It could be one thing if Wilson simply admitted he was stalling the bill to death…but Wilson is running hard for re-election this year on the claim that he's a friend of the environment. And so he wants it both ways.*

In March 1988, Wilson and McCarthy both addressed some 150 California Sierra Club leaders gathered at their spring regional meeting in San Luis Obispo, California. Prior to the meeting, the Sierra Club's executive director wrote to Wilson to the effect that, even though he might not yet be prepared at this time to support Cranston's S. 7, the club's leaders wanted to hear what he *could* support. Wilson remained studiously noncommittal; he said he was still studying the question of desert legislation. McCarthy, the principal Democratic candidate, repeated his support for the Desert Bill. After the June primary, the Sierra Club announced its decision to endorse McCarthy's election. Wilson was angry. He put an abrupt stop to the quiet but serious negotiations between Burroughs and Lacey, and they were never resumed. Cranston told the press that his staff's efforts to present Wilson with a compromise "had gotten nowhere." Wilson responded that Cranston was proposing unacceptably restrictive legislation and had set an unrealistic deadline for reaching agreement on a compromise. In any event, the campaign season was now at hand and the bill was dead in the 100th Congress. In November 1988, Wilson won reelection to the Senate.

It was not clear during the entire first half of 1989 where Wilson stood. In January, the Desert Bill, now S. 11, was reintroduced in the Senate; an identical bill accompanied it in February in the House. It was August 1989 when the *Sacramento Bee* announced that the Senator "finally seems to have wobbled into a position opposing Cranston's measure" after making "Herculean efforts to avoid taking any position at all."[74] A month before the *Bee's* comments, the House Subcommittee on National Parks and Public Lands held its first hearing on the bill. Wilson did not ask to testify. However, by October 1989, when Senator Bumpers held his second Senate subcommittee hearing on the bill, Wilson at last took a firm stand.[75] He was against the bill. More than that, he adopted as his own the rhetoric of the most extreme opponents of the bill. Three times he repeated their absurd shibboleth that the bill "locked" Californians out of the desert, adding with oratorical flourish: "Mr. Chairman, S. 11 proposes to save the desert *from* the people of California. I propose we must save the desert *for* the people of California...."

Wilson made favorable reference in his testimony to the BLM's conclusion that 2.1 million acres of the desert were "suitable" for wilderness designation. Asked by Senator Bumpers if he disagreed both with Cranston's and with the BLM's proposals for desert wilderness, Wilson said: "I approve the BLM proposal." Still, there was a reference in his statement to the desirability of trying to reconcile differences between his position and that of Senator Cranston. He said, "our staffs attempted to do that last year," but he failed to add it was *he* who had called a halt to that effort. Senator Bumpers asked him to "give us a definitive list of your objections to S. 11 or what you would propose as an alternative." Carefully avoiding any agreement on his part to respond to this request, Wilson finally said: "I may introduce a measure of my own." He did neither.

This was for practical purposes Senator Wilson's final word in public on the Desert Bill before he left the Senate.

Despite being quoted in the *San Bernardino Sun* as saying, "You have to look in detail at how different parcels of land will be used,"[76] he was never willing to do this. Nor would he ever permit his administrative or environmental assistants to discuss with spokesmen of the conservation community which proposed wilderness or other areas he thought should be reduced in size or eliminated. Now Wilson no longer had time for consideration of or negotiation involving desert legislation. Not yet two years into his second Senate term, he had decided to devote himself to a run for Governor of California in 1990. But he kept his eye on the Desert Bill, and a short time before the election he successfully maneuvered to keep the Senate Committee on Energy and Natural Resources from holding a markup session on the bill.

Wilson's political fortunes continued to prosper. He was elected Governor of California in November 1990 and would now appoint someone to take his Senate seat. Without any optimism, the conservation community awaited another chance to try to gain the support of both California Senators.

Colorful Local Hearings Give Opposing Sides a Voice

Opponents of the Desert Bill (H.R. 780 in the 101st Congress) had clamored for field hearings on the bill to be held *in the desert* ever since the first House subcommittee hearing took place in Washington. They apparently felt that an overwhelmingly negative response could be guaranteed from the larger audience that would fill a local school auditorium or similar venue. The House Subcommittee on National Parks and Public Lands scheduled the first of three field hearings for such an auditorium at the fairgrounds in Bishop, California, on October 28, 1989. Included on the hearing agenda was a competing desert bill (H.R. 3460, the "California Desert Conservation Act") introduced only two weeks earlier by Representative Jerry Lewis.

The Lewis bill omitted any reference to national parks or monuments. It designated as wilderness only those areas the BLM had found "suitable" in its 1980 Desert Plan, *reduced* by 240,000 acres as the result of the 1982 plan amendments adopted during the tenure of Interior Secretary Watt. Still, the language in Lewis's bill referred to 2.1 million acres of wilderness—the same figure the BLM had initially found suitable in 1980! How could this be, when no change in the boundaries of wilderness acres recommended "suitable" and included in the Lewis bill had occurred between 1982 and 1989?

It was thought that the BLM had discovered large measurement errors when it checked its own maps more carefully. Lewis could thus claim his bill protected 2.1 million acres even though it excluded the acreage cut from the "suitable" category under Watt. But were those 2.1 million acres truly protected? The Lewis bill significantly *reduced* the statutory protections previously enjoyed by all designated wilderness areas. It

- Authorized unlimited motorized access to wilderness for grazers in lieu of the limited access permitted under the Wilderness Act.

- Opened all wilderness areas to establishment of "back country [vehicle] trails" to "provide important recreational opportunities."

- Forbade for 20 years any requirement of a validity exam for a mining exam before mining could be done.

- It included "hard" release language designed to prevent any public land not expressly designated wilderness by the Lewis bill from ever again being considered or studied for possible wilderness designation.

Opponents and proponents lined up to express their views. It was reported that more than 1,000 people attended the Bishop hearing.[77] Some 50 witnesses on each side of the Desert Bill were scheduled to speak. Four hundred and fifty had reportedly asked to do so. Presiding was Congressman Rick Lehman, whose own district included the desert area in Mono County north of Bishop. Four militant Congressional opponents of the bill flanked the presider—Jerry Lewis, leader of the opposition in the House, and Representatives Alfred McCandless

(Republican, California), Ron Marlenee (Republican, Montana), and William Thomas (Republican, California), in whose district the hearing was being held. McCandless and Thomas had both joined in the introduction of the Lewis bill. In a marathon session that lasted almost eight hours, described as boisterous by the press, Chairman Lehman was able to accommodate all the public speakers on both sides of the issue. Many spoke eloquently of the personal experiences that lay behind their views.

California Congressman Jerry Lewis, tireless leader of opposition to the Desert Bill whose 35th District included the largest desert county.

Courtesy of the Office of Congressman Lewis

A week before the Bishop field hearing, Louis Quirarte had called his friend Elden Hughes to suggest that 500 distinctive yellow T-shirts emblazoned with "Yes" be ordered for supporters of the bill who attended the hearing. Hughes wasn't sure there was time, but Louis was sure he could do it if the Desert Committee would come up with the cost, estimated at $2,500. The committee didn't have that much money but, counting on pledges and proceeds from sales of T-shirts, gave the go-ahead. Some 200 of the yellow shirts appeared on supporters when the hearing opened. This first appearance of the yellow T-shirts was just in time, for many of the opponents in attendance sported red ribbons and stickers. When opponents appeared in force at the *next* hearing, *all* had on Day-Glo orange T-shirts. Identifying jerseys were the order of the day from that point on.

The second field hearing was held two weeks later at the Barstow community center in the heart of the Mojave Desert.[78] It drew more than twice the number who had come to Bishop. The opposition was rallying a block away in their orange T-shirts when the center was suddenly opened and nearly 500 yellow T-shirts poured in to occupy most of the center seats. There may have been more orange T-shirts crowded into the back, the sides, and the balcony, than yellow when the hearing opened, but Lady Luck had favored the proponents this time.

The author of the House bill, Mel Levine, presided, flanked by Republican Congressmen Jerry Lewis, Larry Craig of Idaho, and James Hansen of Utah, all rigid opponents of the bill. As is always customary in such hearings, often to the annoyance of participants, each legislator present is afforded the opportunity to speak first. On this occasion, all had courteously shortened their remarks. Not to be outdone by the prior Bishop event, Levine had scheduled 145 witnesses. A field hearing tends to disintegrate into something of a show of numbers present and a demonstration of which side can catcall and applaud the loudest. However, in this case, representation of both sides by actual *witnesses* in the Desert Bill hearings was arranged to be roughly even.

How much can a witness accomplish in two minutes—the time allotted to each public witness at Barstow—in a noisy forum? Not much, except a conclusion and maybe a few facts from personal experience. Peter Burk, author of booklets on the desert, was the only witness to escape from repetition of the usual arguments. His flight of imagination was a guided congressional tour of Mojave National Park in the year 2000. "Ladies and gentlemen," he said,

> *You will be pleased to know that this is the most accessible national park in the country, served by interstate freeways on two sides and crossed by the new mag-lev bullet train. Businessmen are very pleased with the revenues the Park has generated, with visitors from around the world. Last year sales tax revenues from the Park exceeded $6 million. The City of Barstow received over $1 dollars in bed tax revenues from Park visitors. Grass, flowers and native foliage are coming back where the National Park Service has reclaimed mining scars. America has given the world two great ideas—a written Constitution and national parks. The people are grateful to you for passing the California Desert Protection Act just over a decade ago and thank you for your vision and foresight.*

He received applause from half the audience.

The last of the House subcommittee field hearings, scheduled for Beverly Hills, California, was postponed until

February of 1990. Meanwhile, the Congressional Budget Office had come up with an estimate of the cost to the Federal Government of the Desert Bill.[79] It put that cost at from $4 million to $5 million per year over the next five years, including validity examination of mining claims, additional costs of National Park Service management, construction of visitor facilities, and preparation of management plans. This cost estimate was based on Department of Interior data but did not include the costs of land acquisition (if any) for a Mojave National Park. This at last gave Congressman Levine ammunition from a respected source to rebut the outlandish cost estimates claimed for the Desert Bill by the BLM in 1987. At that time the agency, in a fit of hysteria, had asserted it could cost the taxpayers some $400 million just to conduct validity examinations of mining claims.[80] Later it sheepishly lowered this to $75 million—still a gross exaggeration.

Moreover, just two months before the hearing the BLM had decided, in December 1989, to terminate the annual Barstow-Vegas motorcycle race along with three other point-to-point races across BLM desert land because of the inability of the race sponsors to comply with stipulated requirements to limit damage. Enraged motorcyclists and their organizations called for a massive demonstration at Beverly Hills High School. The AMA offered "competitive race points" for attendance, a ploy that drew about 400 cyclists. Estimates placed the total number present at about 2,000 with opponents of the bill outnumbering proponents until late in the seven-hour session, when the cyclists began to drift away.

Minnesota Congressman Bruce Vento, chair of the House Public Lands Subcommittee and strategist in the final campaign.

Courtesy of the Office of Congressman Vento

The hearing was described by many as a shambles, with constant interruptions, catcalls, and heckling of many speakers who favored the Desert Bill. Some proponents reported physical attacks. Subcommittee chair Bruce Vento (Democrat, Minnesota) frequently had to pound his gavel and threaten to terminate the event if the opposing audience did not behave with a minimum of decorum.[81]

Katherine Saubel (properly Katherine Isivayawich Saubel), for years a leading elder of the Cahuilla Indians in the California desert and an authority on food and medicinal uses of desert plants, came to testify for the bill. She was astounded by the rudeness of the opponents. Interrupting the substance of her testimony, she said:

> Some of these people here are so discourteous I cannot believe it. And these people are supposed to be civilized. How can they do that? They were pushing me off the road. The people who were wearing red caps and red shirts, they were pushing me, and I am 70 years old. And I said what kind of people are they? If they cannot have respect for each other, how are they going to respect the environment?

The House field hearings were thus brought to an ignominious end. The raucous demeanor of the bill's opponents at the hearing did not help their cause. If anything, their behavior helped a disgusted but undiscouraged conservation community to redouble its efforts to pass the bill. Quite possibly it had a second important impact which would prove significant in subsequent years; several close observers believe it changed the chairman of the House Subcommittee, Bruce Vento, from skeptic to fervent supporter of the desert legislation.

While the Senate Is Stymied, the House Passes the Bill

The initial introduction of the Desert Bill in the Senate preceded introduction of the House bill by a full year. Cranston, the author, was a senior Senator and the Majority Whip. He had signaled his determination to press for Senate action. Senator Bumpers, chair of the Senate Subcommittee on Public Lands, National Parks and Forests, had indicated strongly in the first 1987 subcommittee hearing that he wanted to move the bill to markup and had subsequently held a second subcommittee hearing on the bill in

1989. Most observers therefore assumed that the bill would move first in the Senate rather than in the House.

When Senator Cranston reintroduced the Desert Bill in January 1989 as S. 11, it contained changes designed to meet many of the questions and objections raised by earlier versions of the bill. The 1989 bill reduced the total area of parks and wilderness by some 82,000 acres to accommodate utility corridors, patented lands, active mines, existing roads, and desirable minor boundary corrections. It added language intended to facilitate military training overflights and land exchanges. Later, at his second subcommittee hearing in the same year, Senator Bumpers invited Senator Wilson to assist the subcommittee in finding further areas of compromise. Wilson did not respond. By mid-1990 Wilson was immersed in his campaign for the California governership. Bumpers determined to move. He obtained authority from his colleague J. Bennett Johnston, chairman of the Senate Committee on Energy and Natural Resources, to proceed to markup in the full committee and to preside over the process. It was, by now, very late—the 101st Congress would come to an end in a few weeks, and national elections would occur early in November. A man of exceptional legislative experience, Bumpers knew there was little chance to finish the markup, let alone make further progress toward passage of the bill, before Congress adjourned. It seems fair to conclude that he wished to make a show of progress in meeting objections to the bill and, in so doing, notch its prospects upward for the next round.

The Senate Committee meeting began on a morning in September 1990 shortly before the full Senate session was to open. Bumpers was ready with amendments.[82] Among other things, these responded to requests from the military for complete freedom to conduct high- or low-level overflights of the desert for training purposes and for withdrawal of wilderness areas in the path of the possible eastward expansion of Fort Irwin. They would be left as WSAs. The amendments also responded to requests of the utility companies for greater flexibility for cross-desert corridors. However, Senator Wallop and his fellow Senators, James McClure (Republican, Idaho) and Conrad Burns (Republican, Montana), opponents of the bill, had determined how they would play their side of this legislative game. There was to be no substantive discussion of proposed amendments to the bill and no votes. All the three Senators needed to do was to talk for no more than two hours at most and each would, of course, make a lengthy opening statement. The three expected Senator Wilson to raise an objection with the Senate Minority Leader on the floor to continuation of the meeting.

It was expected that Wilson would utilize Senate Rule 26, which prevents any committee of the Senate from meeting for more than two hours after a Senate session opens without the consent of both Majority and Minority Leaders.[83] A single Senator's objection registered with his party's leader is almost always enough—the latter will withhold consent and that will put an end to a committee meeting. Normally, as stated in the rule, announcement is made each day on the Senate floor of committee meetings scheduled that day, together with the request of the leadership on both sides of the aisle for unanimous consent to the continuation of such meetings while the Senate is in session. That request is almost always granted without objection.

Wilson performed as expected. The message that the meeting must end was delivered to Senator Bumpers. The Senator so informed the committee and, in a deliberate voice, edged with irritation, he added: "I want everyone to understand that I *have* the votes."[84]

The moment had now come to take stock. Might it be possible in the near future to move the Desert Bill more rapidly in the House? If Senator Wilson lost his bid for governor he would remain in the Senate, a declared opponent of the major provisions of the bill. If he won, he would be likely to appoint someone to replace him who shared his views; that person would not have to run for the office for two more years. As noted previously, opposition by one Senator is usually fatal to the prospects of a bill affecting public land in that Senator's state. But no one believed that a state's delegation in the *House* had to be unanimous, or anywhere near it, to pass a land use bill affecting that state.

Such thoughts passed through the mind of Representative Mel Levine in the few weeks that remained between the date the Senate committee adjourned its effort for the year and the 1990 national election in November. Levine was reelected to his House seat and soon afterward, late fall of that year, sought out his fellow Californian Rick Lehman, also reelected. During the previous year, Lehman had indicated his astonishment that those who opposed Senator Cranston's and Representative Levine's legislation had not come forward with constructive alternatives. However, Lehman was a cautious man; on several occasions he had expressed reservations about Levine's bill and he was not among its co-sponsors. Levine now suggested that the two of them work together on the details of a desert bill that both could support. Lehman agreed.

New Year's Day, 1991, came and with it a new Congress—the 102d—and new committee appointments in both Houses. The grand old man of Arizona, Morris Udall (Democrat), was ill and almost ready to retire as chairman of the House Interior Committee. Without forcing that retirement, the leadership gave Representative George Miller (Democrat, California), chairman-to-be, the full powers of the chair. Miller had built a reputation as a strong and effective leader as well as a conservationist. It crossed his mind that new life might be injected into the Desert Bill if he could figuratively lock Levine and Lehman in a room and hold onto the key until he saw whether they could agree. His strategy was to give an old and dormant subcommittee the new title, "Subcommittee on Oversight and California Desert Lands," broaden it with special responsibility for the Desert Bill, make Lehman (Levine's senior in point of service) its chair, put Levine on it, and tell them he would support whatever they could agree upon. In effect, he challenged the two of them to come together before the bill was reintroduced in the new Congress.

Levine swallowed his pride. It could no longer be "his" bill. Lehman wanted two major changes in the desert bills of the past, namely, to establish a national monument rather than a national park in the Mojave, and to cut substantial acreage (roughly 250,000 acres) from the total area to be protected. He apparently desired this significant compromise on total acreage so he could reach out to Congressional opponents of the bill; he also wanted it understood that additional cuts in acreage might be appropriate if post-introduction negotiations with the opposition showed signs of success. In January 1991, Levine's environmental aide, Betsy Ford, and the chief of staff of the new subcommittee, Melanie Bellar, set to work in earnest on the details of the proposed acreage cut. The two Congressmen asked that their negotiations over the shaping of the bill be a matter of complete secrecy until it could be determined if they would succeed.

Early in January, Senator Cranston reintroduced the Desert Bill, now S. 21, in the Senate, making many changes along the lines suggested by the amendments proposed by Senator Bumpers the previous fall. Cranston's environmental aide, Kathy Lacey, kept him generally apprised of what was going on in the new House subcommittee, and the Senator let it be known he was content to have immediate priority for passage of the bill shift to the House.

California now had a freshman Senator, appointed on January 2, 1991, by ex-Senator, now Governor Wilson. He was John Seymour (Republican), a real estate investor and former state senator from Orange County, California. In 1988, Seymour had received the California School Association's "Legislator of the Year" award. He was appointed to the key Senate Committee on Energy and Natural Resources that had jurisdiction over the Desert Bill. To the surprise of many, the new Senator quickly announced that one of his top priorities would be to work out a compromise with Senator Cranston on the Desert Bill.[85] The conservation community was encouraged; Seymour was deluged with letters from representatives on both sides of the battle. He soon learned from his new colleagues in Washington to pull in his horns.

His initial meetings with Senator Cranston were unproductive. As he had done with Senator Wilson, Cranston told the new Senator that his Desert Bill was in the nature of a broad framework for reform. He was perfectly willing to negotiate over reductions to various protected areas in order to ensure there would be no unnecessary disruption of mining or other legitimate economic uses of the desert. Seymour was unprepared for such detailed negotiations, but it was hoped that his "priority" statement might bring him to the table soon for a discussion of specifics. In February, he engaged Richard Russell as his environmental aide to work on Desert Bill matters. As soon as it could be arranged in March, Elden Hughes and his wife Patty Carpenter took Russell on a five-day trip through the high points of the California desert. It was his first visit to California. Subsequently, proponents of the Desert Bill met with him on numerous occasions to respond to his inquiries and concerns derived from information he had been given by opponents of the bill. He was clearly quite insecure and seemed disinclined to try to develop any specific proposals to deal with the complaints of the opposition forces.

Returning to the House side, Bellar (representing Lehman's new subcommittee) and Ford, representing Levine, remained hard at work through the spring of 1991 on a compromise Desert Bill. For four years Ford had been collecting requests for changes from parties affected in various ways by the prior bills—miners, grazers, utilities, and particularly the ORV community. Changes would have to be made; she and Bellar consulted again with the affected parties and also with principal contacts in the conservation community. Judy Anderson recalls more than one entire eight-hour day on the phone with Ford, who wanted to discuss possible boundary modifications to almost every wilderness area or park boundary map Anderson had prepared. Ford negotiated directly with the big utilities to satisfy their concerns over their cross-desert corridors. Bellar took the lead on grazing issues and revised land exchange language. They collaborated on changes to leave open those areas that had seen substantial use by ORVs and certain of the specific desert routes desired by ORV groups. This ultimately resulted in a reduction of about 74,000 acres in the bill's wilderness areas. As they progressed, Lehman and Levine settled the issues their assistants could not themselves resolve. How long, for example, should grazing be allowed to continue in the Mojave Monument? Levine and Lehman agreed on the lesser of 25 years from date of enactment or the permittee's lifetime. As time passed, it was reported that Lehman was becoming increasingly positive about both the merits of the legislation and the progress of his negotiations with his colleague in the House. He indicated he would like to move the bill to markup as soon as possible that year. Miller, the full committee chair, was as good as his word. He joined Lehman and Levine in introducing the new bill, H.R. 2929, on July 17, 1991. Senator Cranston immediately said he expected to support the Lehman-Levine compromise. Senator Seymour, having now attended the school for new Republican Senators for over six months, quickly expressed his reservations. The reduction in the new bill's protected acreage, approximately 270,000 acres, he dismissed as a mere step in the right direction, adding ominously that the bill "is still a long way from what most people would consider an acceptable compromise."[86]

Rick Lehman had hoped for positive discussions with Jerry Lewis and other opponents of previous versions of the Desert Bill. Such hopes were soon dashed. A relatively few days after the Lehman-Levine Bill was introduced, Lewis introduced what amounted to the Administration's desert bill, H.R. 3066—The California Public Lands Wilderness Act—and firmly staked out his position as its prime supporter. His bill reflected the final recommendation of the BLM for California wilderness that had just been published. It projected 2.3 million acres of new BLM wilderness areas for all of California, including 2.1 million acres in the desert—generally the same desert areas Lewis had included in his earlier desert bill two years before. The Lewis bill's only reference to national parks or monuments was the inclusion of the very minor land additions to Death Valley and Joshua Tree National Monuments agreed to by the BLM in 1989. It eliminated any reservation of water rights for wilderness purposes. Interestingly, it omitted all of the provisions contained in his earlier bill, H.R. 3460, introduced two years previously, that gave ranchers unlimited vehicular access to wilderness, allowed the mining of any claim in a wilderness area for 20 years without demonstration that the miner had a valid claim, opened vehicle routes into or through several wilderness areas, and gave the Secretary of Interior, acting through the BLM, discretion to open additional new roads through wilderness areas. Perhaps these provisions of his earlier bill, which represented a disastrous weakening of the standards established under the Wilderness Act, had proven unpopular with certain of his fellow Republicans.

Following the introduction of the Levine-Lehman bill (H.R. 2929) and the Lewis bill (H.R. 3066), events moved swiftly in the House. Lehman's new subcommittee held its hearing on both bills on September 16, 1991. H.R. 2929 was approved by voice vote in the subcommittee on October 1. The full Interior Committee met on October 16, rejected the Lewis bill and reported H.R. 2929, with amendments, favorably to the House by a vote of 28–16.[87] Intensive campaigning ensued by both opponents and proponents before H.R. 2929 was brought to the floor on November 22. Fourteen amendments were submitted in advance. The House Rules Committee limited debate on each to ten minutes except for Lewis's amendment, which was scheduled first in line and allowed 60 minutes. That amendment proposed to substitute his bill, H.R. 3066, for the committee bill, and it was defeated 150–241. Other significant opposition amendments that were defeated included forbidding any condemnation procedures involving private land in wilderness or park areas (Tom DeLay, Republican, Texas), delaying the bill's effectiveness until the Federal budget was in balance (Dick Nichols, Republican, Kansas), providing that no parcel of land should be designated wilderness until an economic impact analysis had been conducted on each such parcel (William Dannemeyer, Republican, California), and striking all reference in the bill to establishment of the Mojave Desert National Monument (also Dannemeyer). It was on introduction of his second amendment that Representative Dannemeyer, who had announced he would be running for the Senate in the next year, tuned up his oratory. Grandly, he pontificated:

> *There are some organizations that comprise the Environmental Party in American politics...we Americans better wake up to the reality that this*

Environmental Party seeks to change our society to one that worships the creation rather than the Creator. If you wander through life and you do not believe in a hereafter, which I believe the leaders of the Environmental Party do not, what they see in this world is all they ever will see....[88]

The proponents of the Committee Bill submitted a series of amendments passed "en bloc" which included the provisions already in Senator Cranston's bill removing those wilderness areas in the path of possible eastward expansion of Fort Irwin (leaving them in WSA status) and facilitating land exchanges. An amendment submitted by Representatives Ben Blaz (Republican, Guam) and Bruce Vento (Democrat, Minnesota) was passed providing 15-year renewals for two military training areas in the desert and further clarifying the language authorizing low-level military overflights. Representative Blaz, otherwise an opponent of the bill, stated that these amendments satisfied both Air Force and Navy. It was announced that none of the California utilities were opposing the bill. The most disturbing amendment was one by Representative Marlenee, backed by heavy lobbying by the National Rifle Association, which permitted hunting to continue in the Mojave National Monument. It passed 235–193. The conservation community, which had hoped for a national park in the Mojave in the ultimate enactment, had been outflanked and outlobbied. The firm policy of the National Park Service would preclude national park status if the hunting amendment remained in the Desert Bill.

Debate was concluded on November 26, 1991, and the committee bill, as amended, passed the House 297–136, with 45 Republicans, only one of whom was a Californian— Representative Tom Campbell—voting for passage. It was a remarkable victory, a tribute both to the unremitting lobbying efforts of the conservation community and to the skills of the bill's Congressional leaders, Miller, Vento, Lehman, and Levine. The bill benefited from the fact that 1991 was the *first*, not the second session of the 102d Congress, and not an election year—

hence the legislative process could run more smoothly than might otherwise have been the case. As will be seen, a much different sort of process would prevail when the Desert Bill next reached the floor of the House in the closing months of the *second* session of the next (103ᵈ) Congress and shortly *before* an election.

With the Senate Still Stymied, Senators Seymour and Cranston Fade from the Scene

Although Senators Cranston and Seymour had both met and exchanged letters in the summer and early fall of 1991, they seemed to be getting nowhere. Cranston decided to wait and see what the House would do. It had become known that, enmeshed in Senate ethics charges involving his efforts on behalf of Charles Keating and Lincoln Savings, Cranston expected to retire at the end of 1992. Seymour had to bear in mind that the White House was opposed to the Desert Bill and its spokesman had said that if it passed, President George Bush would veto it. Both the Reagan and Bush Administrations had effectively muzzled government employees who might provide aid or support to the bill's proponents. Ed Rothfuss, then Superintendent of Death Valley National Monument, later wrote:

> *The Park Service was told we could not say or do anything to support the desert legislation....The most difficult...were exaggerated claims of what the bill would or would not do...Some of the most painful exaggerations related to NPS management. At meetings, including Congressional hearings, we had to listen to misstatements of how the NPS could not manage bighorn sheep, that they could not patrol the new lands if added, etc. Unfortunately some BLM officials promoted some of these misconceptions. While the NPS took pride in its relationship with BLM, the [Desert Bill] certainly put a strain on some of these relationships.[89]*

Asked about the House bill soon after its passage, Seymour repeated his previous statement that it was only a small step forward and still a long way from an acceptable compromise. Either he had not noticed the significant changes made in the bill before its passage, lessening its impact on consumptive uses of the desert, or his position in opposition was hardening.

California Senator John Seymour— Appointed by Governor Pete Wilson, he fell in line with Wilson's opposition to the Desert Bill.

Courtesy of the U.S. Senate Historical Office

In January and February 1992, the rhetoric between the two Senators escalated. According to the media, Seymour now flatly opposed any provision that would transfer the East Mojave, to the jurisdiction of the National Park Service. "I cannot and will not be flexible on the East Mojave," he said. He reportedly added that he would split the difference halfway with Cranston on the designation of other BLM lands as wilderness.[90] Cranston had written that a Mojave national park or monument was an essential part of the bill and he could not trade it away.[91] Soon, Seymour was telling the press that 20,000 mining-related jobs would be lost under the bill. Informed of this claim, the *Los Angeles Times* made a survey, finding only 356 active mining employees within the boundaries set by the bill.[92] Cranston's reaction was that the bill would not put a single miner out of work since all existing commercial mines would continue to operate.

Shortly after his appointment to the Senate, Seymour had asked that the Senate subcommittee follow the practice of the House and hold a field hearing in the California desert. Chairman Bumpers obliged, and the hearing convened in the Palm Desert High School Auditorium on April 4, 1992. In Chairman Bumpers' absence, Senator Seymour presided and was flanked by Senator Cranston and another new Senator on the subcommittee, Republican Larry Craig of Idaho, who had spent the previous ten years in the House and had from the beginning opposed the bill.[93]

Perhaps stimulated by the fact that opponents of the bill at Palm Desert clearly outnumbered supporters by T-shirt count, Senator Seymour opened with a long statement, constituting, according to the *San Luis Obispo Telegram-Tribune,* "his strongest attack to date against Cranston."[94] Both Craig and Cranston made short statements and more than 200 persons testified, mostly in short bursts of two minutes or so. Outside the auditorium a crowd milled about the many colorful booths where literature was available, including seven men dressed in black and white striped prison garb with "Cranston" across their chests, led by Rick Sieman of the Sahara Club, the organizer of Barstow-Vegas protest rides. They had begun sporting this garb in 1990 at the Beverly Hills High School hearing. After the hearing, Seymour was holding a press conference behind the auditorium when Sieman and his Sahara Club contingent discovered him. They rushed up to attack him for his previously expressed willingness to compromise with Cranston.[95] The Senator beat an instant retreat and disappeared. Jeff Widen of the Sierra Club, who had by chance observed these proceedings, stepped up in place of the Senator and, without revealing his identity, engaged the Sahara Clubbers in a rapid-fire question-and-answer session about the bill and desert protection in general. He hoped the media representatives would drink it all in, and perhaps they did.

Three weeks later Senator Bumpers presided for two more days of subcommittee hearings in Washington, D.C.[96] Senator Seymour's testimony employed the now commonplace catchword of the opposition. He said he believed the desert should be protected without "locking out" the public. He flatly stated the East Mojave appeared to be an irreconcilable issue between himself and Cranston. On that issue he said he would have no flexibility. Cranston informed the committee that he had been willing to cut 1.5 million acres from the 4.5 million acres of BLM wilderness designated in his bill, but that was not enough for Seymour—he wanted a 50% cut. Moreover, Seymour had never been willing to indicate which wilderness areas he supported and which he opposed. Cranston told the subcommittee he would amend S. 21, as introduced, to reflect all significant changes made by the bill as passed by the House.

After the hearing, Seymour reported that Cranston had proposed to him that they try to agree on everything in the bill except provision for a national park in the Mojave and then pass the bill, leaving this issue to be dealt with by the next Congress.[97] Seymour would have none of it. They had now reached the end of the line. At Cranston's urging, Senator Bumpers fixed a date, August 5, for his subcommittee's final vote on S. 21. Seymour let it be known that he would do everything in his power to block all efforts to pass the bill, including mounting a filibuster if necessary should the bill reach the floor.[98] On August 5, 1992, the subcommittee meeting had hardly gotten off the ground when Seymour put an end to it by invoking the same Senate rule— objection to proceeding with a committee meeting when the Senate is in session—that was used for the same purpose two years before by his predecessor.[99] It was no longer possible for the Senate to act before the end of the 102d Congress. Next year, the proponents of the bill would be forced to start again from scratch with fresh bills and another round of hearings in both houses of Congress.

This was Seymour's last hurrah. His opponent in the 1992 Republican primary, the archconservative Representative Dannemeyer (whose oratorical prowess we sampled earlier) took after him unmercifully. "If you put Seymour on trial for being a Republican," he said, "there's not enough evidence to convict him."[100] The conservation community rallied behind his Democratic opponent in the November election, Dianne Feinstein, former Mayor of San Francisco, who had lost the race for Governor of California to Senator Wilson two years before. Feinstein was elected to the Senate.

It was also the end of Senator Cranston's Senate career. Not seeking reelection, he faded away carrying with him the scars of the Keating affair but secure in the knowledge that he had fought the good fight for the desert and would be remembered for it.

*" Stronger than
all the armies in the world…
is an idea whose
time has come."*

—Victor Hugo

Will There Be Victory?

CHAPTER TEN

Senators Feinstein and Boxer—
New Champions for the Desert Bill

During the election campaign of 1992 Dianne Feinstein made it known that she supported the Desert Bill and, if elected, her first action would be to introduce the bill. Under the unusual

California Senator Dianne Feinstein fashioned the final Desert Bill, which passed the Senate Committee and the full Senate to become law in 1994.

Courtesy of the Office of Senator Feinstein

circumstances of that year, she and a fellow Democrat, Barbara Boxer, were both running at the same time for California's two Senate seats. Boxer had defeated Mel Levine in the June Democratic primary and been nominated to run for Cranston's open Senate seat with a full six-year term in prospect. Levine's defeat puzzled his supporters; he had been the author and a consistent champion of a major bill which had passed the House, had shown skill in compromising, had worked hard, grown in office, and was respected by his colleagues. He had had no serious trouble being reelected four times in succession. There was no lack of funds in his campaign treasury. Later, it was speculated that he'd relied too much on TV ads and waited too long for the ads to be shown. Boxer had campaigned with enormous energy and let it be known that she, too, supported the Desert Bill. Finally, there was the luck of the political draw—it was called by some "the year of the woman." A graceful loser, Levine went back to private life with a proud record.

Feinstein had chosen to run against Senator Seymour, the appointed incumbent. Because the seat he occupied had a term of only two more years, she would, if elected, be required to run for reelection after only two years in office. Leading the Desert Bill to passage in the next two years would help in her next campaign. Boxer, although as much a conservationist as Feinstein, graciously agreed to step aside and let her colleague be the author and primary sponsor of the new Desert Bill, assuming both were elected. Boxer would be a co-sponsor and stay in the background.

The election of 1992 set this plan in motion; both were elected, along with a Democratic President who could be counted on to sign the bill if it passed. The conservation community rejoiced. During the previous year, desert advocates had had good reason for concern over a possible compromise between Cranston and Seymour. Cranston might have given up far too much to gain passage of his cherished Desert Bill before leaving the Senate. Now the prospect of such an unpalatable compromise was over. But what would the new Feinstein Desert Bill look like?

Cranston had urged Feinstein to bring Kathy Lacey onto her staff as legislative assistant for environmental matters. Feinstein wisely agreed. Lacey had been of great help to Cranston through the years, had negotiated with both proponents and opponents of the bill, and was respected by both for her unfailing courtesy, knowledge, and discretion. She was the Desert Bill's "institutional memory" that Feinstein needed. In preparing for the introduction of Feinstein's Senate bill, Lacey utilized most of Cranston's final bill including a Mojave National Park plus boundary revisions on the maps resulting from the Levine-Lehman compromise which had passed the House as H.R. 2929. The Senate bill kept the same number in the new Congress, S. 21. New provisions removed the Castle Mountain Mine from within Mojave National Park, authorized grazing there for 25 more years, and made a series of other fairly small downward adjustments in the acreage protected by the bill. It could now be said that there was not a single active mine in the wilderness areas to be established by the bill. The bill was introduced in January 1993 on the Senate floor featuring large blowups of photographs from the desert picture books that had been put together by Elden Hughes back in 1989. Feinstein would use these photographs time and again in the next two years.

At roughly the same time, Representative Rick Lehman introduced a new House bill, H.R. 518. It differed from the new Senate bill principally in calling for a Mojave National Monument instead of a national park. It omitted the hunting authorization for the national monument which had been inserted in the bill by floor amendment when it passed the House in 1991. This was again destined to be a flash point as the bill moved forward in the legislative process. Both House and Senate bills acceded to the military's needs. The chair of the Senate Armed Services Committee, Senator Sam Nunn (Democrat, Georgia), ever zealous for the well-being of the nation's military establishment, was an initial co-sponsor of the Senate bill!

For the moment, the initiative on the Desert Bill shifted to the Senate. Senator Bumpers, again in charge, scheduled an early and final hearing of his subcommittee on Public Lands, National Parks and Forests for April 27, 1993, in Washington, D.C.[101] In contrast to the enormous witness panels of both House and Senate field hearings in prior years, this time the number of witnesses was severely limited. The hearing served mainly to give Senator Feinstein the chance to describe what her bill contained and to respond to questions, and for her colleague Senator Boxer to lend strong support. It also allowed Interior Secretary Bruce Babbitt to express the new Administration's favorable position, the Department of Defense to testify in support "with a few minor modifications," and the bill's inveterate enemy, Representative Jerry Lewis, to repeat his well-worn arguments. Lewis was unimpressed by the fact that Feinstein's bill went well beyond the protected area acreage reductions of the 1991 House bill and included further reductions to accommodate mining, military, and ORV interests. These cut the total BLM wilderness area in Senator Cranston's earliest bill, according to her testimony, by close to 500,000 acres. Lewis was backed up by Gerald Hillier, only six months into retirement from his long service as California Desert District Manager for the BLM, now testifying openly for the principal opposition organization, the California Desert Coalition.

The hearing did not presage smooth sailing for the bill. In the House, it appeared that Lewis would not introduce a desert wilderness bill of his own in the 103d Congress, but he and his followers were as full of fight as ever. Moreover, Representative Lehman let it be known that he would like to see grazing allowed to continue indefinitely in the Mojave and would work for a national monument rather than a national park. The land exchange provisions to facilitate transfer to Mojave National Park of state school trust lands and former railroad checkerboard private lands came in for strenuous objection and were finally labeled unworkable by Senator Bumpers.[102] However, Bumpers was more positive in his assessment of the bill than at any time in the past six years. He clearly thought there had been more than enough hearings and his patience had worn very thin. "Only once," he said, "Morgan Fairchild sat in the front row and made it a little more palatable for me."[103]

The final hearing of Lehman's House subcommittee on June 15, 1993, scheduled more witnesses than did the Senate subcommittee but offered little that was new save the first focused debate on the issue of hunting in the East Mojave.[104] Responding to the NRA representative, Elden Hughes recited his qualifications keyed to the occasion: He had been hunting in the western states for 45 years. His favorite deer hunting area in Utah had been "ruined by yahoos in ATVs." Only wilderness designation, he said, could save Utah hunting (and, by implication, could be helpful to California desert hunters). After this bill passes, he added, the BLM will be managing 4 million acres of designated wilderness in California where hunting would be lawful. "If the BLM manages this vast area for wildlife," he said, "we could have twice as much hunting in the California desert and still have a [new] national park."

Was everything now in order for the full Senate Committee to consider and vote on S. 21? Not quite...

Stephanie Jowers—
Winning the Support of a Southern Senator

Whatever you can do, or dream you can, begin it.

—Goethe

J. Bennett Johnston of Louisiana was a powerful man in Congress. A Senator for 20 years, he chaired the important Senate Energy and Natural Resources Committee. By no stretch of the imagination could he be called a conservationist. And it was he who held a key to the future of S. 21 when it came before his committee for markup and an up or down vote.

His testimony had been brief when he appeared at the subcommittee hearing in April 1993.[105] Immediately, he raised the issue of hunting, saying it was important to him. "In my state," he

said, "we allow hunting in the Jean Lafitte National Historic Park and Preserve." It was the addition of the phrase "and Preserve" which "permitted us to do what we wanted to do there…It is difficult for me to make my way through this issue," he said. It was clear to the proponents of the bill that Chairman Johnston would favor hunting and—for that reason—was very unlikely to be in favor of a national park in the Mojave.

Louisiana Senator J. Bennett Johnston managed the Desert Bill on the Senate floor.

Courtesy of the U.S. Senate Historical Office

The conservation community was not very strong in the state of Louisiana. In 1993 the state had only one land area managed by the National Park Service—the Lafitte Historic Park and Preserve, mentioned by the Senator—and it was a "Historic Park and Preserve," thereby distinguishing it from a "National Park" in the eyes of the National Park Service. Could anything be done?

Enter Stephanie Jowers, age 17, a senior in high school in Destrehan, a suburb of New Orleans. She had learned respect for the natural world from her parents, with whom she also frequently engaged at home in discussions of current political issues. By the time Ms. Jowers was a freshman in public high school she was ready to try to advance what she believed in. She found that the high school did not have an ecology club. How so? She found that it was not lack of interest but simply inertia, an age-old state of affairs. She applied to the school administration for its permission to start such a club. The answer was, "No, you're too young." Undaunted, she went to the school board. The board gave an adroit response. "You may have the club" she was told, "if you can show us a petition with at least

1,000 signatures in favor of your proposal." She got them, and a successful club was born. In time she learned about and joined the Sierra Club. Her future as an activist was on the way.

At the beginning of her junior year of high school in September 1992, Jowers returned an unexpected call from Mark Fraioli, a junior at Brown University and outreach director of the Sierra Student Coalition (the SSC). He had been given her name by a recycling organization in her area. "We're looking for high school students to do national work," he said, filling in the details in a two-hour phone conversation. She agreed to be regional coordinator of the SSC for the southeastern states. Barely a month later, she received another call, this time from Adam Werbach, age 19, a sophomore at Brown University, director of the SSC and its founder when he was a high school senior in Los Angeles. (Four years later, in 1996, Werbach became the youngest national president in the history of the Sierra Club.) Would Jowers come to Providence, Rhode Island, to help set up an SSC office there? She took several weeks off from school to do it. During subsequent discussions with Werbach, he told her that the California desert was the most important conservation challenge of the day and discussed with her the status of the Desert Bill in Congress. It was to be the first national campaign of the SSC. Would she help the campaign in Louisiana whose senior Senator chaired the Committee that must pass on the bill?

Ms. Jowers had never been in the desert but that made no difference—it was the challenge that intrigued her. During the winter of 1992–93 she got her ducks in a row and then began calling on students in her own and other Louisiana high schools and colleges. Over the spring and summer of 1993, she amassed some 5,000 personally signed postcards and letters to Senator Johnston from young Louisianans, all expressing deep concern about protection of the California desert and asking his support for the Desert Bill.

She had surmised that these communications would have a greater impact if they were "bundled" and delivered to the

Senator's office as a package, so she kept them together for the propitious moment. Thus she demonstrated political sophistication far beyond her years. Meanwhile, she had learned that Senator Johnston had a daughter, Mary, who was in law school at Tulane University. She talked with Ms. Johnston, explained the national park and hunting issues, and found a sympathetic ear. Ms. Johnston volunteered that she loved the Lafitte Historic Park and Preserve but had been fearful of the guns of hunters. She promised to call her father about this and did so.

Shortly before the Senate Committee was scheduled to meet in late September, the package of postcards and letters was delivered. The Senator was astonished. He called Jowers to express his amazement that so many of his young constituents felt so strongly on the subject. She came to Washington to be present for the hearing and had an appointment to see the Senator. Urgent business kept the Senator busy but she had a long talk with the committee's majority counsel, David Brooks, discussing the "student perspective." Brooks, who was in charge of Desert Bill matters for the Senator, was positive about the impact of the work she had done. He had talked with the Senator and was very confident that Johnston had been won over. He was right, and to a degree that proved truly astonishing. During the unexpectedly contentious committee debate, which took parts of two days before a final vote could be taken, Senator Johnston informed the committee that he was one who enjoyed the "blood sports" as much as any man. But, he said, we must recognize that some people are not at all comfortable when guns are being used. My daughter has told me, he said, that although the Lafitte Historic Park and Preserve is one of her favorite places, she would not go into it during hunting season. There are lots of other places in the Mojave Desert to hunt, he added, and the East Mojave Scenic Area deserves to be a national park with no hunting.[106]

This committee meeting proved critical for passage of the Desert Bill. It's fair to say that the Desert Bill might never have emerged from the Senate Committee in anything like its present form had it not been for Senator Johnston's conversion. That conversion can be traced to the work of Stephanie Jowers. Credit must also go to Adam Werbach, who convinced Ms. Jowers of the importance of the California desert as a national conservation issue. The SSC, his baby and, in a sense, hers as well, is now 30,000 strong, and growing.

Stephanie Jowers is intelligent, attractive, and energetic, but she possesses an additional quality that arguably overshadows these three—the ability to take bold action. "Boldness has genius, power and magic in it," says the second sentence of the quotation from Goethe that appears at the beginning of this subchapter. Jowers would answer the call to action again in October 1994, when the chips were down and help was needed to insure Senator Kerry's presence for the decisive vote. On that occasion, in the last agonizing moments, Senator Carole Moseley-Braun finally reached the Senate Chamber to cast her deciding vote for the Desert Protection Act. She had been delayed by a malfunctioning garage door opener. The Sierra Student Coalition's appreciation was conveyed to the Senator in a colorful gift package containing—did you guess it?—a *new* garage door opener.

The Senate Struggles to Escape from its Shackles

In the spring and summer of 1993, proponents of the Desert Bill continued their efforts without resting. Frequent bursts of lobbying, orchestrated by Debbie Sease of the Sierra Club in Washington, D.C., were focused on seeking additional co-sponsors in both House and Senate. As he had in years past, Nobby Riedy took on the task of organizing the pro-bill testimony for the last two subcommittee hearings. No new developments of any note occurred without press releases to all the major media, particularly in California. Op-ed pieces were frequently sent to the papers; magazines were pelted with ideas for articles, pictures to use, and offers of help, including a trip to see the high points of the desert, if desired. When a favorable editorial appeared it was circulated to co-sponsors and potential co-sponsors. Whatever might encourage the fighting spirit of Senator Feinstein for the battle ahead was promptly sent to Kathy Lacey, her environmental aide.

BLM policy had long been one of flat opposition to anything in the way of California desert wilderness legislation beyond the agency's own much reduced list of "suitable" wilderness and the relatively small areas (minuscule in the case of Joshua Tree National Monument) which the agency had informally agreed to give the Park Service as additions to Death Valley and Joshua Tree. Staff members of the BLM were actively discouraged from discussing the wilderness boundaries proposed in the Desert Bill with the bill's supporters, although supporters—and, in particular, Judy Anderson and her mapmakers—realized that the boundaries laboriously mapped for the bill undoubtedly contained errors. They were anxious to see these corrected. Correction, might of course, tend to reduce opposition to the bill. With this in mind, "don't give an inch" seemed to be the BLM's marching orders. But it gradually dawned on the California BLM that the Desert Bill might be on the road to passage. At last, its California resource area offices were instructed to review the Desert Bill's maps to locate possible errors and develop reports suggesting boundary changes that would make for easier administration and enforcement. They were ordered not to share any of this information, however, until all reports were complete and a decision was made as to whether or not to let the Desert Bill's proponents see them.

In the fall of 1992, a change had occurred that brought the matter to a head. Gerry Hillier, who it appeared was the author of the "no talk" order, left as manager of the BLM's Desert District. He soon resurfaced as spokesman for the most vocal organization opposing the Desert Bill. Henri Bisson, from the Arizona office of the BLM, replaced him. Bisson did not reach the California desert until close to the end of the year. He quickly assessed the situation. His reaction was the opposite of Hillier's: He wanted to schedule a meeting with the leaders of the California Desert Protection League as soon as possible. Sensibly, Bisson told his staff that the meeting would discuss more manageable boundaries for the bill's wilderness areas "irrespective of whether the BLM believes such areas should be designated as wilderness." Anderson, Dodson and Hughes sensed the change of attitude with pleasure and suggested Harvey Mudd College in Claremont, California, as an appropriate neutral ground for the meeting. George Barnes and Nobby Riedy joined them. Present for the BLM were Bisson, several senior staff members, and all of the desert resource area managers and "wilderness specialists."

The Harvey Mudd meeting convened at 8 a.m. and ended over 13 hours later at 9:15 p.m. on January 8, 1993. Much was accomplished. The proponents of the bill agreed to recommend numerous revisions of wilderness boundaries in order to use existing roads or natural landmarks wherever these made sense, eliminating hard-to-patrol lines on topographic maps. For example, a boundary along the old route of the Coachella Canal needed to be shifted—a section of the Canal had been rebuilt. On the other hand, when the BLM asked for removal of part of the Jacumba Wilderness area, because it contained two county roads, the conservationists were able to respond that there were no roads in any of the wilderness areas in the bill, including the Jacumba. Joseph Monroe of Victorville, a volunteer, documented this information. He had used county records to examine *all* the proposed wilderness areas for county roads. The Jacumba and other wilderness areas remained intact, thanks to Monroe.

As it turned out, this constructive meeting had occurred too late to be of immediate value. Details of the changes accepted by all participants were prepared without delay and relayed to Kathy Lacey in Senator Feinstein's office. But the Senator had just introduced her bill. In effect, the Senator responded: "How can you expect me to do this now? It would look as if I didn't know what I was doing if I came up with a whole bunch of changes right after introducing the bill!" So the potential changes were temporarily put aside. Most were later included in "en bloc" amendments or otherwise found their way without objection into the ultimate Conference Report.

It was not long before Senator Feinstein was fully engaged, preparing for the Senate Energy and National Resources Committee markup session. Debbie Sease aptly described this as the bill's "most difficult test of all." On the full committee were 11 Democrats and nine Republicans. Feinstein was not one of them and when she counted the votes it was very, very close. One Democrat, Richard Shelby of Alabama, was in doubt; many expected him to vote against the bill. If he did, and if no Republican voted for it, the bill would lose on a 10–10 vote.

It is theoretically possible for a bill to be passed even if the committee with primary jurisdiction has not previously approved its major provisions. Such an event, however, is a great rarity and would at best involve long delay. Feinstein *had* to get no less than one Republican vote in committee *and* make certain that she did not lose another Democrat.

The American Motorcyclist Association had prepared a list of desert routes that it wanted open to its members and took that list to Kathy Lacey. Senator Feinstein carefully reviewed the list and agreed to some but not all the requests. The association took the remainder of its list to Senator Ben Nighthorse Campbell of Colorado, a Democrat, an AMA member, and the only Native American in the Senate. He was on the committee. He told Feinstein that if this request was accommodated he was prepared to vote for the bill. She promised, as she had to. The conservation community would have to bite its collective lip. In return, the AMA agreed to withdraw its objections to the bill and it did so.

Senator Mark Hatfield of Oregon, a Republican, had long taken an uncompromising position in favor of the timber interests in the Northwest forests when they were confronted by those endangered varmints, the spotted owls. This had soured the largest part of the conservation community in his state and elsewhere. Why not, then, win points by co-sponsoring a bill that was high on the conservation agenda, that directly affected only southern California, that would certainly do no harm to his Oregon constituents and could even be of some value to those who might perversely wish to journey south from their lush forests and spectacular snow-capped volcanoes to see a sunburnt desert? It made good sense and so, several years before, he had agreed to co-sponsor one of Senator Cranston's Desert bills. He had not, however, co-sponsored Feinstein's bill when it was introduced. He was a member of the committee. Where did he stand now? Would he provide the critical Republican "yes" vote? He conferred with Feinstein. Yes, he would, provided she made several changes, principally to take out the provision that gave assistance to Catellus Corporation in exchanging its private lands in the Mojave National Park for other government property, even property in states other than California. Hatfield was one of several Senators who questioned this provision. It might strip their states of government property that could be useful for a similar purpose. She agreed. He wanted a commitment from George Miller, chair of the House Natural Resources Committee, that the House would not try to reinstate the Catellus provision. She got it for him.

Feinstein early on determined to shore up her position by dealing with other objections which did not go to the heart of the bill. For this purpose she went to Senator Bumpers, who had personally steered the bill through at least five subcommittee hearings in four Congresses. Would he, acting on her behalf, offer an amendment at the outset of the hearing in the form of a substitute bill that could take care of these objections and then serve as the original text for consideration of further amendments? He gladly did so. When the committee met for its markup session on September 29, the amendment was agreed to without objection.[107] It made miscellaneous boundary adjustments. Consistent with the deal struck with the AMA, it deleted one major wilderness area the conservation community had hoped to preserve—the South Algodones Dunes. Although a Desert Plan WSA, the BLM had allowed it to become an ORV play area. It shifted to WSA status proposed wilderness areas that stood in the way of possible eastward expansion of Fort Irwin, pending resolution of the expansion issue which, at this writing, is still pending. So long as they were WSAs, they would be protected until Congress acted on their final status. It gave vehicular access to California's Fish and Game authorities for maintenance of bighorn sheep "guzzlers" within wilderness, and to law enforcement agencies in wilderness along the Mexican border for the interception of illegals. It excluded an additional small area of the proposed Mojave National Park south of Interstate 15 containing mining claims of the Mountain Pass Rare Earth Mine. Finally, before the committee met, Feinstein had agreed to strike the entire Catellus provision to make sure of Senator Hatfield's vote. She counted more than 50 changes from the last Cranston version of the Desert Bill which she had made to satisfy her fellow Senators. Now would they give her the votes she needed?

At particular risk was what she had referred to as the centerpiece of her bill, the proposed Mojave National Park where hunting was not allowed. Thanks to Stephanie Jowers, she now had the vital support of the committee's chair, Senator Johnston. An amendment to eliminate such a park and substitute a Mojave National Monument administered by the BLM, with hunting allowed, was the first of nine amendments offered by Senator Wallop, leader of the Republican opposition to the bill. It was defeated by the narrowest of margins, a vote of 9 for, 10 against. After that, with one exception, the votes—though narrow—were expected. The Catellus provision was deleted. At least two amendments designed to kill the bill outright were offered by Frank Murkowski (Republican, Alaska) to force condemnation of all private lands in protected areas and by Robert Bennett (Republican, Utah) to make the bill null and void unless all such private lands were acquired by the government within five years. The Murkowski amendment was defeated. Bennett withdrew his amendment in the face of the argument that it would make any new national park hostage to any single landholder who did not wish to sell, or who wished to exact a ransom from the government. He indicated he would reword it and offer it again on the floor. Senator Murkowski also offered an amendment to redesignate Mojave National Park as a "Park and Preserve" so hunting could be allowed, hoping, perhaps, to garner Senator Johnston's vote by suggesting an analogy to the Jean Lafitte National Historic Park and Preserve in his home state of Louisiana. It didn't work. But one very dangerous amendment was offered which did pass by one vote and turned into a monster, gobbling up some 290,000 acres in the very heart of Mojave National Park.

This came to be known as the "Lanfair Bite." Interior Secretary Babbitt had earlier advised the committee that he wanted to propose an "innovative approach" to the Lanfair Valley, a scenic valley in the far eastern portion of the park which had been heavily homesteaded in the early 1900s during an unusual period of wet weather. It was largely abandoned when more typical climatic conditions returned. Now less than a dozen structures remained in the valley, many infrequently used, excluding the facilities of Gary Overson's OX cattle ranch. The problem centered on what to do about the many small parcels of land that remained in private ownership. The BLM had proposed in 1988 that some 30,000 acres of such private land be acquired over time, to "reduce the potential for worst-case development." Pending an opportunity to put this excellent program into effect, Secretary Babbitt proposed that San Bernardino County and the National Park Service jointly develop a plan both to promote park purposes and to afford the landowners "maximum flexibility." When the plan was adopted, the Interior Department's authority to condemn private lands in the area would be suspended.

Idaho Senator Malcolm Wallop, leader of opposition forces in the Senate.

This somewhat complicated proposal did not gain favor. Senator Feinstein included a far simpler version in the substitute bill that had been adopted at the start of the session. Senator Wallop rejected both ideas. To him, the quick and easy solution, consistent with his objective to eliminate the national park, was simply to delete the Lanfair Valley entirely from the park. The bill's proponents resisted this simplistic approach since the historic Lanfair Valley was bounded by mountain ranges entirely within the park, and its location, ecological and scenic values, and the approach previously taken by the BLM, all argued for its retention in the Park. It was expected that this Wallop amendment would lose. The bill's proponents were taken by surprise, however, when Ben Nighthorse Campbell, for reasons which have

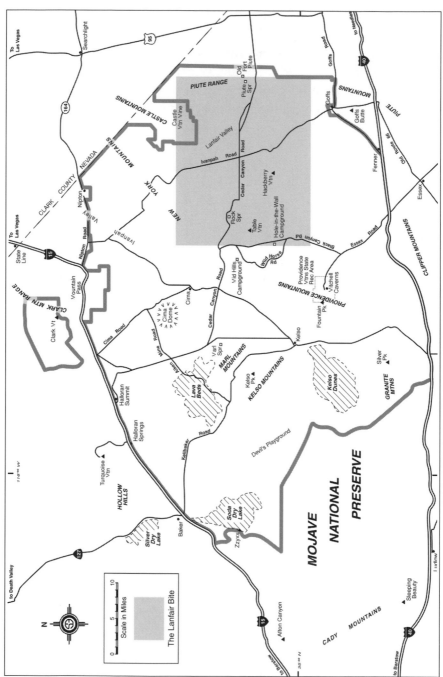

The Mojave National Preserve showing the Lanfair Bite which was ultimately placed back into the preserve.

remained obscure, voted "yes". Thus it was adopted by a margin of 10–9. Only then was the question asked in the committee room: "What did we do? What (for legislative purposes) is this Lanfair Valley?" A map appeared somewhat mysteriously. The committee proceeded to attach this map to the bill. No one on the committee or its majority staff appears to have taken time to ask anyone in a position to know precisely what was being done.

To the horror of the conservation community, it was discovered that this map went far beyond the actual Lanfair Valley. It reduced the total area of the park by well over 20%—a tremendous rectangular "bite" ranging all the way from the park's eastern border, where it included Piute Creek and historic Fort Piute, westward to the campgrounds and grottos of Hole-in-the-Wall, taking in such gems as Table Mountain, the Woods Wash petroglyphs, Rebirth Rocks, and Caruthers Canyon (shown on map opposite page). The BLM had considered Lanfair Valley to consist of approximately four half-townships (or an aggregate of two townships). The map now attached to the bill covered 12 townships, some of them much larger than the typical 23,040 acres in size. An error of huge proportions had been made.

At the end of two long markup sessions described as "brutal" by Jim Dodson, the bill with amendments came to a final committee vote on October 5. It passed 13–7. Two of the favorable votes surprised the proponents—those of Senators Shelby and Bennett. It was hard to explain Senator Bennett's vote since his amendment, which he withdrew, was thought to have been an effort to kill the bill. Could his vote have been pure mistake? A senior member of his staff, who was present, later explained that although he opposed the bill, the Senator believed that if both Senators of a state favored a bill dealing primarily with that state, such a bill should, as a courtesy to those Senators, be allowed by the committee to reach the floor of the Senate.

The conservation community now had an urgent goal of the greatest importance—to reverse the damaging "Lanfair Bite." Could this be done when the bill reached the Senate floor? Could the "Bite" be kept out of the House Bill? The second objective *should* be possible. If the first objective failed and the second did not, would the ConferencereCommittee take the Bite out? Would it become an insidious trading chip? The Desert Bill's proponents went to work to educate the media on the problem, successfully seeking editorials which would be helpful, examining the implications for management of the park, doing everything possible to persuade Senator Feinstein that this problem *had* to be solved. Members of conservation organizations were urged to write to Senators, particularly Feinstein. The bill's proponents anxiously tried to take Senator Feinstein out to the desert to show her, on the ground, what the results of the Bite would be. A trip was scheduled in December but had to be canceled.

When it became clear that Feinstein would be unable to join the desert volunteers for a close look at the Lanfair Bite, something needed to be done quickly to make clear to the Senator the gravity of the impending loss. Elden Hughes went through all the photographs taken by himself, Jim Dodson and many others, which were contained in the picture books that had already proven useful to the Senator. He selected those which displayed prime features of the park that would be lost as a result of the Bite, keyed each to a map of the Bite, included descriptions of each picture, and sent it off to Washington. Kathy Lacey confirmed that it had been instrumental in persuading the Senator not to give in on the Lanfair issue and useful in persuading others that a serious error had been made.

In the previous year, Feinstein had taken a trip, hosted by the BLM, to the proposed Mojave Park area. On this trip, she was much taken with the two principal ranching families in the East Mojave, the Blairs and the Oversons. It became known that she had told Rob Blair she was persuaded that their grazing permits should be continued indefinitely, rather than being phased out in 25 years, as the Senate Committee Bill provided. It proved impossible to change her mind. But it seemed likely that rancher Gary Overson, who owned land which would lie outside the park if the Lanfair Bite prevailed, would prefer to have his land included in the park. It would then be more likely that at some point his interests could be well sold. Hughes contacted a friend at the Trust for Public Land who had previously negotiated a purchase of land from Overson. If this were Overson's preference, would he express it in a letter to Feinstein? The friend called Overson who promptly wrote the Senator that, "from my point of view, Lanfair Valley should be included in the proposed park." Feinstein was later able to quote from that letter on the Senate floor.[108]

Now Senator Feinstein was ready to request Senate floor time for the bill. On March 25 Senator Mitchell moved to proceed with consideration of the bill but also said he had been informed by the minority leadership of an intended filibuster against the motion and was therefore filing a petition for cloture to stop the filibuster. He proposed and received consent to hold the cloture vote on April 11, immediately after the Easter recess.[109] Proponents of the bill were dismayed to learn of the projected filibuster and immediately went to work to flood the Senate with calls and letters during the recess, urging a favorable vote for cloture.

On April 11 Senator Wallop irritably complained that he had no intention of filibustering the motion to proceed. Those on the scene concluded that he had checked his hand during the recess, determined that he fell far short of the votes needed to defeat cloture, and did not wish to suffer an early setback. After an hour or two of preliminary debate on the motion to proceed, including a long, rambling speech against the bill by Wallop and speeches by Feinstein and Johnston in its defense, Feinstein secured unanimous consent to cancel the scheduled cloture vote. At last, the bill was before the full Senate.[110]

Serious proceedings began on April 12 with submission of a motion by Senator Johnston who, as committee chair, would lead the effort to pass the bill for adoption of a series of amendments en bloc.[111] Most of these resulted from discussions held by Johnston and Feinstein with other committee members, including Senator Wallop, the previous evening. They included changes that permitted grazing to continue indefinitely in Mojave National Park and in the areas added to Death Valley National Park. The amendments removed Great Falls Basin wilderness (because of an adjacent mining company's objections) and the Cady Mountains (because of a proposed waste dump) from wilderness designation but retained them as legislated WSAs. They modestly modified wilderness and park boundaries in five areas and established a Mojave Park Advisory Commission. All were later passed by unanimous consent.

Wallop now offered his major amendment to eliminate the Mojave National Park and launched into his argument for keeping the East Mojave under the BLM. Its single thrust was that Congress hadn't appropriated enough money for proper management of existing national parks, and it was therefore foolish to add another one. Senator Johnston complimented Wallop on this argument with a touch of irony, saying, "I hope my colleagues will listen to the Senator's plea not to starve the National Park Service. I expect to support him." Unspoken was the comment, "when and if the Senator should do anything significant to raise NPS appropriations." He went on to add that the Senate had before it "almost the most thoroughly considered bill we've ever had." Senator Feinstein then rose in response to the Wallop argument and they engaged in a spirited debate. Senator Boxer spoke eloquently in support of her colleague. Senator Ben Nighthorse Campbell rose to state that Feinstein had acted on all his concerns. The Wallop amendment was defeated 35–62.

The only other amendment to receive extended debate was Senator Bennett's revision of the one he had offered, then withdrawn, in the Committee markup hearing. Now he wanted to withhold all authorization to designate parks or wilderness in the desert unless, within ten years, the Federal government acquired 90% of all private land in the protected areas. The lawyer in Senator Johnston could not resist the chance to employ his skill in taking apart this flawed proposal. He took the floor to carry the argument against the Bennett amendment. The amendment lost 34–64.

Senators Murkowski, Craig, and Warner all offered amendments, then withdrew them. What was going on? Senator Johnston presented an amendment to add, as Title IX of the bill, an extensive piece of legislation to carry out projects in the Lower Mississippi Delta recommended by the Delta Development Commission, including the support of education, a heritage and cultural study, support of minority museums and cultural centers, a musical heritage program, a Delta antiquities survey, and the like. He reminded the Senators that this "Delta Bill" had already passed the Senate. Obviously he had prepared the way by conversations with his colleagues for such a motion. His proposal to attach it to the Desert Bill, presumably because he expected the Desert Bill to be passed by both Houses and to become law, was agreed to unanimously. A short while later, he offered a second amendment to add Title X to the bill, establishing a New Orleans Jazz National Historical Park. This, he said, incorporated a bill already reported out of committee, which would cost only $1 million a year or less. He said that he "knew of no objection to it on the floor." Johnston received unanimous agreement to *its* adoption.

He then stated that no further motions were anticipated that afternoon. The bill's proponents were aghast. What could have happened to Feinstein's amendment to eliminate the Lanfair Bite from the bill, an amendment she had clearly signaled that very morning that she expected to propose? It was later learned that opponents of the bill had informed Johnston they would stop attempting to amend the bill and let it pass if the proponents offered no more amendments. Implicit in this proposal was the threat that otherwise the opponents could, by offering more and more amendments, delay the bill from coming to a vote until much later. Johnston's advice to Feinstein was to drop her Lanfair amendment so the final vote on the bill could be taken the next day. He had in mind the fact that the House had not as yet held even a committee markup session on its bill, much less brought it to the floor. She had reluctantly taken his advice.

Before the first day concluded with agreement to vote on the bill the next day, Senator Harry Reid (Democrat, Nevada) who had so far been silent but was aware of what had happened, rose to make a statement deploring the consequences of failure to eliminate the Lanfair Bite from the bill and of his hope that this would eventually take place. He spoke of being raised as a youngster just across the California-Nevada border from Piute Spring and the New York Mountains, two treasures of the Mojave that were excluded from the park by the Bite. In a light-hearted passage, he said:

> *Mr. President, I have been to Yellowstone and the national parks around the country. I am ill-at-ease, frankly, near pine trees and lots of water and green things. But here, this is home. This is where a national park should be. There is no place on earth that has better scenery than this. This area is as unique as any place in the world. I recognize I am bragging about California but I really claim this as being part of Nevada anyway.*

Next day, the vote was tallied. It was 69–29 for passage. Taking to the floor once more, Chairman Johnston complimented Senator Feinstein and chivalrously thanked Kathy Lacey of Feinstein's staff. Feinstein was unrestrained in her tribute to Senator Johnston for his leadership; she also paid tribute to Senator Bumpers. Without Bumpers' help, she said, the bill could never have moved ahead as it had through the years. Thanking Kathy Lacey, she added, "My nickname for her is 'Britannica' because she retains facts and figures in a way I would never have thought possible."[112]

"Filibuster by Amendment" Fails in the House

Hardly two weeks after the Senate had acted on the Desert Bill, House Interior Committee Chairman George Miller called his committee's markup session to order on May 4, 1994.[113] The committee now had before it both the Senate bill (S. 21) and its own bill (H.R. 518), a modified version of H.R. 2927 which had passed the House by a large majority before the previous (102d) Congress ended in 1991. The bill just passed by the Senate included a Mojave National Park without hunting. The new House bill had a Mojave National Monument without hunting. In its most important test of the day, the House Committee agreed not to change this provision of the bill.

Both the House bill and the bill that passed the Senate had shifted three important wilderness areas to WSA status to make way for possible expansion eastward of Fort Irwin. This was approved. In deference to the Senate, the committee also shifted the small Great Falls Basin wilderness area to WSA status but did not follow the Senate in further reducing the size of the mighty Kingston Mountains wilderness. Matching Senate action, the committee voted to permit cattle grazing to continue indefinitely in the Mojave and the additions to Death Valley National Park. Provisions in the House bill, similar to those rebuffed in the Senate, which facilitated the exchange of Catellus Corporation lands in the Mojave Park for public lands elsewhere in California and even in other states, were retained by the committee. The extraordinary circumstances surrounding the Senate Committee's action in cutting 290,000 acres from Mojave National Park—the Lanfair Bite—and, almost as extraordinary, the absence of any effort to correct that action on the Senate floor, were noted. Representative Lehman, asserting his complete disagreement with what had happened in the Senate, offered an amendment which he urged, would be sensitive to the interests of small landholders in the area of the Lanfair Valley but retain protection for the remainder of that area. His "Lanfair Nibble," which passed the committee by unanimous consent, kept in the park most of the area of the Lanfair Bite but excluded from the park all private land (except for State and Catellus holdings) in the Bite, amounting to some 59,000 acres. This, he hoped, would for practical purposes eliminate the risk that the Senate's Lanfair Bite would be retained when and if the two Desert Bills came to conference. It responded concretely to the arguments for private property rights advanced by Senator Wallop in support of his successful Lanfair Bite amendment but greatly reduced that amendment's largely unforeseen and drastic consequences. The conservation community was concerned about problems that would be created by even the Lanfair Nibble but there was little choice—it would have to be accepted. The issue did not arise again during the House floor debate.

Acting with surprising swiftness, the committee voted the same day 28–14 to pass the bill as amended. Neither Jerry

Lewis nor his cohorts, Republican Representatives McCandless, Duncan Hunter (California), and Thomas were members of the committee; hence, they could not attempt to delay the committee's deliberations nor did committee members who were in opposition to the bill try to do so. It was anticipated, however, that when the bill reached the floor, a coalition of opponents might try to bottle it up by proposing large numbers of amendments both before and during debate. Chairman Miller asked the Rules Committee to take that danger into account in establishing its rule for debate.

The House Rules Committee is a unique institution.[114] Nothing quite like it exists either in the Senate or in the state legislatures. Small but extremely powerful, the Majority and Minority Leaders appoint its members, in a ratio of approximately 2–1. In essence, it acts on behalf of the Majority Leader as a traffic manager for bills on that leader's agenda. No bill can come to the floor unless the Rules Committee has given it a "rule." Not surprisingly, the committee has on rare occasions exercised its powers perversely to stop a bill from ever coming to the floor during an entire session of Congress!

The rule will fix a time limit, usually one hour, for general debate and will always specify if, and how, amendments to a bill are to be debated. Sometimes a specific time is fixed for debate on each amendment, as was done when the House previously voted on the Desert Bill in 1991. In most cases, debate on amendments is limited by the "five minute rule," under which no member may talk more than five minutes on a given amendment. This limitation is frequently breached by the device of having an ally who does not wish to talk yield his time to the member whose time has expired, or by having another member request unanimous consent, usually granted, to allow his colleague another two or three minutes. Even so, indulgence by other members has its limits, and House rules do not expressly permit a Senate-style filibuster with unlimited debate.

As to amendments, an "open rule" is quite common; members are free to offer germane amendments at any time while a bill is under consideration. A "closed rule" would not permit amendments to be offered either before or during debate. With the Desert Bill, the Rules Committee dealt with a complex piece of legislation containing dozens of individually mapped geographic areas. It would be hard for almost any member to grasp the significance of an amendment dealing with a part of one of those areas offered for the first time in the midst of floor debate, and dozens of such amendments could possibly be submitted to delay progress. It would not seem a grave hardship for members with serious amendments to ask them to submit their amendments for advance printing before debate began and to limit amendments to those so printed in advance and available for advance review. This would allow responsible staff personnel to warn against error or surprise. Such at least was the reasoning of the majority on the Rules Committee. The rule it adopted was a cross between an open and a closed rule and required advance printing of all amendments.

This was exactly what Jerry Lewis did *not* want.

If Lewis could muster the opponents of the bill to keep offering amendments throughout the floor debate, and if he could also persuade a sufficient number of his allies to use the quite stretchable five minutes each was allowed for discussion of each amendment, then even if all such amendments were eventually voted down, the bill might never be passed in time. Adjournment of the second session of the 103d Congress was not far off and many appropriation bills were coming to the floor, taking precedence over any other legislation. A strategy of "filibuster by amendment," carried on as long as possible, could do the trick. Lewis could count on weeks of further delay if the filibusters permitted under the Senate's rules could hamstring subsequent Senate procedures. Events would show how close to success this strategy came, even if crimped by the Rules Committee's requirement that only amendments printed in advance could be offered on the House floor.

Lewis and his cohorts, angered as they were, still managed to submit for preprinting the great majority of the 45–50 amendments copied into the *Congressional Record* the day before debate began. Among the Lewis amendments were his old substitute for the entire committee bill and such killers as: the act shall not take effect until the Federal budget is balanced, and the act shall take effect only when the Park Service has reduced its nationwide backlog of desired land acquisitions by 50%.

On May 17 the full House began debate with one hour, equally divided, for consideration of the rule submitted by Representative Anthony Beilenson of California on behalf of the Rules Committee. Then there would be one hour for general debate on the bill before amendments were debated.[115] Only preprinted amendments would be considered and these under the five-minute rule. "Second degree" amendments, or amendments to amendments, were permitted without limit. Beilenson urged adoption of the committee's rule. The amendments that had already been submitted and printed, he observed "covered a wide range of issues and would give members the opportunity to discuss every conceivable controversy."

Representative David Drier (Republican, California), a member of the minority on the Rules Committee and a Lewis ally, rose to urge defeat of the pending resolution "so I can offer an honest, open rule that will allow for open debate." Defeat of the resolution would mean the end of debate until the Rules Committee met again to pass a new rule. The rule offered by Beilenson, said Dreier, "would allow the Natural Resources Committee to perpetrate a textbook case of legislative abuse." By requiring pre-printing of amendments, "it continues a scheme to prevent the bill from being fully scrutinized and debated." Having thus set the tone of debate on the resolution, Drier yielded the balance of his time to Lewis.

An elaborate punctilio of address established over time by tradition in the Houses of Congress seeks to restrain members from personally attacking the motives or character of their colleagues. A notable illustration of that custom came years ago when Speaker John McCormick (Democrat, Massachusetts), seeking a way to express his low opinion of a fellow House member, commented, "I must say I have a minimum high respect for the gentleman."

But it can be hard for tradition to control the expression of strong feelings when an issue is highly emotional. Representative Lewis had fought the Desert Bill for eight long years. At last, he had a strategy that might kill the bill if he could put it into effect. The Rules Committee had drastically reduced the potential impact of that strategy. He could barely contain his frustration. "This bill," he said, "has been handled in the most outrageous fashion of any legislation that it has been my experience to deal with.... It is outrageous to think that the Chairman would actually go so far as to ram legislation in this fashion through without even bringing in those members [referring to himself and Messrs. McCandless, Hunter and Thomas, all of whom represented parts of the California desert] for personal consultation about their districts. It is unbelievable...." When Lewis had finished, Beilenson yielded the balance of his time to Miller. The latter, his gorge rising, observed:

> A great deal has been said in a short time about the procedures used in the Committee and by the Chairman of the Committee, which happens to be me, and I have got to tell the House that...it simply is not true. I find it rather interesting that if this was [so important] to the gentleman and to his colleagues from California, they would never ask me for an appointment to have a substantive discussion on this matter, they would never send me an amendment or a note or a request for any change in the five years since I have been Chairman of the Committee and we have had this under discussion.... We are here on an open rule. We are simply asking for management.... Now the gentleman has decided to make this personal and impugn the integrity of the Committee and me as the Chair....

Lewis: "The gentleman would probably like to be informed that I did sit...with the author of the bill [Lehman] just a week ago to discuss some of these possibilities. He is the author."

Miller: "Reclaiming my time, the gentleman was talking about *me*. You were referring to the Chairman of this Committee."

Lewis: "Let me just complete the statement. The response of the author of the bill was 'Jerry, I am not going to be able to help you on this. The Chairman is going to do exactly what he wants to do with this bill...he is going to roll right over me.'"

George Miller, chair of the House Interior Committee and field marshal of the House forces seeking passage of the Desert Bill.

Courtesy of the Office of Congressman Miller

Miller: "Reclaiming my time, how long has the gentleman been in this body?"

Lewis: "I am not sure that is relevant, but long enough."

Miller: "Well, are you incapable of having a face-to-face conversation with another member? Are you incapable of coming over and asking me whether that characterization is accurate or not?..."

Lewis: "Your style is always so gentle."

Miller: "Don't tell me about my style."

After an hour or more of this sort of thing, the vote was taken on the motion to adopt the rule and it took effect, 248–165. The chair then declared that the House had "resolved itself into the Committee of the Whole House on the State of the Union for consideration of H.R. 518." Such was the quaint but historic formula for calling the House to order to actually consider a bill! The rest of the time available on May 17 was taken up by the prescribed hour of general debate.

Now began a process under which the Desert Bill became, in Miller's words, "hamburger helper."[116] A product is actually found on grocery shelves today under that name. Appropriation bills would have first call on the floor time, and the Desert Bill could be debated only in extra time not required by the Appropriations Committee. This was the best that could be done for it. Lewis and his cohorts did not have the entirely open rule they wanted, but they still had plenty of time to burn. For starters, further debate could not be scheduled until June 10.

How to use up the time on June 10? Lewis and his friends gave a classic demonstration. The first amendment that day was offered by Representative Thomas to delete one square mile of wilderness for a possible quasi-military installation. This was acceptable to the bill's proponents with one small modification and could have been passed quickly. Thomas, however, spent his allotted time complaining about how badly the subcommittee had treated him. Lewis then discussed in detail how the Desert Bill bypassed the BLM's 1980 Desert Plan, the importance of NASA's Selene program, the unfortunate treatment of Thomas, the arbitrary treatment of everyone by the committee. When his time ran out he asked and got three more minutes and yielded them to others; when these ran out Dreier asked that Lewis be given three more minutes, most of which he yielded to Thomas. Again he was given three additional minutes, then two additional minutes while Thomas and McCandless continued a dialogue. At last this ended and Chairman Miller offered the correcting amendment to the amendment on the floor. A debate then ensued between Representatives Lewis and Vento, mostly dealing with Lewis's complaints about the committee's procedures. James Hanson of Utah, an opponent of the bill, appearing somewhat frustrated, rose to support Miller's amendment to the amendment indicating that the minority accepted it and it should be passed. Did that end the debate? By no means. Debaters now dealt with objections to the entire bill: to the definition of wilderness, to the size of the bill, with Congressmen Bill Emerson (Republican, Montana), Duncan Hunter and Randy Cunningham (Republicans, California) expatiating on the bill's economic impacts and with Cunningham yielding part of his five minutes to Lewis so the latter could describe the virtues of his substitute bill, which had yet to be offered. At last, after the entire morning had been consumed, the chairman

California Congressman Bill Thomas, a vigorous opponent of the Desert Bill, whose 20th District included Death Valley in the early '90s.

Courtesy of the Office of Congressman Thomas

asked if the Miller amendment to the Thomas amendment was agreed to. It was.

The chairman then put the Thomas Amendment, as amended, to a vote and announced "the ayes have it." Lewis demanded a recorded vote. Further delay to record the vote, typically taking 20 minutes to half an hour. The vote was 396 to 1.

California Congressman Duncan Hunter, a consistent opponent of the Desert Bill, his 45th District included the desert in San Diego and Imperial Counties.

Courtesy of the Office of Congressman Hunter

Representative Hunter had an amendment that authorized law enforcement and border patrol operations by vehicle or aircraft in desert wilderness areas. After his speech on behalf of his amendment, and a response to a question of clarification, Miller and Hanson rose to state that the majority *and* minority both accepted the Hunter amendment. One would think a vote would ensue, but no; Lewis, McCandless and Hunter then entered into a long discussion of the drug war, quoting passages from letters received from three county sheriffs and a patrol agent on the subject. When the Hunter amendment was finally put to a voice vote, the chairman predictably announced, "the ayes have it." Then Hunter demanded a recorded vote on his own amendment that had just passed! After further delay, the vote was announced: 398 to nothing.

And so it went. After two other amendments were dealt with, the day was over. On June 13, the interminable talkfest permitted only one amendment to be considered. Thereafter, no time for debate was available until July 12, a solid month away.

By July 12 Anna Eshoo, a freshman Democratic Representative from the San Francisco Bay area, had had enough and decided to tell her colleagues exactly what she thought. Her statement was:

Mr. Chairman, after almost two months of needless debate and delays, the House once again takes up the California Desert Protection Act....A small group of members are trying to kill it by literally talking it to death....Mr. Chairman, we must end this filibuster and once and for all advance this critical legislation....I urge my colleagues to rescue this bill from being sandbagged by its opponents' tactics.

Possibly this was heard by some of her colleagues and, for a brief moment, things seemed to move a bit faster. One Congressman, James Bilbray (Democrat, Nevada), who introduced a relatively noncontroversial amendment, actually requested unanimous consent to limit debate on *his* amendment (and any amendments thereto) to ten minutes, five minutes for each side. With laughter (or relief, it is suspected), his request was granted without objection. Alas, this was not to be the norm. The House moved on to long debate on the contentious amendment of Congressman Larry Larocco (Democrat, Idaho) to shift Mojave National Park to the status of a preserve with hunting. It passed 239–183. Although a great disappointment to the conservation community, this was not terribly surprising in view of the similar vote on the House floor in 1991.

Next came another troublesome amendment, offered by Representative DeLay of Texas, to deny the authority of the Interior Secretary to condemn for public purposes any private land in the Mojave Park. The largest landholders were excepted. This prompted an extended and vigorous debate with both sides participating. The amendment was defeated 145–274. Apart from one additional amendment that had been agreed to in advance, that finished the day.

The following two days were also available for the bill. Miller could begin to see light at the end of the tunnel, although it would probably not be possible to address all further amendments in two days. On July 13 there was a long debate over the military overflights amendment, largely unnecessary as the committee version prevailed without a recorded vote. Other amendments were noncontroversial and handled fairly quickly. On July 14, a Thomas amendment to force the Interior Department, within one year of acquiring any land for purposes of the Desert Bill, to dispose of Federal land of equal value, called forth substantial debate, but it, too, was rejected without a recorded vote. Then came the longest debate of the entire affair on an amendment submitted by W.J. "Billy" Tauzin (Democrat, Louisiana) requiring any land acquired by the government pursuant to the bill to be appraised without regard to the existence of any endangered or threatened species which might be found there.

On its face, this was an effort to deal with an enormously complex issue of eminent domain, one which had thoroughly confused the courts as well as policymakers, and to treat it within the narrow context of a portion only of the public land in a single state. It was an issue that impacted all government operations which might involve land acquisition—the military, highway construction, government office needs, flood or fire control measures and, so on. The Tauzin amendment's supporters had seized the opportunity to strike a blow at the Endangered Species Act before that act was before the House, urging unfairness if any reduction in the value of land occurred prior to its condemnation because it was included in a critical habitat designation. What about other actions, such as zoning, which may adversely affect the value of land, asked one congressman. Another asked: could not the same question of fairness be turned on its head if the government has built a road adjacent to the land, created a popular park next door, or made irrigation water available, thereby causing a sizable *increase* in the value of land to be condemned? By the same reasoning, shouldn't the fair market value of the land be reduced to its previous value for condemnation purposes? Questions such as these went unanswered as emotion swept reason aside in the unfocused debate. Miller tried several times to gain consent to limit further debate to an hour, or to a "time certain." Everyone, however, wanted to be heard and recorded at length in defense of private property, and the

Tauzin forces, sensing victory, rejected any limitation. At the end of the day they succeeded, 241–148.

Two weeks had to pass before the bill could again be taken up on July 27. First on the agenda was a Lewis amendment introduced by Ken Calvert (Republican, California) designed to kill the bill by providing that it should not take effect until the Park Service land acquisition and construction backlog had been reduced by 50%. It was, Lewis said, a simple question of fiscal responsibility. When Lewis reached his five-minute limit on this subject and wanted more, Miller, for the first time during the entire debate, objected, indicating that in an effort to move the debate forward he would hereforth object to any extensions of time on both sides of the aisle. Lewis slipped neatly past the objection by the device of having any ally who began his allotted five minutes and immediately yielded to Lewis. Supporters of the amendment continued to speak for an hour or more; the amendment finally lost by a recorded vote 138–288.

It was now nearly noon. Miller asked for unanimous consent that further debate on amendments to the bill close at 2 p.m. McCandless, predictably, objected. It appeared that at this rate, the debate might be stretched into the next month. Rarely does the manager of a bill on the floor suddenly ask for a vote of the House to limit debate beyond the limitations adopted by the Rules Committee. Miller sensed, however, that many of his colleagues were fed up, or close to it. He decided to strike. He moved that all debate close at 2 p.m. The opponents of course demanded a recorded vote. The motion won 246–179! Lewis was incensed. He would soon claim the opportunity to speak once again.

California Congressman Alfred McCandless, a staunch opponent of the Desert Bill, whose 37th District in the early '90s included a major part of the desert.

Courtesy of *Riverside Press-Telegram*

Two more amendments remained but both were now doomed. The first was rejected without a vote although it consumed at least three-quarters of an hour of debate. The last was the Lewis substitute bill in the form of an amendment—the same substitute he had unsuccessfully introduced during the 1991 floor debate in the House. It gave him one more chance to argue that the present bill was a breach of faith with the process that had produced the California Desert Plan. After his cohorts had supported him, using almost all of the remaining time available, he lashed out at Miller, saying, "I do not remember on the floor when we had a motion to limit debate. It may have occurred sometime in the last 15 years. But this is an outrageous exercise one more time of the kind of control [the committee] likes to exercise." He then *withdrew* his amendment!

Miller exercised his right to close debate. When his time had expired, Lewis asked that his antagonist be given two additional minutes. Jerry, was that you? It was, in fact. He had, perhaps for amusement or perhaps to stretch out the proceedings one last time, changed his tune for the moment. Miller refrained from comment. The final vote on the bill was 298–128, exceeding by one the similar favorable vote on the House floor in 1991. New members of Congress had not perceptibly changed the weight of opinion in the House, either pro or con, attesting to the value and necessity of the constant lobbying pressure maintained by the conservation community.

More than ten weeks had elapsed between the opening day of debate and final passage of the House Bill. As can be imagined, during those weeks the anxiety of the conservation community was intense. What could concerned individuals do? It was essential both to encourage existing Congressional supporters of the bill and continually to seek new support. By the summer of 1994, all the major newspapers in California had endorsed the bill. Every editorial, every favorable magazine article was copied and sent to supporters in Congress and to those it was hoped would join them. Debbie Sease, Marty Hayden, and Leslie England of the Sierra Club's Washington staff, together with Nobby Riedy and Nancy Green of the Wilderness Society's Washington office, acted as a general staff to focus the efforts of the troops. As adverse amendments came up for a vote, volunteers from around the country who could come to Washington were pressed into service and given lists of the most important Representatives and their staff members to try to reach in person. Contributions were sought to pay the transportation of those who could not readily afford it. Before Congress took its August recess, Jim Dodson managed a week in Washington to lobby, as did Elden Hughes. Many wrote letters when they could not come. The trio of Anderson, Dodson, and Hughes were again communicating almost daily with each other and with Hayden in Washington, who was in constant touch with the leadership of conservation organizations supporting the bill.

It was very late when the House finally "rose" on July 27, having passed the bill. Each of the houses of Congress had now passed a roughly similar Desert Bill. A little over two months remained before the anticipated adjournment of Congress—not only of Congress but, more ominously, of the second session of Congress. When that *second session* came to an end, the bills passed by each house but not yet submitted to and reported out by a Conference Committee, and every Conference Committee Report not yet approved by *both* houses, would vanish into thin air. Proponents of these vanished bills would be required to start all over again when the next Congress convened the following January.

The Desert Bill's supporters around the country who were not fully aware of the pitfalls ahead celebrated with enthusiasm the victory in the House, having previously celebrated victory in the Senate, and innocently anticipated a swift end to the long road traveled by the bill. Those with more experience in the workings of Congress tightened their belts and prepared for the most intense period of work in the history of the desert legislation.

"It Ain't Over Till It's Over"

The environment is democracy's biggest challenge—but democracy is the environment's best hope.

—William H. Ward

How would one describe what happened in Washington from the end of the August recess in 1994 until mid-September of that year?

One might use Shakespeare's favorite stage direction, "Alarums and Excursions," for the ins and outs of battle just before its climax.

During late August and early September both Senator Wallop and Congressman Lewis floated somewhat different ideas for compromise involving a small national park in the East Mojave, about one-third the size of the proposed Mojave National Park, with the remainder of the area of the proposed park a preserve managed by the BLM. This was not Senator Feinstein's idea of an acceptable formula and she turned it down. Meanwhile, proponents of the bill, mindful of the House action and doubtful that it would be possible to gain Conference Committee acceptance of a full Mojave National Park, toyed with the somewhat similar idea of keeping a core area in the East Mojave as a national park surrounded by a National Park Service preserve where hunting would be allowed. Marty Hayden, Nobby Riedy, and Nancy Green all thought this might be feasible and discussed it with California volunteer leaders Anderson, Dodson and Hughes. All three were in agreement that to have a chance of success, such a proposal would have to come from the National Park Service. Wonder of wonders, almost immediately Hughes received an unexpected call from Brian Culhune of the Park Service, indicating people in the Service were thinking along the same lines. Would the Californians draft a map?

Anderson and Hughes called Peter Burk to ask if he would like to prepare the draft. He said he could not—it would be like cutting up a baby. In the end, Hughes went to work on a map, ran it by Anderson and Dodson, and sent it to Hayden. By that time, however, the Park Service had gotten a case of cold feet and dropped the idea. It was probable that the House provision, a National Park Service Preserve in the Mojave with hunting, would be the likely outcome, but it remained imperative to seek elimination of the Senate's Lanfair Bite which would cut the heart out of the preserve.

Throughout these weeks in late August and early September, the threat of a Wallop filibuster, or series of filibusters, as will be seen, lay like a black cloud over the Desert Bill. Since the late 18th century, the privilege of unlimited debate has been a Senate tradition.[117] By the mid-19th century, the misuse of that privilege came to be called a "filibuster," originally a French word for a pirate or freebooter. Only the word was new—it has been observed that legislative obstruction is as old as the Roman Senate, but nowhere has it achieved the notoriety it has gained in our own senior legislative body. A record may have been set in 1893 in the fight for repeal of the silver purchase law when 64 Senate business days were consumed by continuous speech making. In 1917 a filibuster against the armed ship bill brought a stinging rebuke of the Senate from President Woodrow Wilson, accompanied by great public outrage. This led to the first cloture rule, which provided that debate could be shut off by a two-thirds majority of the Senators. If cloture was voted, each Senator could still speak for one hour before a vote could be taken, and each Senator continued to be the sole judge of the relevancy of his remarks.

So weak was this rule that successful filibusters continued without much restraint. They were particularly likely to prevail near the end of a second session of Congress or when the participants were numerous enough to be able to talk as long as necessary, thereby in both instances preempting other vital business. Efforts to effect a change to a majority vote for cloture got nowhere, so holy was the tradition of unlimited debate. The Senate came to be referred to as a "legislative boneyard." In 1975, after bitter debate, the required vote was finally changed to three fifths of all Senators, or 60 votes, on all measures except changes in the Senate's own rules. At some point a limit of one hour per Senator but no more than a total of 30 hours was agreed upon for post-cloture debate. A petition to invoke cloture continued to require 16 signatures and could not be brought to a vote until the third day after it was filed.

One might think that a filibuster would only be permitted on a motion to *adopt* a bill. Not so. *Any* motion before the Senate is subject to a filibuster. The Desert Bill illustrates the impact of this. Under Senate rules, once both Houses have adopted a bill with somewhat different terms it must, of course, go to a Conference Committee. Three motions must be adopted on the floor of the

Senate before this can happen. First, a motion must be made and passed "to reject the House version [of the bill] and insist on the Senate version." If that is adopted, a motion "to go to conference" must be made and passed. The third essential motion is "to appoint conferees." Only then can the Majority Leader exercise his appointment power and the appointed Senate conferees meet with those of the House. *Three* required motions, *each* subject to a filibuster, and *each*, if a filibuster is threatened, necessitating a cloture petition, a waiting period, a cloture vote, and finally, up to 30 hours of debate before that motion can come to a vote!

Needless to say the three motions almost always take up no time whatsoever, being adopted by consent without objection. What then is their purpose? Is it to serve the noble ends of good government? Or to lie dormant, available for a Senator and allies to use when circumstances are ripe for a deathblow to be given a bill that the large majority of Senators might well wish to see adopted. Not surprisingly, a reaction of utter disbelief and amazement was expressed by many ordinary citizens who were interested in passage of the Desert Bill but not actively involved in the campaign when they learned how the Senate's rules would apply to it.

Certainly, it is useful to have two Houses of Congress in order to lessen the chance that unwise legislation will be passed in haste. Argument can even be advanced for a policy of unlimited debate when a bill is up for adoption, provided there is some ultimate mechanism for bringing that debate to a close. But to allow three opportunities for unlimited debate on a bill before the question of its adoption even comes before the Senate seems bizarre at best. How can it fail to undermine the respect in which thoughtful citizens would prefer to hold the country's most honored legislative body? Is it too much hope that the rules in question might one day be reexamined?

So much for the challenge that now confronted the Desert Bill's supporters. All efforts were concentrated on reducing the chance that filibustering could defeat the bill in the few remaining weeks before the scheduled October 7 adjournment.

Early in September, the bill's proponents organized the first of several nationwide phone banks intended to put their constituents directly in touch with the offices of all Senators who might be favorable to cloture. Lists of the members of the major conservation organizations from every state were gathered in Washington, purged of duplication, and sorted by state and by zip code, the latter to enable callers to reach their own Representatives in the House when that became necessary. These lists were placed in the hands of experts whose task it was to reach the persons listed and ask them to call their own Senator with a constituent's eloquent plea not to let the Desert Bill be blocked by filibuster. Before the final day in October, in addition to steady phoning by California volunteers, several additional nationwide phone banks had been organized with funds scraped together from every possible source. Proponents of the bill proudly state that 70% of those asked—some several times—to call their Senator, agreed to do so.

Senators Wallop and Johnston were talking about possible compromise. Was this a Wallop ploy to delay further progress until his filibusters were sure to kill the bill before adjournment? By mid-September, Senator Feinstein was becoming much alarmed. In the House, Miller indicated to Johnston that he was opposed to compromise. Finally, Johnston gave up and was ready to move. To Feinstein's great relief, Senate Majority Leader George Mitchell was prepared to help.

On September 20, Senator Mitchell filed a petition for cloture on the first of the three motions needed to get the bill to conference—the motion "to reject the House version."[118] The cloture vote was scheduled for Thursday afternoon, September 22, following the mandatory delay. As it turned out, Thursday was a fortunate day on which to schedule that vote. Wallop could *lose* the cloture vote and still claim up to 30 hours on the floor during which he and his allies, each using one hour of time, could voice their objections, or recite poetry or the Bible if they chose, before the motion could come to a vote. Mitchell, however, indicated that if Wallop insisted on doing this, he would keep the Senate in session throughout the weekend. His fellow Republicans let

Wallop know that they would like to spend their weekend at home; in fact, nearly one-third of them needed the weekend to campaign for reelection. They persuaded him to forego the post-cloture debate and to permit the cloture vote, if successful, to be followed immediately by consent to the motion.

September 22nd might be regarded as a historic occasion. It may have been—Senator Mitchell thought it was—the first time in history when it was necessary to invoke cloture to permit the Senate to act on a motion to reject the House version of a bill! Sixty votes were needed and the cloture motion passed 73–20.[119] Senator Wallop did not even bother to come to the chamber and vote— delay was his sole objective. On the same day, by the rarest of coincidences, cloture was also successful on a motion to reject the House version of the 1994 Campaign Finance Reform Bill. That bill was doomed, however, and later died when cloture failed on the next motion needed to get it to a Conference Committee.

Friday, September 23rd, Monday the 26th, and Tuesday the 27th came and went with the clock ticking ominously. The bill's supporters waited tensely for the filing of the next essential cloture petition. None was filed. What had happened? On September 28, Senator Feinstein spoke at length on the Senate floor to express her utter dismay and frustration over "holds" on the Desert Bill that had been registered with Senator Dole, the Minority Leader, by several Senators whose names she could not know for sure.[120] Senate practice permits any member to express objection to proceeding with a motion or bill, customarily registering that objection with his or her party leader. That leader, unless the Majority Leader, will inform the Majority Leader that objection has been raised but keep the maker of the objection secret. Known as a "hold," this device prevents consideration of a motion or bill so long as it remains in effect unless the Majority Leader determines that the bill cannot wait and he must invoke cloture. It *may* be employed for legitimate purposes. For example, a member may wish to seek an answer to a question, may not yet have had the opportunity to read the bill, or may expect to speak on the bill and need time to prepare. Or, the member may simply be trying to stop a motion or bill from coming to the floor at all. Feinstein obviously believed that was the case when she gave her impassioned speech.

At last, those outside the halls of Congress learned that a critical negotiation was in progress between Senators Mitchell, Dole, and Wallop. In order to avoid a weekend on the Senate floor, the three Senators agreed on September 28 that the last two pre-conference motions would be adopted by unanimous consent without formal cloture votes. This was not without cost—consent would be delayed by the number of days the three Senators estimated it would have taken to "age" two hypothetical cloture petitions, take two hypothetical cloture votes, and hold some hours of hypothetical post-cloture debate on each of the two motions. Hence, the next steps toward a Conference Committee would not take place until the morning of Tuesday, October 4. On that morning, in accordance with the deal struck September 28, the motions to request a conference and appoint conferees were adopted and Mitchell was at last able to appoint the Senate's conferees.

Wallop had achieved the delay he had sought. Now it was up to his allies in the House to quit their trenches and move against the enemy. Led by Congressman Lewis, their powder was dry and they were ready.

At 1:20 p.m. on that same day (October 4), Congressman Miller brought to the House floor a motion, fortunately simpler than the several motions required in the Senate, to insist on the House amendments and agree to a conference.[121] Under House rules, each side was entitled to 30 minutes for debate. Could Lewis and his allies string out that debate for the rest of the day, making it more difficult to finish work on the bill before adjournment? The skill with which they accomplished this goal deserves to be recorded. (Lewis's allies are referred to as "opponent.")

- Opponent presented a point of order that the main motion was out of order because the Committee on Merchant Marine, which had secondary jurisdiction over the bill, had not authorized it. He argued long and hard.

- The Speaker pro tem ruled against the point of order.
- Opponent then asked for a vote on whether or not the main motion should be considered at all.

Vote was taken and the Speaker announced, "The ayes have it."

- Opponent demanded a recorded vote. It won 268-148.
- The Speaker asked if there was objection to laying on the table a motion to reconsider that vote.
- Opponent objected.
- Miller moved to reconsider the vote on the motion to consider the main motion.
- Proponent moved to lay the motion to reconsider on the table.

Vote was taken and the Speaker announced, "The ayes have it."

- Lewis demanded a recorded vote. It won 271-150.

One hour of debate on the main motion then ensued and the time expired.

- Miller moved the previous question on the main motion.
- Lewis moved to table the motion for the previous question.
- The Speaker ruled that the previous question could not be tabled.
- Lewis then moved to table the main motion.

Vote was taken and the Speaker announced, "The noes have it."

- Lewis objected to the vote.

A quorum was rounded up and a recorded vote was taken. It lost 144–259.

The next question was on ordering the previous question on the main motion.

Vote was taken and the Speaker announced, "The ayes have it."

- Opponent demanded a recorded vote.

A recorded vote was taken; it won 265–144.

- Opponent moved to reconsider the vote by which the previous question was ordered.
- Miller moved to table the vote to reconsider.

Vote was taken and the Speaker announced, "The ayes have it."

- Opponent demanded a recorded vote.

A recorded vote was taken; it won 273–143.

- Opponent moved to commit the main motion to the Committee on Merchant Marine.

Vote was taken and the Speaker announced, "The noes have it."

- Opponent demanded a recorded vote.

A recorded vote was taken; it lost 141–277.

- Opponent moved to reconsider the vote by which the House did not agree to the motion to commit.
- Miller moved to table the motion to reconsider.

Vote was taken and the Speaker announced, "The ayes have it."

- Opponent demanded a recorded vote.

A recorded vote was taken; it won 280-141.

The question was now on the main motion.

Vote was taken and the Speaker announced, "The ayes have it."

- Lewis demanded a recorded vote.

A recorded vote was taken; it won 283-140.

- Opponent moved to reconsider the vote by which the main motion was agreed to.
- Miller moved to table the motion to reconsider.

Vote was taken and the Speaker announced, "The ayes have it."

- Opponent demanded a recorded vote.

A recorded vote was taken; it won 282–140.

It was now exactly 5:00 p.m. Almost another hour was consumed by roll call votes on a motion to instruct the House conferees before the Speaker could finally appoint them.

The day was not yet over. During the past several days, Senators Johnston and Feinstein and Representative Miller had taken time to carefully discuss what each of them wanted in the Conference Report, Johnston and Miller considering the politics of the situation while recognizing Feinstein's primary interest. They agreed on the National Park Service Preserve in the Mojave with only the House Lanfair Nibble left out of the preserve. Feinstein had now done all she could; she was not on the Conference Committee and had to leave it in the hands of her able colleagues. The meeting had to wait until a specified time after the final House vote. It was now announced on the floors of both Houses that the Conference Committee would hold its public meeting at 6:30 p.m. Key members of the committee from both Senate and House, including Senators Johnston and Bumpers and Representatives Miller, Vento, and Lehman, gathered *very* promptly at 6:30 p.m., selected a chair (Senator Johnston), and agreed to accept the chair's recommendations. Having completed their business in a little over two minutes, they adjourned, turning over to the majority staffs of the House and Senate Committees, as was customary, the job of preparing the Conference Report,[122] getting it printed, and carrying it around for signature by a majority of the conferees. When the rest of the appointed conferees dribbled in, they found the meeting was over!

"I know that
every good and
excellent thing in the
world stands,
moment by moment,
on the razor edge
of danger and
must be fought for."

—Thornton Wilder
in *Skin of our Teeth*

The
Miracle

CHAPTER ELEVEN

"We've reached the edge

of the precipice—so hang tight," reported Martin Hayden from Washington to others around the country with whom he communicated daily. It was Wednesday morning, October 5, 1994. Barely three days remained before final adjournment of the 103d session of Congress on Friday, October 7.

The fate of the Desert Bill hung in the balance. Hayden was front-line scout for the Sierra Club on the Congressional battlefield. Other staff members of major conservation organizations acting in similar capacities, and sharing fast-breaking information, were Norbert Riedy for the Wilderness Society and Thomas Adams for the National Parks and Conservation Association. That morning, their news was good. Despite the delaying tactics of opponents of the act, the Conference Committee to resolve differences between the bills, previously passed by large margins in both House and Senate, had been able to meet the previous evening. Its Conference Report, embodying a final bill, had been filed. All that remained, one would think, was to put the Conference Report to an up-or-down vote in both House and Senate.

So near, but yet so far! Under its rules, the Senate would not act on the Conference Report until the House had voted. Senator Wallop had made clear his intent to drag out Senate debate by filibustering the Senate vote on the Conference Report. A swift House vote on the report, under procedures that did not permit a filibuster, was the only hope. But no such vote could take place, of course, until the House Rules Committee established the necessary "rule," or program for House debate. The Rules Committee had been scheduled to meet Tuesday night, after the meeting of the Conference Committee, but Representative Jerry Lewis, deadly opponent of the Desert Bill, was reported to have threatened to delay other House business if this schedule was adhered to. The Rules Committee therefore met Wednesday morning and quickly adopted the usual rule for Conference Reports—one hour for debate on the report and no amendments. The committee waived its requirement that its rule must "age" until the third day after its adoption before debate could take place in view of the closeness of the adjournment date. Floor time would now have to be obtained for the House to vote. After that vote, the necessary cloture petition to shut off Senator Wallop's filibuster in the Senate would have to be filed, followed by adoption of the cloture motion by the necessary 60 votes, and, finally, the Senate would have to approve the Conference Report. Could these intricate procedures be completed in time?

It seemed impossible. Under the Senate's rules, a full legislative day had to intervene between the filing of a cloture petition and the cloture vote itself. That petition, with its minimum of 16 signatures, could not even be filed until the House had acted. The press of end-of-session business in the House would likely prevent the House from acting on the Conference Report until sometime on Thursday. Even if the House took final action by Thursday night so that the cloture petition could be filed in the Senate Friday, the cloture vote would have to wait until Sunday, October 9, *two days* after the date scheduled for Congress to adjourn and for its members to go back to their home states.[123] And if cloture was adopted, the Senate's rules permitted opponents of cloture a *further* 30 hours of debate before there could be the final vote on the Conference Report!

Throughout the country, supporters of the act had only three remaining resources at their disposal: prayer, the telephone, and the fax machine. All were feverishly put to work. Could such slender resources prevail in the chaotic atmosphere of Washington at the very end of a Congressional session?

Miracles do happen, however. California Congressman George Miller, leader of the House conferees, finally obtained floor time from the Speaker for debate on the Conference Report to begin whenever possible *after midnight* on Thursday. Thus the debate would take place in the early hours of the day of adjournment, October 7. The Conference Report finally came to the floor of the House shortly after 1:00 a.m. with one hour permitted for debate. That hour was taken up by complaints from opponents of the bill about the speed with which the Conference Committee had acted and about the waiver by the Rules Committee of its "Germaneness Rule."[124] This waiver had allowed inclusion in the Conference Report of the Mississippi Delta and New Orleans Jazz Festival amendments so dear to the heart of Senator Johnston. (No germaneness rule hampers amendments in the Senate; hence it is customary for the House rule to be waived in order to permit the conferees to consider non-germane Senate amendments.)

Finally, at 2:10 a.m. the report was agreed to without objection. This time, Jerry Lewis did not insist on a recorded vote or, for that matter, any vote at all. Everyone was exhausted. A quorum of House members who supported the bill had stuck with it to the very end. At last they could go home, with adjournment that day uppermost in their minds.

Maine Congressman George Mitchell, the Majority Leader who held the Senate past adjournment day to vote on the Desert Bill.

Courtesy of the U.S. Senate Historical Office

The final hope now rested with Senator George Mitchell (Democrat, Maine), the Senate Majority Leader. Few Senators in recent years had earned greater respect from their colleagues on both sides of the aisle. Long before, Mitchell had announced that he would retire at the close of this session of Congress. His colleagues knew this was to be his last day. Would he be able to hold the Senate in session past adjournment and into the weekend, if necessary, in order to make possible a vote on the bill? It was an election year and national elections were a bare month away. Many of his colleagues, up for reelection, wanted in the worst way to get home to campaign.

On the floor of the Senate Friday morning, Mitchell asked Wallop if he would be willing to allow the vote on cloture and on the Conference Report to take place that day. Wallop refused. In fact, he asserted his right to have the entire 60-page Desert Bill read aloud in the Senate chamber, taking two-

and-a-half hours of precious time. Mitchell then played his last card and announced that he would keep the Senate in session as long as necessary to take the required votes. His action was wholly in character—in his mind, it did not befit the dignity of the Senate to fail to vote on a bill clearly favored by a sizable majority of his fellow members.

Certain Republican Senators, several up for reelection, called on Senator Wallop during the day to moderate his insistence on the prescribed delay before the cloture vote could be taken. They did not wish to ignore Mitchell's last request but wanted to get home as soon as possible. Under heavy pressure from his colleagues, Senator Wallop at last consented to the holding of the cloture vote on the Conference Report at 10 a.m. Saturday morning, rather than insisting that it wait until Sunday under the rules. A "time agreement" fixing the date and time for that vote, and specifying that a vote on the Conference Report would immediately follow if the cloture motion were approved, received the unanimous consent of the Senate on Friday evening.

Already, a trickle of Senators had departed Washington for home and more were in the process of leaving. Victory was possible if—and only if—most of the Senators who had previously voted for the bill would appear in the Senate Chamber Saturday morning. Senator Mitchell, along with the act's principal sponsor, Senator Dianne Feinstein of California, their staffs and staff members of conservation organizations headquartered in Washington, went to work on the phones Friday evening and into the early hours of Saturday morning, attempting to reach Senators who had voted for the bill in April, asking them to remain in or return to Washington for Saturday's vote. After midnight Friday, Senator Mitchell was observed on two phones at once, talking with a Senator on one line and, on the other, trying to arrange a private charter flight to bring him back.[125]

Senator John Kerry (Democrat, Massachusetts) was getting ready to leave Friday evening. Marty Hayden knew that Stephanie Jowers, who had done much to gain the support of Senator J.

Bennett Johnston of Louisiana, had just come from her home state of Louisiana to Tufts University in Massachusetts as a freshman. Hayden tracked her down at the university. She immediately went to the campus center, through the dining halls and into the dorms, giving out Senator Kerry's number. The old alchemy that had worked for the bill in Louisiana did so again. Calls began to pour into Senator Kerry's Washington office. If the Senator's harried staff failed to answer, an urgent message was left on voice mail that the Senator *must stay* in town for the vote on Saturday. One student told Stephanie he had somehow managed to reach the Senator directly; the Senator told him he had changed his mind and would not leave Washington.

Senator John Chafee (Republican, Rhode Island) called fellow Republicans late Friday evening to urge them to stay and vote for the bill. In several instances those who had left town by the time a call reached them drove or flew back Friday night or early Saturday morning. Senator James Sasser (Democrat, Tennessee) had gone back to his home state to campaign for his political life. Before dawn on Saturday morning he flew back to Washington on a chartered plane to cast his vote. It was almost his last vote as a Senator, for he lost the election a month later. Senator William Roth (Republican, Delaware) had given his commitment to a constituent, Tim O'Connor, a member of the Sierra Club's Delaware chapter, that he would cast his vote for the bill. At 7 a.m. Saturday he drove from his home in Delaware to the Capitol to be present "for the only vote," he told his staff, "I could not miss."[126]

The Saturday morning session opened at 9 a.m. for one hour of debate before the cloture vote.[127] Many supportive Senators were still not present. They dribbled in while Johnston and Feinstein addressed the Senate for the last time in support of the bill and Wallop and Senator Larry Craig of Idaho delivered their final attack upon it. The hour of ten o'clock ended the debate.

The roll was called on the cloture motion. Onlookers in the gallery held their breath. Would there be 60 "aye" votes present?

Many Republican Senators had previously voted in favor of the act. Now, their votes were in doubt. Senator Dole, the Republican leader, had called a caucus meeting of Republican Senators early that very morning in the interest of garnering a "no" vote. Representative Jerry Lewis and his cohorts were invited to the meeting to make their appeal to Senators who had previously supported the bill. Would these Senators now vote their consciences or would they bow to pressure from their leadership and withhold their votes?

As the roll call proceeded, seven strong-minded Republican Senators rejected that pressure and voted "aye." They were Chafee of Rhode Island, William Cohen of Maine, Dave Durenberger of Minnesota, Judd Gregg of New Hampshire, Mark Hatfield of Oregon, James Jeffords of Vermont, and William Roth of Delaware. Without the votes of *all* of the above there would very likely have been no Desert Protection Act. Eight other Republican Senators who had previously voted *for* the bill stood by on the sidelines. None cast a vote for cloture. The tally reached 59 and hung there. The time for voting on the motion for cloture under the rules expired. There would be a few minutes' grace under the tradition of Senatorial courtesy if another vote was to be expected. But was it?

The atmosphere was thick with tension. Years of work, hopes, disappointments, compromises, successes and defeats hung in the balance. A telephone call came in. Senator Carole Moseley-Braun (Democrat, Illinois) was on the line. Her garage door opener had failed to work that morning and she was finally on her way by taxi. Hayden, who was at the entrance, watched her sprint up the steps of the Capitol, throwing her coat to an aide. She burst into the chamber with both hands held high. Hers was the essential 60th vote.

The rest was anticlimax. The seven remaining Republican Senators (John Danforth of Missouri, Pete Domenici of New Mexico, Charles Grassley of Iowa, Nancy Kassebaum of Kansas, Richard Lugar of Indiana, Arlen Specter of Pennsylvania, and John Warner of Virginia) who had all supported the bill in April but had withheld their votes at the behest of their leadership on the roll call for cloture, now quickly stepped forward to vote "aye." Thus, the final cloture vote was 68–23.

The Conference Report was agreed to without a further recorded vote. The members of the most important legislative body in the nation, if not the world, whose procedures might on occasion belie its greatness, had only to resolve a few leftover issues before they could grab their bags and leave for home.

★   ★   ★   ★

This is an instance where federal legislation, passed by over 60% majorities in both houses of Congress, came within an ace of being killed by one Senator through the use of the Senate's own filibuster rules. The question remains: Is this, or is it not, a process that serves the public's interest?

Winston Churchill, that old practical philosopher, tells us that "democracy is the worst form of government—*except* for all the others." Fortunately for all of us, as the case of the Desert Bill demonstrates, democracy is capable of occasional miracles— seeming miracles that are, in truth, the outcome of long, persistent efforts that are sometimes forgotten. Such a seeming miracle surely occurred in the first few days of October 1994. But the story of the Desert Bill is not quite finished, as the Epilogue will show.

"Difficulty Gives
Value to Things."

—Montaigne

EPILOGUE

On October 31, 1994,

President Bill Clinton signed the California Desert Protection Act in the presence of lawmakers, Administration officials, and several of those notable men and women whose voluntary efforts brought the act into being. Moments after he laid down his pen, four baby desert tortoises and their older brother made their way slowly across the President's desk to greet him.

In the aftermath of the Desert Bill's passage, even *Cycle News* markedly softened its rhetoric. On October 26, 1994, it published a statement by the president of the Motorcycle Industry Council, "putting the Desert Bill in perspective" and announcing distribution of a map of motorcycle play areas and routes open in California. "The map shows," he said, "that virtually all traditionally-used OHV areas, including nearly half a million acres of desert terrain, remain open and accessible....When you look at the total picture as represented on the map, there is no reason to see anything but a very positive future for OHV recreation in California."[128]

Others continued to predict the worst. "It's going to tear California apart," said Dana Bell, Western States Representative of the AMA. "These are our public lands and they've been taken away."[129]

Celebration of the Republican victory in the '94 Congressional elections was barely over when an old foe of the Desert Protection Act began looking for a way to undercut its most striking feature—establishment of the new Mojave National Preserve. By virtue of his seniority, Congressman Jerry Lewis was a high-ranking member of the House Appropriations Committee. He asked that a rider be added to the House Interior Department Appropriations Bill for the ensuing fiscal year which, in effect, transferred management of the preserve from the National Park Service to the BLM by limiting the Park Service to the expenditure of $1.00 (one dollar) for management of the Preserve in fiscal year 1995–96, while providing $599,999 to the BLM "to manage the Preserve." The Committee did what he asked.[130]

How can this sort of substantive lawmaking be done by an Appropriations Committee without reference to the committee of Congress appointed to deal with the subject, without any hearing conducted by that committee and without formal input from the governmental agency involved, the scientific community, or the public? "That's just the way it's done in Washington," a cynic from the Beltway would say.

And where did Lewis get his aggregate figure of $600,000? The Mojave Preserve superseded the East Mojave National Scenic Area previously under the management of the BLM. Prior to the Desert Act's passage, one or more Congressmen had asked the Interior Department for the annual cost of the national scenic area. The BLM had responded with the figure of $600,000. But that figure was the direct cost of only three programs in the scenic area—cultural resource protection, visitor service, and management of WSAs. It failed to include other costs, such as a share of the Bureau's very substantial indirect costs of general land management. Was the House Appropriations Committee going to appropriate less than half of the funds needed to do the job, regardless of which agency did it? Realizing the problem, the Department of Interior requested the Committee's approval for an interim transfer of additional Park Service funds to use in managing the preserve. The transfer was blocked.

Lewis, long-time leader of the House opposition to the Desert Bill, had remained extraordinarily bitter over its adoption. But *this* went far beyond bitterness. The conservation community hoped that the Senate Appropriations Committee would reject an action by the House that was, at best, an egregious slap in the face of the National Park Service. However, the Senate Committee meekly went along with the House.

During the spring and fall of 1995, wrangling in House and Senate delayed voting on the appropriations measure, to which the new Republican majority in Congress had added a string of other riders weakening or removing existing laws protecting the environment. Short-term funding measures were passed by both Houses to permit the government to function temporarily on the basis of the prior year's appropriations. However, the Park Service, now thoroughly alarmed, took drastic action to reduce its management expenses associated with the Mojave Preserve. At the low point (which lasted for months), the Preserve was reduced to a superintendent and three other employees.

Finally, on December 14, 1995, the rider-encumbered appropriations bill was passed and sent to the President. Four days later, citing the $1.00 cap on the appropriation for Park Service management of the Mojave Preserve as one of his reasons, the President vetoed the measure. The Christmas holiday season had now begun and Interior Department operations, including national parks and preserves, had to be largely shut down. Not quite, however—winter visitors were encamped at Hole-in-the-Wall and Mid Hills campgrounds in the Mojave Preserve. Mary Martin, the Superintendent, and her daughter Jennifer, home from college for Christmas, went out to both campgrounds and emptied the trash.

It is well known that the public did not take kindly to this situation. As for the Lewis ploy, the *Riverside Press-Enterprise* had opined in the previous year: "It reduces lawmaking to legislative vandalism, the level of a college prank."[131] After the veto, the *San Diego Union-Tribune*, generally regarded as quite conservative in the media spectrum, observed:

> *Lewis' battle against the Mojave [Preserve] is getting ridiculous...the people who live and work around the [Preserve] want the National Park Service to run it, not the BLM. The Chambers of Commerce in Barstow, Baker and Newberry Springs all support the National Park Service instead of the BLM. Individual business owners in the Desert area, such as hotel and restaurant owners...say that Lewis' action will hurt their communities.... The President needs to continue to stand firm against an appropriations bill with Lewis' rider attached to it.*[132]

Efforts in Congress to override the President's veto failed. Now the Congress had to face growing public disfavor. On April 25, 1996, one day before the last short-term spending measure expired and a third partial government shutdown was about to begin, Congress approved a bill which had the effect of eliminating almost all of the anti-environmental provisions in the appropriation bill for the year. It also granted the Park Service $1.1 million in new funding for the Mojave Preserve—still inadequate, but a start. The standoff was at an end, perhaps only temporarily.

As the foregoing events were unfolding, the few employees of the Park Service still at the Mojave Preserve did what they could. Superintendent Martin was able to borrow help from parks in Alaska, Death Valley, and from the Lake Mead National Recreation Center to perform a minimum of essential services. It had been necessary for the preserve to operate with only one interpretive ranger, none for law enforcement. Now, at last, key staff positions could begin to be filled.

As for the BLM, its partisans had long urged that it needed a better chance to show that it, too, could manage special areas of the public lands to preserve their wildness. It had not done so with the East Mojave National Scenic Area. Now, it had a second chance. Thanks to the Desert Protection Act, the BLM's California Desert District found itself one of the largest managers of wilderness areas in the lower 48 states. It had full responsibility for training the staff to care for these areas and to develop careful plans for their management.

Suddenly, the BLM in Utah was handed the greatest management opportunity in the agency's history. This was the President's action in September 1996 establishing, in the southern Utah desert, the new Grand Staircase/Escalante National Monument—1.7 million acres of natural magnificence.[133] Breaking with precedent, President Clinton left the BLM in charge and did not turn the area over to the National Park Service. In effect, he challenged the BLM to demonstrate that it was capable of protecting a very special area—the first National Monument it has been given to manage—and educating the public to enjoy it but not harm it.

Can the BLM do it? Will it adopt policies for the new monument similar to those tried and tested by the National Park

Service in managing other national monuments throughout the West, including outstanding *desert* national monuments such as Death Valley and Joshua Tree in California? The challenge is clear. One can only hope it will be met.

APPENDIX A:

Basic Provisions of the California Desert Protection Act

First: The Act established the Mojave National Preserve, modestly smaller than the East Mojave National Scenic Area it replaced. As the result of remeasurement after the Act was passed, it turned out to be between 1.5 and 1.6 million acres in size, even after deletion of the Castle Mountain Mine and its associated claims in the northeastern quadrant and the "Lanfair Nibble," 59,000 acres of small, private lands in the Lanfair Valley. (This was subsequently referred to as the "Lanfair Valley Exclusion Area"). Of critical importance, the Act provides that the preserve will be managed by the National Park Service under the same standards applicable to national parks, subject to the following special provisions: hunting (as regulated by the State of California) and grazing of domestic livestock (at no more than the level when the Act was adopted) continue to be permitted. Of the total preserve acreage, 695,000 acres were designated wilderness.

Second: The Act established Death Valley National Park, including the area of the present monument plus additional adjacent lands together totaling approximately 3,368,000 acres, and designated 3,158,000 of those acres as wilderness. Grazing at no more than the level when the Act was adopted continues to be permitted in the additions to the former monument.

Third: The Act established Joshua Tree National Park, including the area of the present monument plus additional adjacent lands, together totaling approximately 795,000 acres, and designated 132,000 of the added land as wilderness. (A substantial portion of the former monument land had been designated as wilderness in 1976.)

Fourth: The Act establishes 69 wilderness areas in the desert to be managed by the BLM, comprising approximately 3,570,000 acres. Approximately 95,000 acres of Forest Service land and approximately 9,000 acres in Havasu and Imperial National Wildlife Refuges were also designated as wilderness. Eight areas totaling approximately 326,000 acres (seven of which were designated as wilderness in earlier versions of the Act) were left as WSAs for later Congressional consideration.

Fifth: The Act transferred approximately 20,500 acres of BLM land to Red Rock Canyon State Park and created a Desert Lily Sanctuary of approximately 2,000 acres.

Sixth: The Act authorized appropriations to the National Park Service and Bureau of Land Management of not more than $36 million over that provided in fiscal year 1994, for additional administrative and construction costs in fiscal years 1995 through 1999, and $300 million for all land acquisition costs.

Seventh: The Act withdrew from mining and mineral leasing 6,000 acres to create the "Bodie Bowl" with its old mining town in far northeastern California. The Act included the lower Mississippi Delta Development provisions and established a New Orleans Jazz National Historical Park.

APPENDIX B:
Glossary

ACEC: Area designated by the BLM as an "Area of Critical Environmental Concern"

AMA: American Motorcyclist Association

ATV: All-Terrain Vehicle

BLM: Bureau of Land Management

"Brown bill": Bills introduced in Congress by Representative George Brown in 1978–79 to establish a Mojave National Park

CDCA: California Desert Conservation Area

CDPA: California Desert Protection Act (Desert Bill)

CDPL: California Desert Protection League

Cloture, Motion for: Passage of a cloture motion is the usual process for terminating a filibuster in the U.S. Senate. It requires 60 affirmative votes and its passage limits further debate on the bill or motion under consideration.

Conference Report: Report of the Conference Committee appointed to resolve differences between the House of Representatives and the Senate on bills in each House dealing with the same subject. The report sets forth the language of a final bill to be submitted to each House for a final vote (no further amendment being allowed).

DEIS: Draft Environmental Impact Statement

Desert Committee: The Desert subcommittee of the Sierra Club's Southern California Regional Conservation Committee

Desert Bill: California Desert Protection Act of 1994 and the legislative bills that preceded it

DPC: Desert Protective Council, Inc.

EA: Environmental Assessment, a preliminary environmental analysis under the National Environmental Policy Act (NEPA) leading to a decision to prepare an Environmental Impact Statement (EIS) or to a finding of no significant impact (FONSI)

Earthjustice Legal Defense Fund: An independent nonprofit public interest law firm representing organizations attempting to protect environmental values. It was formerly named Sierra Club Legal Defense Fund.

EIS: Environmental Impact Statement, an environmental analysis required under "NEPA" when a significant impact on the environment is anticipated

EMNSA: East Mojave National Scenic Area

Filibuster: Action taken by one or more Senators in the U.S. Senate in order to delay a vote of the whole Senate by "talking a bill to death." The House of Representatives does not permit filibusters.

FLPMA: Federal Land Policy and Management Act of 1976

FONSI: A "finding of no significant [environmental] impact" by a government agency

GAO: General Accounting Office (U.S.)

ICMP: Interim Critical Management Program for California desert

IMP: BLM's Interim Management Policy and Guidelines for Lands under Wilderness Review (December 1979)

MUC: Multiple Use Class, as defined in the California Desert Plan of 1980

Class C (Controlled Use)

Class L (Limited Use)

Class M (Moderate Use)

Class I (Intensive Use)

NEPA: National Environmental Policy Act of 1969

NOA: National Outdoor Association

NPS: National Park Service

ORV: Off-road vehicle (a general category)

ORVAC: Off-Road Vehicle Advisory Council, organized by Russ Penny, California State Director, BLM

Phantom Duck: Adopted nickname of Louis McKey

PLLRC: Public Land Law Review Commission.

SCRCC: Southern California Regional Conservation Committee of the Sierra Club (now SCNRCC, reflecting the addition of Nevada)

Sierra Club Legal Defense Fund: Former name of Earthjustice Legal Defense Fund.

WSA: Wilderness Study Area

APPENDIX C:
Some of the Players in the Drama

The California Desert Protection Act, as introduced and reintroduced in five sessions of Congress, is referred to as "the Desert Bill"; the Federal Land Policy and Management Act of 1976 is referred to as FLPMA.

American Motorcyclist Association—Strongest opponent of the Desert Bill which, in the end, gained its objectives sufficiently to withdraw its opposition.

Anderson, Judy—Organized the enormous task of mapping wilderness in the desert as a California volunteer leader; chaired the California Desert Protection League; a strategist throughout the campaign.

Audubon Society—National supporter of the Desert Bill.

Babbitt, Bruce—Secretary of Interior who developed the Clinton Administration's position supporting the Desert Bill.

Barnes, George—Lifelong desert explorer whose annual monitoring of the Barstow-Vegas motorcycle race helped to make the case for its termination.

Bellar, Melanie—Staff chief of the new House subcommittee on California Desert Lands in 1991 who helped to develop and draft the first version of the Desert Bill to pass the House that same year.

Berry, Dr. Kristin—Independent-minded BLM expert on the desert tortoise. She ceaselessly worked to protect her favorite creature.

Brown, Congressman George (California)—Gave public notice that there was a treasure in the California desert by introducing a bill for a Mojave National Park long before the Desert Bill came into being.

Bumpers, Senator Dale (Arkansas)—Chair of the Senate subcommittee with jurisdiction over the Desert Bill through five sessions of Congress. He presided over many hearings of his subcommittee and praised Hollywood star Morgan Fairchild for making at least one of them "palatable."

Burk, Peter—With his wife Joyce, in 1976 issued a call to arms from the midst of the Mojave Desert in Barstow by founding Citizens for Mojave National Park. He supported the cause by publishing many booklets arguing the case for desert protection.

California Desert Coalition—Active and effective organization in opposition to the Desert Bill.

California Desert Protection League—Formed in 1994 to develop support for a Desert Bill. It ultimately included over 120 member organizations.

Carpenter, Patty—With husband Elden Hughes, raised the "littlest lobbyists," baby desert tortoises, which went to Congress under her care.

Cates, Robert—His efforts gained over 1,300 of the 1,600 scientists and teachers as endorsers of the Desert Bill.

Chapman, Howard—Chief, Western Division, National Park Service, whose Division conducted a study that concluded that the East Mojave, Death Valley and Joshua Tree qualified for national park status. It was rejected in Foggy Bottom.

Citizens for Mojave National Park—(see Burk, Peter).

Crandell, Harry—As a leading staff member of the Wilderness Society, organized the successful testimony that brought provisions for BLM wilderness into FLPMA.

Cranston, Senator Alan—Volunteered to sponsor the Desert Bill, assisted in its development, introduced it in four successive Congresses, and was its principal Senate spokesman for seven years.

Desert Protective Council, Inc.—Active supporter of the Desert Bill.

Dodson, James—Perhaps the intellectual leader and one of the strategists in the campaign for the Desert Bill; major volunteer spokesman for conservation organizations in development of the California Desert Plan.

Earthjustice Legal Defense Fund (formerly Sierra Club Legal Defense Fund)—Volunteer legal counsel for conservation organizations in many court battles over desert protection.

Feinstein, Senator Dianne (California)—Dauntless negotiator and orator who fashioned a final Desert Bill that overcame all obstacles to pass the Senate in 1994.

Ford, Betsy—Legislative assistant for the environment on the staff of Representative Mel Levine. She helped to develop and draft the first version of the Desert Bill that passed one of the Houses of Congress in 1991.

Gaston, Lyle—Scientist and desert explorer whose leadership in organizing desert study trips led to his early chairmanship of the Sierra Club's Desert Committee.

Hastey, Ed—Chief of the BLM in California during the campaign for the Desert Bill; an able opponent of the Bill.

Hattoy, Robert—Southern California Field Representative of the Sierra Club; very active in the campaign for the Desert Bill.

Hayden, Martin—Tactician and communicator for the Sierra Club in Washington, D.C., during the final days of the Desert Bill campaign.

High Desert Multiple Use Coalition—Important, active opponent of the Desert Bill.

Holden, Bill—Founder and first chair of the Sierra Club's Desert Committee, originator of desert study trips.

Hoover, Vicky—Tireless volunteer who coordinated phone banks for the Desert Bill and succeeded in gaining its endorsement by a large number of California cities and counties.

Hughes, Elden—West Coast volunteer leader in the campaign for the Desert Bill; prime media spokesman and a strategist in the campaign.

Hunter, Congressman Duncan (California)—Staunch opponent of the Desert Bill from the time of its introduction; represented part of the desert.

Izaac Walton League—National supporter of the Desert Bill (though its largest chapter in California bowed out).

Jennings, Robert—as District Assistant to Congressman Bob Mathias, conceived and helped to draft the first Congressional bill for a California Desert Plan.

Johnston, Senator J. Bennett (Louisiana)—Chair of the Senate Committee with primary jurisdiction over the Desert Bill. He skillfully managed the bill in the Senate (and gained two "Kewpie dolls" for his home state in the process).

Jowers, Stephanie—High school senior in Louisiana and member of the Sierra Student Coalition who brought messages of support from thousands to Louisiana's powerful Senior Senator Johnston.

Kari, Douglas—Co-founder of Desert Survivors; became a lawyer partway through the Keynot Mine case and carried it forward to a successful conclusion.

Lacey, Katherine—Much-respected legislative assistant for conservation on the staffs of Senator Cranston and his successor, Senator Feinstein.

Lehman, Congressman Rick (California)—Chair of the special House Subcommittee on Oversight and California Desert Lands which led the way to House passage of the Desert Bill in 1991.

Levine, Congressman Mel (California)—Introduced the Desert Bill in the House in 1987 and was its principal House spokesman through the next five years.

Lewis, Congressman Jerry (California)—Tireless leader of the opposition to the Desert Bill in the House from the time of its introduction. He represented a major portion of the desert.

Mathias, Congressman Bob (California)—Introduced the first bill in Congress for a California Desert Plan in 1971.

McCandless, Congressman Alfred (California)—Staunch opponent of the Desert Bill from the time of its introduction. He represented part of the desert.

McKey, Lewis—Leader of motorcyclists protesting closure of the Barstow-Vegas Race. Styled himself, "The Phantom Duck of the Desert."

Miller, Congressman George (California)—Chair of the House Committee with jurisdiction over the Desert Bill. He skillfully managed the Desert Bill in the House.

Mitchell, Congressman George (Maine)—Senate Majority Leader whose efforts and prestige brought the 60 essential Senate votes for the Desert Bill to the floor a day after Congress was scheduled to adjourn.

Morton, Rogers C.B.—Secretary of Interior who supported the earliest California desert planning efforts.

Moseley-Braun, Senator Carol (Illinois)—Broke the anguished suspense on the Senate floor to cast the most crucial vote of all.

Moss, Larry—Senior staff member of the Sierra Club, and later of the Wilderness Society, who gave critical advice on desert legislation.

National Parks and Conservation Association—National supporter of the Desert Bill.

Penny, J. Russell—Chief of the California BLM 1967–1974, who wangled the mighty sum of $25,000 from his agency to begin planning for "people management" in the California desert.

Pettis, Congressman Jerry (California)—Only 25 days behind Congressman Bob Mathias of California in introducing a second bill in the House for California desert planning in 1971.

Pettis, Congresswoman Shirley (California)—Carried on her deceased husband's fight for a California Desert Plan and following his untimely death, helped to pass FLPMA (which included that plan).

Reames, Deborah—Cut her teeth as a lawyer for Earthjustice Legal Defense Fund representing conservation organizations in lawsuits for desert protection.

Riedy, Norbert—Point man for the Wilderness Society in the campaign for the Desert Bill.

Schifferle, Patty—California field representative of the Wilderness Society 1986–1990); active in the campaign for the Desert Bill.

Scott, Douglas—Sierra Club Conservation Director; converted to the Desert Bill and then helped draft it.

Sease, Debbie—Sierra Club Director of Public Lands and manager of lobbying for the Desert Bill from her office in Foggy Bottom.

Seymour, Senator John (California)—Appointed in 1991 by Governor Pete Wilson after the latter left the Senate; became an opponent of the Desert Bill when his proposals to revise it failed to gain support.

Sherwood, Michael—Senior lawyer for Earthjustice Legal Defense Fund; active in Barstow-Vegas and other desert cases.

Sieman, Rick—Editor of *Dirt Bike* Magazine, Founder of the Sahara Club and its newsletter opposing restrictions on desert motorcycle racing; author of *Monkey Butt* (1995), a saga of life with motorcycles.

Sierra Club—National supporter of the Desert Bill; volunteers associated with club were a major factor in passage of the bill.

Silver, Larry—Senior lawyer for Earthjustice Legal Defense Fund who represented conservation organizations in much early desert litigation; presently Project Attorney for California Environmental Law Project, Mill Valley, California.

Sopher, Terry—Spokesman for the Wilderness Society in Washington, D.C., during the time the Desert Bill was put together.

Thomas, Congressman William (California)—Staunch opponent of the Desert Bill from the time of its introduction; represented part of the desert.

Vento, Congressman Bruce (Minnesota)—Chair of the House subcommittee with jurisdiction over the Desert Bill during most of the years of campaigning; became a strong supporter.

Wallop, Senator Malcolm (Idaho)—Indefatigable opponent of the Desert Bill in the Senate from the time of its inception.

Watt, James—Secretary of Interior when the Desert Bill was conceived; had a hand in the conception.

Widen, Jeffrey—Sierra Club Southern California Field Representative. Worked tirelessly for the Desert Bill.

Wilderness Society—National supporter of the Desert Bill.

Wilson, Senator Pete (later Governor of California)—Shifted from neutral to determined opposition as the Desert Bill gained co-sponsors in the Senate.

FOOTNOTES

Preface

1. John Charles Fremont, *Report of the Exploring Expedition to the Rocky Mountains in the Year 1842 and to North Carolina in the Years 1843–1844* (Washington, D.C., Senate Executive Doc. 174, 28th Cong., 2d Sess., 1845) 256

2. Hearing before the Senate Subcommittee on Public Lands on S. 63, *A Bill to Establish the California Desert National Conservation Area* (93d Cong., 2d Sess., February 19, 1974) 43

3. Hearing before the Senate Subcommittee on Public Lands, National Parks and Forests on S. 7, *To Provide for the Protection of the Public Lands in the California Desert* (100th Cong., 1st Sess., July 21 and 23, 1987) 504–05

Chapter One

4. California BLM Circular No. 2257, 34 Fed. Reg. No. 13, January 18, 1969

5. Report of the 1970 Annual Meeting of the BLM California State Advisory Board, 22

6. *Federal Land Policy and Management Act of 1976* (FLPMA), Statutes at Large, 2743; 430 US Code § 1701 (1976)

7. California BLM Instruction Memo: *Special Land Use Permits for Off-Road Vehicle Events*, August 1972

Chapter Three

8. Public Land Law Review Commission (PLLRC) *One Third of the Nation's Land* (Washington, D.C., U.S. Govt. Printing Office., 1970)

9. The principal bills in Congress which eventually led to FLPMA, together with the relevant Committee Reports discussing the content of those bills and their interpretation, are found together in a single volume, *Legislative History of the Federal Land Policy and Management Act of 1976* (Publication 95–99, Washington, D.C., U.S. Govt. Printing Office, 1978)

10. FLPMA, n. 6, 90 Statutes at Large § 603, 43 US Code § 1782

11. Opinion of the Solicitor of the Interior Dept. *Interpretation of Section 603 of The Federal Land Policy and Management Act Of 1976*, February 13, 1979

12. Department of Interior *Final Wilderness Inventory, California Desert Conservation Area*, March 31, 1979

13. BLM *Interim Management Policy and Guidelines for Lands Under Wilderness Review*, December 12, 1979, 10–11

Chapter Four

14. Memorandum to Howard Chapman, National Park Service Western Regional Director, from the Director, BLM Desert Plan staff, June 5, 1979, with attached Preliminary Study

Chapter Five

15. Wilderness Act, 16 US Code 1131 (1964), § 2

16. House Subcommittee on Interior and Insular Affairs, Report to Accompany H.R. 13777 (104th Cong., 2d Sess., May 1976) 17

17. *Final Wilderness Inventory*, n. 12

18. FLPMA, n. 6, 90 Statutes at Large, § 103(c), 43 US Code § 1702(c)

19. Editorial in the *Los Angeles Times*, June 25, 1988

20. FLPMA, n. 6, 90 Statutes at Large, § 601(a), 43 US Code § 1781

21. Chambers, *California Desert Plan 1976-1980, a Draft Monograph*, BLM California State Office (undated) 35

22. Senate Subcommittee on Public Lands, National Parks and Forests, n. 3, 690

23. Chambers, n. 23, 50

24. Report of the American Arbitration Association in the files of the BLM's Riverside, California office

25. California BLM, *California Desert Conservation Area Plan* (1980) 93–94, 128

26. *American Motorcyclist Ass'n et al v Watt*, 534 F. Supp. 923 (D.C. Cal., 1981)

27. *American Motorcyclist Ass'n et al v Watt*, 714 F2d 962 (9th Cir., 1983)

Chapter Six

28. Statement of Secretary Watt at the Western Governors' Association Conference in Jackson Hole, Wyoming, September 11, 1981

29. California BLM, *1982 Plan Amendments to the California Desert Plan* Record of Decision, May 17, 1983, 25

30. *Wilderness Society et al v BLM*, Interior Board of Land Appeals, 90 IBLA 221, January 30, 1986

31. *1982 Plan Amendments to the California Desert Plan,* n. 29, 28

32. *1982 Plan Amendments to the California Desert Plan,* n. 29, 28; Final EIS, 2–2, 2–3 and 2–7

33. Rulings and observations of the District Judge in this case are unpublished

34. Principal Brief on Appeal of the Sierra Club and others in *Sierra Club v Clark* (D.C. Cal, 1983) 13–23

35. Unpublished Opinion of the District Judge

36. *Sierra Club v Clark*, 774 F2d 1406 (CA 9, 1985)

37. 47 Fed. Reg. 58, 372 (December 30, 1982)

38. *Sierra Club v Watt*, 608 F Supp 305 (DC Cal., 1985)

39. Memorandum to Howard Chapman, n. 14

Chapter Seven

40. Article in the *Los Angeles Times*, "Video Will Dramatize Foes' Attack on Bill to Preserve Desert Areas," December 16, 1987

41. Interview with Linda Kulik

42. BLM's Response to *Failure in the Desert*, December 22, 1986

43. Associated Press Release, "California Senate Race Tops $25M," Los Angeles, December 7, 1986

44. Editorial in the *San Bernardino Sun*, January 15, 1988

45. Article in the *San Bernardino Sun*, "Teacher Pursues Decade-Old Dream," January 10, 1988

46. Editorial in the *Sacramento Bee*, August 5, 1989

Chapter Eight

47. Memorandum to Howard Chapman, n. 17

48. Senate Subcommittee on Public Lands, National Parks and Forests, n. 3, 509–513

49. Hearing before the House Subcommittee on National Parks and Public Lands, Committee on Interior and Insular Affairs, on H.R. 780, *California Public Lands Wilderness Act of 1989* and H.R. 3460, *California Desert Conservation Act of 1989* (101st Cong., 1st Sess., July 27, 1989) 521

50. Hearing before the House Subcommittee on General Oversight and California Desert Lands, Committee on Interior and Insular Affairs, H.R. 2929, *California Desert Protection Act of 1991* and H.R. 3066, *California Public Lands Wilderness Act* (102d Cong., 1st Sess., September 16, 1991) 169–171, 218–219

51. California BLM Final Management Plan and Environmental Impact Statement for the East Mojave National Scenic Area, Appendix B (May 1988)

52. Memorandum of the Acting Director, National Park Service, to the Legislative Counsel, Department of Interior, dated June 5, 1987

53. Editorial in the *San Bernardino Sun*, October 4, 1988

54 California BLM, *The Monuments*, Final EIS (May 1989)

55. California BLM, *Castle Mountain Mine*, Final EIS (August 1990), and Record of Decision (October 31, 1990)

56. California BLM, Draft EIS, East Mojave National Scenic Area Management Plan (April 1987) 1

57. Press Release of Earthjustice Legal Defense Fund on the Castle Mountain Mine, October, 31, 1990

58. California State Director's Instruction Memorandum CA 95–32, November 30, 1994

59. FLPMA, n. 6, 90 Statutes at Large §§ 302(b) and 601(f) 43 US Code §§ 1732(b) and 1781(f)

60. California BLM, *California Desert Conservation Area Draft EIS and Plan Alternatives* (February 1980) 22

61. Memorandum of the Secretary of Interior, January 6, 1997

62. Dialogue captured in *Desert Under Siege*, half-hour film distributed by The Video Project, Oakland, California

63. Darlington, *The Mojave* (Henry Holt, 1996) 311

64. *Ibid.*, 259–274

65. Dept. of Interior, Fish and Wildlife Service, *Emergency Determination of Endangered Status for the Mojave Population of the Desert Tortoise*, 54 Fed. Reg. 32, 326, 32, 327 (August 4, 1989)

66. Undated 71-page California BLM *Barstow-Vegas Post Race Report* to the Desert District Manager, 5

67. California BLM Policy Paper on *Barstow-Vegas Race*, February 21, 1990, 4

68. Article in the *San Diego Union*, "Judge Authorizes Desert Cycle Ride," November 29, 1991

69. Dept. of Interior, Fish and Wildlife Service, Desert Tortoise Proposed Rule 54 Fed. Reg. 42270 (October 13, 1989); and Desert Tortoise Final Rule 55 Fed. Reg. 12178, 12180 (April 2, 1990)

70. Dept. of Interior, Fish and Wildlife Service, *Determination of Critical Habitat for the Mojave Population of the Desert Tortoise*, 59 Fed. Reg. 5820 (February 8, 1994)

Chapter Nine

71. Senate Subcommittee on Public Lands, National Park and Forests, n. 3, 57, 58, 61, 74, 101, 649–53

72. Article in the *California Journal,* "Will Cranston and Wilson Duel on the Desert?," January 1988, 27–28

73. Editorial in the *Sacramento Bee,* July 12, 1988

74. Editorial in the *Sacramento Bee,* August 5, 1989

75. Hearing before the House Subcommittee on Public Lands, National Parks and Forests, Committee on Public Lands, National Parks and Forests on S. 11, *To Provide for the Protection of the Public Lands in the California Desert* (101st Cong., 1st Sess., October 2, 1989) 99–102, 112–113

76. Article in the *San Bernardino Sun* "Wilson Is Looking for Compromise," January 10, 1988

77. Hearing before the House Subcommittee on National Parks and Public Lands, Committee on Interior and Insular Affairs on H.R. 780, *California Desert Protection Act of 1989 and H.R. 3460, California Desert Conservation Act of 1989* (101st Cong., 1st Sess., October 28, 1989)

78. Hearing before the House Subcommittee on National Parks and Public Lands, n. 77 (101st Cong., 2d Sess., November 11, 1989)

79. Congressional Budget Office Cost Estimate (January 29, 1990)

80. BLM Response to Briefing Book on S. 7/H.R. 371 (July 1988)

81. Hearing before House Subcommittee on Public Lands, National Parks and Forests, Committee on Interior and Insular Affairs, on H.R. 780 and H.R. 3460 (101st Cong., 2d Sess., February 10, 1990)

82. Informal list of Senator Bumpers's Amendments distributed at the Committee hearing. (The hearing was attended by Elden Hughes but was not officially reported.)

83. Senate Manual containing Standing Rules [etc.] of the U.S. Senate (U.S. Govt. Printing Office) Rule 26.5(a)

84. Interview with Elden Hughes who was present at the aborted hearing, observed the action and heard Senator Bumpers's statement.

85. Article in the *Los Angeles Times,* "Seymour Caught in Whirlwind of Change," January 27, 1991

86. Senator Seymour's "Statement on the Lehman/Levine Bill," July 1991

87. House Committee on Interior and Insular Affairs, *To Designate Certain Lands in the California Desert as Wilderness*, [etc.] (102d Cong., 1st Sess., November 4, 1991) 73

88. 137 Cong. Rec. H. 11 371 (Daily Ed., November 26, 1991)

89. *Proceedings of the Fourth Death Valley Conference on History and Prehistory*, February 2–5, 1995, Death Valley National History Association (1996) 168

90. Editorial in the *San Bernardino Sun*, May 17, 1992

91. Letter from Senator Cranston to Senator Seymour dated September 11, 1991

92. Article in the *Los Angeles Times*, "Desert Bill's Impact on Mining Jobs Disputed," March 20, 1992

93. Hearing Report of the Senate Subcommittee on Public Lands, National Parks and Forests, Committee on Energy and Natural Resources, on S. 21 *To Provide for the Protection of Public Lands in the California Desert* (102d Cong., 2d Sess., April 4, 1992)

94. Article in the *San Luis Obispo Telegram-Tribune*, "Sparks Fly on Packed Hearing on Desert Issues," April 6, 1992

95. Article in the *San Bernardino Sun*, "Desert Bill Debate Draws Thousands," April 5, 1992

96. Hearing Report of the Senate Subcommittee on Public Lands, National Parks and Forests, Committee on Energy and Natural Resources, on S. 21 (102d Cong., 2d Sess., April 29–30, 1992) 8 and 13

97. Article in the *Riverside Press Enterprise Desert*, "Park Deal Between Senators Collapses," July 31, 1992

98. Article in the *Los Angeles Times*, "Seymour Maneuver Bottles Up Desert Bill in Committee," August 6, 1992; also article referred to in footnote 97

99. *Ibid.*

100. Article in the *San Francisco Chronicle*, "Seymour Calls Himself an Outsider," March 31, 1992

Chapter Ten

101. Hearing Record of the Senate Subcommittee on Public Lands, National Parks and Forests, Committee on Energy and Natural Resources, on S. 21, *To Designate Certain Lands in the California Desert as Wilderness* [etc.] (103rd Cong., 1st Sess., April 27–28, 1993)

102. *Ibid.*, 141

103. *Ibid.*, 142

104. Hearing Record of the House Subcommittee on National Parks, Forests and Public Lands, Committee on Natural Resources, on H. R. 518, *To Designate Certain Lands in the California Desert as Wilderness* [etc.] and H. R. 880, *To Withdraw Certain Federal Lands in the California Desert for Military Purposes* [etc.] (103d Cong., 1st Sess., June 15, 1993) 271–275

105. Senate Subcommittee on Public Lands, National Parks and Forests, n.101, 93

106. Report from those who were present at the markup sessions from late September 1993 through October 5, 1993. No Hearing Record published

107. "Legi-Slate" Status Report for the 103d Congress on all actions on S. 21 since introduction, including the Senate Committee markup sessions September 22 and 29 and October 5, 1993. (No Hearing Record was published.) See also Report on S. 21 of the Senate Committee on Energy and Natural Resources, 103d Cong., 1st Sess., October 13, 1993 for further details.

108. 140 *Cong. Rec.*, S 4059 (Daily Ed., April 11, 1994)

109. 140 *Cong. Rec.*, S 4036 and S 4047 (Daily Ed., March 25, 1994)

110. 140 *Cong. Rec.*, S 4054–4061 and S 4063–4068 (Daily Ed., April 11, 1994)

111. 140 *Cong. Rec.*, S 4102–4158 and S 4167–4176 (Daily Ed., April 12, 1994)

112. 140 *Cong. Rec.*, S 4190–4195 (Daily Ed., April 13, 1994)

113. "Legi-Slate" Report of the House Committee markup session May 4, 1994. See also Report of the full House Committee on Natural Resources, *California Desert Protection Act of 1994* (103d Cong., 2d Sess., May 10, 1994)

114. Siff and Weil, *Ruling Congress*, Viking Press, 1975, 119–129, and interviews

115. 140 *Cong. Rec.* H 3476–3492 (Daily Ed., May 17, 1994)

116. 140 *Cong. Rec.* H 4299–H 4332 (Daily Ed., June 10, 1994); H 4367–H 4383 (Daily Ed., June 13, 1994); H 5491–H 5524 (Daily Ed., July 12, 1994); H 5558–H 5589 (Daily Ed., July 13, 1994); H 5668–H 5691 (Daily Ed., July 14, 1994); H 6303–H 6310 (Daily Ed., July 27, 1994)

117. Burdette, *Filibustering in the Senate*, Princeton University Press, 1940; Cummings, *Capitol Hill Manual*, Bureau of National Affairs (Washington, D.C. 1976), 64–65; Standing Rules of the Senate, Rule 22

118. 140 *Cong. Rec.* S 13029 (Daily Ed., September 20, 1994)

119. 140 *Cong. Rec.* S 13256–13257 (Daily Ed., September 22, 1994)

120. 140 *Cong. Rec.* S 13559–13560 (Daily Ed., September 28, 1994); Cummings, *Capitol Hill Manual*, n. 117, 63–64

121. 140 *Cong. Rec.* H 10695–10731 (Daily Ed., October 4, 1994)

122. Conference Report (House Report 103–832) to accompany S. 21, *California Desert Protection Act of 1994*, (103d Cong., 2d Sess., October 4, 1994); see also 140 *Cong. Rec.* H 11124 (Daily Ed., Oct. 6, 1994) remarks of Representative Drier

Chapter Eleven

123. Standing Rules of the Senate, Rule 22

124. 140 *Cong. Rec.* H 11126–11131 (Daily Ed., October 7, 1994); Cummings, *Capitol Hill Manual*, n. 117, 69–70 (House Germaneness Rule)

125. Article in the *Los Angeles Times*, "Filibuster Broken. Senate OKs California Desert Protection," Oct. 9, 1994. It should be noted that soon after he retired, George Mitchell was asked to go to work on the toughest job of all—the attempt to bring peace to Northern Ireland. His diplomatic skills were put to their highest test and his success will be well known to readers of this book.

126. Recalled by John Duncan, of Senator Roth's staff in 1994.

127. 140 *Cong. Rec.* S 14963–14970 (Daily Ed., October 8, 1994)

Epilogue

128. Article in *Cycle News*, "Putting the California Desert Bill in Perspective," October 26, 1994

129. Article in the *Riverside Press-Enterprise*, "Uniqueness of Desert Now Will Be Preserved," October 30, 1994

130. Editorial in the *San Francisco Chronicle*, "Austere Landscape, Austere Budget," October 30, 1995

131. Editorial in the *Riverside Press-Enterprise*, June 22, 1995

132. Editorial in the *San Diego Union-Tribune*, January 20, 1996

133. Proclamation by the President on Establishment of the Grand Staircase/ Escalante National Monument, released September 18, 1996

CHRONOLOGY:
Important Events in the Fight for California Desert Parks and Wilderness

MAJOR EVENTS:

RELATED EVENTS
AND OBSERVATIONS:

1967–69

- June 1967—Russ Penny appointed California State director of the Bureau of Land Management (BLM)

  ◆ Astonished by photographs of the infant Barstow-Vegas motorcycle race, Penny persuades his Washington office to let him have $25,000 with which to study the resources of the California desert and how they might be protected. He puts together a team from his office and the National Park Service (NPS) to conduct the study.

- November 1968—Publication of "The California Desert, a Preliminary Study"

  ◆ Penny puts his tiny desert study staff to work on an expanded second study.

- June 1969—Penny organizes Off-Road Vehicle Advisory Council (ORVAC) to advise him.

  ◆ ORVAC report recommends a plan designating "open areas," "restricted areas" and "non-use" areas for ORVs.

1970–71

- January 1970—Penny publishes second desert report, observes "the California desert, your desert, is on the brink of an environmental disaster."

- June 1970—Publication of the Report of the Public Land Law Review Commission (PLLRC)

  ◆ PLLRC Report recommends inventory of BLM lands for potential wilderness designation.

- Fall 1970—First Sierra Club Desert Committee organized; an ambitious program of desert study trips is undertaken to acquaint more people with sensitive desert resources.

- July 1971—California Congressman Bob Mathias introduces bill for a funded California desert plan; Congressman Jerry Pettis follows suit with a separate bill of his own.

  ◆ Penny and his staff assist in developing the Mathias bill. Mathias and Pettis bills languish in committee.

1972–75

- May 1972—Secretary of Interior Morton withdraws from sale or other disposition 2.4 million acres of the California desert nominated in Penny's first desert report for protection as "special recreation areas."

- August 1972—California's Senator Alan Cranston introduces a California desert plan bill similar to the Mathias/Pettis bills.

  ◆ Cranston gains a subcommittee hearing for his bill, something neither Mathias nor Pettis were able to do; subcommittee approves it unanimously and recommends it be incorporated in the pending full committee bill for a BLM organic act; full Committee approves this unanimously.

- December 1974—Russ Penny retires.

- Fall 1975—Permit for the Barstow-Vegas race denied for the first time, based on a study of the 1974 race conducted by Penny's staff.

1976–80

- July 1976—Peter and Joyce Burk adopt the goal of a Mojave National Park, form "Citizens for Mojave National Park."

- October 1976—BLM organic act adopted. Work by the BLM on California Desert Plan and California wilderness area inventory begins.

  ◆ Called "Federal Land Policy and Management Act" (FLPMA) it includes Cranston's California Desert Plan provisions and requires BLM to study and recommend wilderness study areas (WSAs).

- December 1980—Final Desert Plan adopted; conservationists disappointed; decide not to attack plan in the courts but seek its amendment.

  ◆ Desert Plan staff's views on suitability of East Mojave for national park status rejected by Management; East Mojave is made a "National Scenic Area" under BLM. Only 2.1 million out of 5.7 million acres of WSAs are declared "suitable" for wilderness designation.

  ◆ Plan is attacked in the courts by ORV organizations and others but their attacks fail.

1981

- Summer 1981—New Interior Secretary James Watt attempts to eliminate protected status of two-thirds of desert WSAs in California. He is ultimately unsuccessful.

  - ◆ Appalled by this action, California desert leaders begin mapping the desert for possible wilderness legislation.

  - ◆ BLM approves enormously destructive Keynot Mine in the Inyo Mountains WSA; through the efforts of volunteers and lawyers, the project is eventually halted.

1982–83

- September 1982—BLM proposes amendments that severely weaken the Desert Plan, including reopening Barstow-Vegas race.

  - ◆ Despite heavy protest, the amendments are largely adopted in 1983. Conservation organizations appeal the race reopening in Federal Court, are unsuccessful.

- December 1982—Secretary Watt publishes order reducing WSA acreage nationwide.

  - ◆ Watt's order is eventually rolled back after years of litigation. The California conservationists are now convinced of the necessity of legislation to protect the desert.

  - ◆ Proposal for California desert legislation is held up pending negotiation and passage of California Forest Service Wilderness Act for California in 1984.

1984–85

- December 1984—Senator Cranston agrees to sponsor a California Desert Protection Act (the "Desert Bill").

  - ◆ Mapping work is stepped up, as are desert study trips; California Desert Protection League is formed to support the Desert Bill.

1986

- February 1986—First version of the Desert Bill (S. 2061) introduced in Senate.

1987

- January 1987—Senator Cranston and Congressman Mel Levine introduce second version of Desert Bill in both Houses (S. 7 and H.R. 371).

  ◆ In January 1987, Western Regional Office of the NPS submits to Washington a report supporting the Desert Bill's proposal for a Mojave National Park, redesignation of Death Valley, and Joshua Tree as national parks, and their expansion. The recommendations are rejected.

  ◆ Campaigning for and against the Desert Bill grows, in print and other media, and in local governmental units.

  ◆ In December 1987, conservation organizations appeal BLM's approval of a great open pit gold mine in the East Mojave National Scenic Area (the Castle Mountain Mine); substantial environmental benefits are negotiated.

1988

- May 1988—California office of BLM publishes final plan for management of East Mojave National Scenic Area; considered unacceptably weak by conservationists.

1989

- July 1989—BLM proposes the transfer of minor additions of its land to Death Valley and Joshua Tree Monuments, much less than NPS had requested.

  ◆ After several years of inaction, the proposed transfers are incorporated into the Administration's substitute for the Desert Bill. The House Committee rejects it.

- October 1989—Negotiations between Senator Pete Wilson and Cranston fail; Wilson then opposes the Cranston bill as "locking" Californians out of the desert.

- December 1989—BLM announces an end to the Barstow-Vegas race.

  ◆ The announcement cites "the cumulative environmental impact of these events over the years and the sponsor's continuing problems in managing them."

1990

- September 1990—Senator Wilson, now campaigning for Governor of California, nevertheless blocks Senate Committee from meeting to mark up the Desert Bill.

◆ Wilson uses Senate Rule 26, preventing any committee from meeting over two hours after a Senate session opens except with consent of both the Majority and Minority leaders.

1991

- July 1991—Congressmen George Miller, Rick Lehman and Mel Levine introduce a new version of the Desert Bill (H.R. 2929). A product of intensive negotiations between Lehman and Levine it reduces wilderness acreage and proposes a "Mojave National Monument," not a park.

◆ California's new Senator John Seymour (appointed to take Wilson's place by newly elected Governor Wilson) states that the House bill "is a long way from what most people would consider an acceptable compromise," signaling his likely opposition.

- October 1991—House passes H.R. 2929, amending it to permit hunting in the proposed Mojave National Monument.

◆ Senator Cranston hails the House bill and promises to support it. Seymour rejects its terms.

1992

- Year 1992—Cranston and Seymour fail to reach a compromise; the latter vows to take all possible steps to prevent the bill's passage.

- August 1992—Using Rule 26, Seymour blocks the Senate subcommittee from taking action on the bill.

- November 1992—Seymour defeated by Dianne Feinstein; Cranston retires; Levine suffers defeat; Boxer is elected to the second California Senate seat; Clinton is elected President.

1993

- January 1993—Senator Feinstein introduces a somewhat modified Desert Bill; Congressman Lehman introduces its counterpart in the House.

◆ New administration signals support.

- October 1993—Senate Committee approves the Desert Bill.

  ◆ To the conservationists' horror, the bill is amended in Committee to remove 20% of the territory of Mojave National Park—the "Lanfair Bite."

1994

- April 1994—Full Senate adopts the Desert Bill as amended in committee.

  ◆ The Lanfair Bite is *not* eliminated; amendments are adopted adding a Mississippi Delta project and a New Orleans Jazz National Historic Park to the bill at the behest of the Committee's chairman.

- May 1994—House Committee approves House version of the Desert Bill.

- July 1994—Full House again passes the Desert Bill.

  ◆ By virtue of opposition tactics, ten weeks and many separate hearings are required to reach a final vote.

- September 20 to October 4, 1994—Threatened filibusters by Senator Malcolm Wallop, requiring cloture processes, delay appointment of Senate's conferees until October 4.

- October 4, 1994—House agrees to a conference and appoints conferees. Conferees meet and quickly agree on Conference Report eliminating the Lanfair Bite but including a Mojave National Preserve (managed by the NPS) with hunting.

  ◆ House is required to act first on the Conference Report. Time cannot be allocated for House debate on Conference Report until after midnight, October 7.

- October 7, 1994, at 2:10 a.m.—House approves Conference Report.

  ◆ Congress is scheduled to adjourn October 7; Senator Wallop refuses to permit the Senate to vote on the Conference Report by exercising his right to filibuster; cloture petition is filed; House adjourns. Majority Leader George Mitchell holds the Senate over for the cloture vote; agreement is reached to take that vote the next day.

- October 8, 1994—The Senate votes cloture without a single vote to spare, then approves the Conference Report by a voice vote.

  ◆ Cloture requires 60 votes; the 60th vote comes in at the last moment; thereafter, other Senators who had previously refused to vote pile on for a 68-23 final cloture vote.

- October 31, 1994—President signs Desert Bill.

1995–1996

- Spring 1995—House Appropriations Committee, at the behest of Congressman Jerry Lewis, appropriates $1.00 to the NPS and $599,000 to the BLM for management of the Mojave National Preserve for fiscal year 1995-96, in an attempt to shift management to the BLM.

- Fall 1995—The Senate agrees; the appropriation bill is sent to the President; it is vetoed in December 1995. Efforts to override the veto fail.

- January 1996—Management of the Mojave Preserve shrinks to four regular employees, including the superintendent and one interpretive ranger, none for law enforcement.

- April 1996—Faced with public anger over park closures nationwide, Congress passes a revised appropriations bill granting NPS $1.1 million in new funding for management of the preserve. The standoff is over.

INDEX

Note: Omitted from the Index are matters to which frequent reference is made throughout the book, e.g. California Desert Plan, Mojave National Park (subsequent Preserve), California Desert Protection Act (the Desert Bill), Federal Land Policy and Management Act (FLPMA), Bureau of Land Management, National Park Service, Department of the Interior, and major conservation organizations such as the Audubon Society, Wilderness Society, Sierra Club (and its chapters and committees), National Parks and Conservation Association.